Pyramind

TRAINING SERIES

MW00448903

Music Theory, Songwriting, and the Piano

Production & Training

Pyramind

evolving sound

Alfred

Alfred Music Publishing Co., Inc.
Los Angeles

Alfred Music Publishing Co., Inc., Los Angeles

Copyright © MMXIII by Alfred Music Publishing, Co., Inc.
All Rights Reserved.   Printed in USA.

ISBN-10: 0-7390-7193-9 Book & DVD
ISBN-13: 978-0-7390-7193-9 Book & DVD

Cover photograph by Trevor Traynor.

Produced in Association with Lawson Music Media, Inc., Nashville, TN
www.lawsonmusicmedia.com

Contents

Acknowledgments

Everyone at Pyramind knows that we're part of a larger musical community. As a part of that whole, we've learned that no art is created alone—it's the people around us that make the art special. This book, and all of the books in the Pyramind series, is the result of all the good people in the Pyramind community. From the authors, the graphic designers, and audio collectors, to all of the support staff that keeps the place humming day in and day out, these works represent the collected efforts of our entire team. There are some teammates that deserve special mention for their extra effort and dedication on this particular book. It's been a pleasure to work with all of them at Pyramind and I am extremely proud of every contributor. I've listed them here to give them a heartfelt thanks for everything they've done, both for this project and for Pyramind every day.

Thank you!

– Matt Donner, author, teacher, producer, coach, CAO, and COO at Pyramind, project manager, and a few hundred other things

At Pyramind

Lynda Arnold, contributing author, pianist, teacher, artist
　　(www.divasonic.com)
Anthony Michael Peterson, contributing author, guitarist,
　　teacher, jazz artist
Daniel Blum, graphics creator, drummer, artist
　　(www.tumbleweedwanderers.com)
Charles Geoghegan, photographer, DVD author
Steve Heithecker, content contributor
Jay Wiltzen and Alex Blue, content contributors

At Large

Jordan Rudess, touring artist, keyboard virtuoso, producer,
　　technologist, wizard (www.jordanrudess.com)
Mike Lawson, acquisitions editor
Link Harnsberger, Editor-in-Chief
Sam Molineaux-Graham, copyeditor

Preface

Over my 17-year career, I witnessed radical changes in all the many aspects of the sound industry. The artistry has changed, the business has changed and the technology has certainly changed—the only thing that hasn't changed is sound itself!

These days, technology has never been so powerful and affordable. Newcomers to music and audio production have the lowest cost of entry ever with more power per dollar coming every year! We're continually bombarded with cool new hardware products that become "must-have" items for studios and producers, and much of that hardware stays valuable for life. In fact, some of the most-prized studio microphones and outboard processors are more than 50 years old! On the other hand, manufacturers of digital software tools debut amazing new versions every eight to twelve months, so keeping up is both an exciting and challenging process! While each version may only last a year or so, the tools become more powerful and easier to use with each release. Fortunately, many newcomers to audio production are already technically savvy, and can readily understand the software and achieve solid results quickly.

This is an exciting time to become involved with music/audio production due to the access to such power, yet there's never been a harder time to get started. The tools are affordable; building a professional music and audio production studio used to cost millions of dollars for the gear alone—never mind the cost of building the space! These days, a professional rig can be assembled for roughly $25,000 and semi-professional and hobbyist studios (we call them "project" studios) can come together for less than $5,000! But just because you can build it, doesn't mean they will come. You've got the same tools as 25 other producers on your block, but what makes you so special? Why should someone pay you?

The world of music and audio production is like a diamond—it may be dazzling and brilliant, with dozens of facets to stare at, but it's really only one stone. If you stare at one facet only, you'll miss the others. By simply twisting the diamond a bit, a whole new set of colors is presented, making it seem like a whole new stone—but it's not. Once you've seen the whole stone, facet-by-facet, you truly understand what you're seeing.

Many people in our industry simply stare at one facet thinking they have the diamond nailed. Most often, it's the technology facet. Users get lost in the features and functions of their gear and forget about the listener. But simply having the tools does not make you successful—you need to understand the whole process behind productions that succeeded before making it a career. In other words, you've got to keep twisting the diamond to see all the facets before truly knowing it.

We Made These Books for Producers

To describe the producer's role, you have to describe the production process. It usually starts at the artist with the song. Good producers work the song with the artist to script the flow of the song, the instruments that will play and the performance nuances so a certain sonic goal can be achieved. From the rehearsal space, the producer takes the artist and project into the studio to work with an audio engineer. Afterwards, the producer takes the final product and moves it to the market. This can be in conjunction with a label or manager, but isn't always that way. Long and short, the producer's job is to take this song idea, produce a recording and then market it.

This is not what an audio engineer does. Audio engineers have a fairly clear job description. They're responsible for the capture, manipulation and delivery of audio. That job starts and ends in the studio while the producer's job started long before the studio and ends long after it. Producers have the widest responsibility set and they usually take a good portion of the song and production ownership for their efforts and risk. Theirs is also the most complex, as it involves aspects of songwriting, engineering, marketing, sales and a whole lot of personality management—to name a few!

We at Pyramind have been doing this a long time and already made the mistakes most producers make as they begin their careers. What makes us unique? We offer a world-class training program, partnered with the industry's leading manufacturers and we produce music and audio all day, every day. We practice everything we preach for our clients because it works. Now, we are presenting our knowledge to you here in these books.

Why Create a Book Series?

☛ Getting information is easy but getting the right information is hard. The Internet has no shortage of "how to" examples. However, for every 20 free videos, you'll be lucky if one will give you a clue about what to do in your situation. There's no way to get personalized coaching from videos—especially free ones! That's why we hire coaches and mentors, go to school, etc. Books can be hard to learn from because they "tell you," rather than teach you. Knowing what something is doesn't tell you how to use it—these books are meant to give you the tools to using the information. After all, the results are all that matter so knowing the tech talk is useless until you can actually use it!

☛ We want to be your "on-call" coaches. We've done this long enough to know that there are no right answers for every situation and the only method that really works for you is yours. We always say there are four ways to do things—the right way, the wrong way, the Pyramind way and your way. Good coaches help you develop your own sense of workflow based on your creativity so that you can make the right call every time. Until the time when you're ready to craft your own workflow, you can just use ours to get through—they work every time.

☛ Writing these books helps us give back to our community in ways we weren't lucky enough to have when we were learning this stuff! From our self-earned knowledge, we've become excellent at teaching—a very different skill from simply knowing or even doing. A good teacher creates a framework for you to operate under until you're ready to operate on your own. These books offer just that framework.

☛ Selfishly, we want better producers out there. Music and audio production is a glorious art form and we all deserve great art. We also believe that there's an artist in each of us. Having the tools and simply stapling loops together doesn't make great art—it makes collage art. We want to hear what you think—not what the presets think.

☞   We want to buck the "starving musician" category. We make great music that everyone should enjoy. Music makes our lives richer and artists should be paid for their works. This is not a podium rant on the state of file sharing; rather it's the overall comment that says "music is valuable" and creating it can be a viable career. In fact, some people become wildly rich in our business! It's not just a pipedream—there are real opportunities out there if you're willing to bust your hump to get it.

How to Use These Books

When completed, this series comprise nine books in three levels—beginning, intermediate and advanced—with books on creative, technical and business in each group. We believe that the blend of all three of these disciplines is the key to success in our industry. Having wild creativity won't move your career forward if you can't execute your ideas. And if you can execute your wild ideas, if you misunderstand the music-purchasing marketplace, you won't earn any money. And without money, you can't buy more gear.

The best way to use these books is to have them all, one level at a time. You can't separate the creative and technical aspects of a project—these must work together to achieve a goal. You can't separate the creative and business sides, either—making something great and selling it to no one does nothing for your career. Having a great idea for a piece of music and having the market to sell it to won't do you any good if it doesn't sound good when you release it. We know–we've made all of these mistakes ourselves and we see others making the same mistakes every day.

Having each of the three disciplines (creativity, technology and business) in an easy-to-digest form with references to each other is the best way to provide the teaching and coaching we want to give. We love to teach, we're extremely focused on giving real-world, practical, highly effective training to our students and we wanted to offer the same approach here.

These books are written in plain language—we're not trying to dazzle you with facts, figures or overly technical information in an effort to show you how smart we are. In fact, how smart we are doesn't even matter! The only thing that matters is your results—making you smarter about how and "why" you work. The language is used to help you get into the information easily and put it to use. Knowing the difference between dB SPL and dBfs is great—as long as it has some application that can make your productions sound better. Otherwise, it's just jargon—words that get tossed around at conferences to make people look like they know what they're doing.

Keep in mind that some information will be duplicated across the three. This helps reinforce the commonality of the subjects and the information itself.

One of our training techniques is cross-referenced learning, which means that hearing the same thing three times from three teachers in three different classes should tell you that something is true—and it's something your really need to know. By covering the same subject across each of the books, your understanding of the material (the "why") is much greater than just reading it once.

By that same reasoning, some of the same material is occasionally covered more than once within each title. In this case, you're getting the same information—or something similar—from two or more sources. Each book has several authors covering the subject, each presenting facets of the diamond in their way.

We hope that you enjoy these books and more importantly—that you find them useful. If this first series covers information you already know, then congratulations—you're ready for the next series! It's likely that even if you already know this information, there's bound to be a few nuggets of wisdom that you didn't have at the start. We always have students who already have a lot of experience, yet we find that their body of homegrown knowledge is made up of little "bubbles" of knowledge with thin connections between them. These books are the perfect for these folks to help erase the boundaries of the little bubbles and make one big bubble out of them. So even if you know many of the pieces, these books should help you wrap all of this knowledge up into a single body of knowledge you can use every day.

And we hope that your productions shine as brightly as a diamond!

—Matt Donner

Introduction
Welcome to Music Theory

We've seen a lot of up-and-coming producers through Pyramind. Many who come to us are technically quite savvy—they can manipulate software and GUIs[1] easily to achieve a sonic result. Loops and libraries are aplenty in the digital world and it's not that hard to push a few buttons and make something happen. Sometimes, the results are even kind of fun! Using common DAWs,[2] nearly anyone can grab a collection of loops and "glue" them together to make a piece of music.

Couple that with all of the fix-it tools such as quantizing and pitch correction and it's easy to glue together pieces of music without actually contributing anything *unique* to the piece, other than the acts of choosing and organizing the sounds.

Many people feel that this approach, and the resulting music, is like a child's school project where pictures cut out of magazines are simply glued to a page. It's called collage art and my kids are really good at it.

To them, each picture represents a story or emotion—or at least an interpretation of an emotion. Combining multiple items or emotions on a single page allows them to express a larger inner feeling out of prefabricated pieces. Occasionally, something outstanding is created this way, but usually it just looks like a bunch of pictures glued to construction paper.

It's not the *unique* expression of the artist at all.

Most of the success of the Pyramind Training Method is how we marry the use of these prefabricated sounds and computer-based tools to the *language* of music. We train our students how to communicate *their* emotions (or the emotion requested by their clients) through the use of both this language and the tools.

In creating our curriculum, we felt (and still feel) that it's not enough to combine prefabricated loops together, conform them to a common tempo, and call it personal expression. For this to happen, there must be an effective *communication* of emotion *from* the producer *to* the audience.

---

1   GUI = graphical user interface
2   DAW = digital audio workstation

All of us have an inner feeling that we try to express with music. We want to produce music to link ourselves to our audience. In fact, many people feel that this should be the primary goal of music production—to make the audience feel the same emotion as the producer themselves! If you're reading this right now, my guess is that your inner emotions are more complex than can be expressed fully by cutting out pictures and gluing them together—unless you happen to be five years old.

Over and over, we've heard people claim that learning music theory will stifle their creativity. For those people, this may be a ruse to avoid doing the hard work required to learn this language. Perhaps they feel music theory is the exclusive language of old folks, classical music, and boring, trite pop tunes from decades ago, holding no relevance to their preferred styles of music.

We disagree.

Knowing theory does *not* precipitate writing boring, old music. Music theory is just the language—a tool of emotional communication. It is the *application* of the music theory that determines the emotions being communicated.

There's an old saying - "You can't break the rules until you know the rules..." The "rules" of music theory do not limit one's creativity—they *liberate* one's creativity.

We hear the application of music theory in lots of today's music, be it hip-hop, R&B, house, breaks, electro, folk, drum 'n' bass, dubstep, rock, pop, or whatever. It works. It always has and always will. A person's unwillingness to learn this language is an utter contradiction—how can anyone think that they could be better at expression with a language if they don't speak the language?

So how *does* one learn this language? If it's so important, why doesn't everyone learn it? Is it *really* that hard? Is it necessary to study for years before "getting" it? The truth is, it's not that hard to learn. It just takes discipline, repetition, and memorization—the same for any other endeavor.

Consider how you learned to ride a bicycle or catch a ball. At first, there was fear—fear of falling off or of being hit by a bad throw. After fear came the first attempts at riding or catching. Overwhelmingly, the first result was failure. This reinforced the fear and doubt, making it even harder to be successful. But you stuck with it and kept trying, and eventually you had success. Once you knew that you *could* do it, the desire to *keep* doing it and to get better at it grew until it was second nature and you were just riding or catching every ball.

It's the same with music. The fear is that you won't be *able* to learn it. It's just too hard and, by trying, you'll feel stupid and will be demotivated. Playing an instrument is basically muscle memory—muscles in your hands on your instrument, but also muscles in your brain. By *hearing* things more acutely, you'll find your ear develops right along with your hands. You will start to dissect songs simply by hearing them, once your ears, mind, and hands know enough.

Think about it—you will hear a song and be able to reproduce the heart of that song instantly. Playing the same song over and over eventually "burns in" the ability to play the song without thinking—it becomes a part of you.

To this end, learning theory and applying it must be coupled with an instrument so you can develop this muscle memory and let the music become a part of you. In today's DAW-centric music production world, the most important instrument is the piano. It is known as the mother of all instruments, after all. We all use the piano to play parts, create MIDI tracks, and develop and execute chords, bass lines, and even drum parts. While drum pads are great for playing drum parts like a drummer, it's very difficult to use them to create chords.

So we're going to teach you how to play piano here too. And you might ask, "As if theory wasn't hard enough, you're going to teach me piano at the same time?"

Yes.

Remember that learning the theory needs to be tied to playing an instrument—the piano in our case. You should also know that we use a lot of cross-referencing at Pyramind. That means you're likely to be learning the same thing from several sources at once, which we find makes learning happen deeper and faster than only learning things sequentially. For example, you might learn about editing in a DAW class one day, then hear it again in an audio class the next, then in a production class on the third day. By the end of the week, you'll have a deeper understanding of editing.

So, yes, we're going to teach you theory and the piano at the same time. We'll also use specific exercises to practice, so you can apply the theory directly while *using* the piano. It will work too. We know it will work because we've seen it happen over and over.

What's the catch, you say?

You have to work at it, as well. Consistently. Passionately. Unrelentingly.

Most students cover this material in anywhere from four to eight months so it's OK to give yourself at least that much time to work through this book. It's a language, after all and you can't learn a language without practice and memorization (which takes time) and, most importantly, without *using* it. Just like it was with the bicycle and the same with the ball and glove.

That's the bad news—you have to actually work. Yes, work.

Now's a really good time to ask yourself a question: "Are the loops I'm using doing my music justice?

If you're satisfied with the loops, put this book down—it won't do a damn thing for you. Just buy more loop CDs and glue more pictures on construction paper. I'm sure the teacher will give you a gold star and a smiley face for your efforts. If you're really good, maybe your mama will take you out for ice cream!

If not, strap in, buckle up, and get ready to get dirty. There will be work to do and a lot of practice required, but in the end you'll be making *real* music—in any genre you like. You'll have the power to express yourself completely and create the emotions in your audience that you feel in yourself.

Isn't that why you wanted to produce music in the first place?

Section 1
Rhythm

What Is Rhythm? The Up and Down of It All

Generally referred to as "the beat," rhythm is what gives a song movement, speed (or tempo), and creates the momentum of the emotional intent (the emotion that the composer is trying to create in the listener) of the piece. Rhythm makes us move our bodies, nod our heads, tap our feet, or shake our hips. We all know the beat when we hear it and when we feel it, but… how do we create it? More to the point, how do we *learn* to create it?

Listen to the click track on **Audio Track 1** and as you do so, follow along with the pacing of the clicks until you feel comfortable with the tempo. Can you clap along to the clicks? Does your rhythm fall out of sync with the click? Concentrate on your clapping by listening to the click *and* your clapping and trying very hard to make the two perfectly in sync. Each of the clicks is called a *beat*, short for *downbeat*. Now listen *between* the clicks—how long is the silence? Even silence within a piece of music has its own rhythm.

 **Audio Track 1:** 30 seconds of a quarter-note metronome playing at 120 bpm (beats per minute).

> **Beat**
> The basic time-unit of music. In common time, or 4/4 time, this beat is 1/4 of the measure or a quarter note. It is most commonly found as the "click" sound on a tempo track—also known as the click track.

Coach's Corner: Understanding the Beat

The term *beat* can be a bit confusing here for some. For the majority of this book and in general, the term refers to each pulse in the music—the quarter note in 4/4 time. There's a tick on your watch each second and if your watch was a click track, the ticking would be the beat. The term *beat* has been used generically to mean the overall piece of music, especially in dance music and hip-hop where a fully produced track is often called "a beat"—but as we're just getting started here, let's just accept that the term *beat* as referring to the "ticking" of the music and not a finished rhythmic piece of music.

Clap along with Audio Track 1 and make sure your clapping lines up with the click three times in a row—*perfectly*. If you can't make it happen three times in a row perfectly, keep trying until you can (my first music teacher told me ten times but we'll go easy on you this time). This will be a repeated theme—three times *perfectly* means you've got it. Any less and you need to keep working it.

Coach's Corner: The Metronome

The metronome is a great tool for measuring your success with the rest of the book's lessons. As you get started, start with a metronome that is fairly slow—say 60 beats per minute. As you become better practicing at slower speeds, slowly raise the metronome as you improve. Work at the slower speeds until you attain success then continue with consistent tempo increases as you can get better. For example, if you jump from 60 to 65 bpm, upgrade to 70 next, then 75, and so on. Before long, you'll be upping the tempo by larger increments as you become faster and faster, moving from 100 to 110, then 120 and beyond.

You may have noticed on Audio Track 1 that one click is different than the rest—the first one. The accented beat is called the "1" as it's the first in each bar. You can always hear where you are in the rhythm by identifying the "1" and counting from there. In our case, you'd count "1…2…3…4…" and with the accenting, "**1**…2…3…4… **1**…2…3…4…," and so on. Right now, we're working with rhythm that contains four beats per measure, or per repeat. That is, after the fourth beat is over, it's straight back to the "1." Don't count the next beat as the "5"— even if it is the fifth beat.

Rhythm has a wave to it; there is both a "down" energy and an "up" energy. Think of it in terms of breathing—exhale and inhale. The downbeat represents exhale and the upbeat represents inhale. If there are four downbeats per measure, then there are also four upbeats *in-between* the downbeats.

Now listen to the click from Audio Track 1 again. This time, begin clapping *between* each click and **not** on the click itself. Can you fit your claps in evenly between the clicks? Are you clapping too early or too late, making the downbeats seem off time from your claps? It's much harder to clap in-between the beats as there isn't a click to clap to—you've got to fill in the gap yourself based on the tempo.

The trick here is to *only* clap when there isn't a click—on the upbeats *only*. In addition, try to make it feel as though the pace of the click is twice as fast, with you clapping on the upbeats—that is, keeping the feel of the tempo smooth and consistent. This will ensure that you are clapping right in-between and not too close to the beginning or the end of the upbeat.

This is the beginning of learning about rhythm: noticing that the beat *and* the space in-between the beat are important parts of rhythm in creating the groove, the tempo, the pace, *and* the feeling you want your listener to have when they hear the piece. You should also notice that by clapping on the upbeats, you've effectively cut the time between each beat in half. When creating rhythm patterns we often fill the measure with sounds both on—and in-between—the basic beat and then vary these parts over time to create movement and interest.

As we begin to study rhythm, we'll start by seeing it written as music. All music (including rhythm) can be written on special paper called *staff paper* which has several groups of five horizontal lines on it. When writing music, a vertical line is drawn from the top line to the bottom line of the staff after each four beats. This is called the *bar line*. The music between the bar lines is designated as the *measure* or *bar* and each has only four beats… for now.

Rhythm is measured in a few ways—the number of beats per measure being one and the beats per minute being another. Only the latter is referred to as *bpm*—beats per *minute*. Note that both measurements have the acronym bpm (measure or minute). There is another term for the number of beats per *measure*; we call that the song's "meter."

Bar Line
The vertical line on staff paper denoting the end of one rhythmic section and the beginning of the next.

Measure
The division of music into equal rhythmic portions, usually four beats per measure.

bpm
Short for *beats per minute*, the bpm is a metronome measurement of the pacing or tempo of rhythm (how fast the music plays). Not to be confused with beats per measure.

Meter
Meter is the definition of the beats per measure along with the definition of the length of the main beat. When written, the top number refers to the number of beats in a measure, such as 3/4 or 4/4. 3/4 time, for example would mean that there are 3 beats per measure. The lower number refers to the length of each beat.   3/4 time has 3 beats per measure where each beat is a quarter note.

Subdivisions of the Beat (or note durations)

Beat and Beat Subdivisions
The length of the note played and the smaller durations available between the beats.

When you clapped on the beat, you were clapping what are called *quarter notes*. There are usually four beats in a bar and each is worth 25% of the measure, or a quarter of a measure—quarter notes. Simple enough, right? You're already used to counting this—it sounds like "1…2…3…4… 1…2…3..4." In trance and house music, this rhythm would be played by the kick drum and would sound like **Audio Track 2**. This is often called the *four on the floor*, as the rhythm is four beats in the low frequency range (kick drums are also placed directly on the floor). If we divide the quarter note in half, we get the *eighth note.* It takes two eighth notes to complete the duration of a single quarter note. When you were clapping in-between the notes on Audio Track 1, you were clapping along with four of the upbeat eighth notes. If you clapped to both the quarter notes *and* the upbeat eighth notes, you were clapping to all eight of the eighth notes. As you might guess, there are four quarter notes in a standard bar and there are eight eighth notes in a standard bar. You can see this in **Figure 1.1**.

Audio Track 2: A kick drum played on each quarter note (a.k.a. the "four on the floor") at 120 bpm.

Eighth Notes

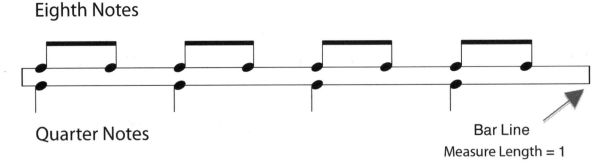

Quarter Notes

Bar Line
Measure Length = 1

Figure 1.1: The staff of quarter notes and eighth notes showing the bar line and measure length.

Now begin counting to yourself, "1…*and*…2…*and*…3…*and*…4…*and* " and clap along to Audio Track 1 again. The "*and*" part of the pulse is commonly called the *upbeat*, the second half of the quarter-note pulse—the eighth note in-between the quarter notes. The resulting sound is that there will be one clap and number for each beat ("1" with a clap) but only the "*and*" for the in-between upbeat. Clap and verbalize the quarter notes as numbers while only verbalizing the eighth notes with the "and" until you are comfortable with the click and can play it perfectly three times in a row. Feel free to create your own track and speed it up to get comfortable feeling the pace of quarter notes and eighth notes in any rhythm.

This subdividing the beat in half continues a few more times. The quarter note is the most popular note duration and the eighth note is right behind it. In fact, the ubiquitous house music beat perfectly exemplifies this quarter- and eighth-note relationship as heard on **Audio Track 3**. The four-on-the-floor kick drum plays each quarter note while the slightly opened hi-hat plays the eighth note upbeat rhythm. Notice that the hi-hat *only* plays the upbeat eighth and not the downbeats. In other words, it onlay plays eighth note 2, 4, 6, and 8 while the kick drum plays the downbeat eighth notes 1, 3, 5, and 7. You'll see this as well in **Figure 1.2**.

Audio Track 3: A standard quarter-note and eighth-note house beat where the kick drum plays the downbeats and the hi-hat plays the upbeat eighth notes only.

Hi Hats   (upbeats)

Bass Drum (downbeats)

Figure 1.2: A written notation of the house beat from Audio Track 3 where the lower quarter notes represent the kick drum and the higher eighth notes represent the upbeat (in-between the beat) hi-hats.

Now let's try a new rhythm—something called the *triplet*.

> **Triplet**
> The triplet is a note duration value where each note of the triplet counts for one third the length of a beat.

A triplet is a collection of three notes played equally on one beat. The way you would clap it would be "*one*-two-three, *two*-two-three, *three*-two-three, *four*-two-three," and so on. If you think of polka music, this would be a similar count to the familiar *boom-cha-cha, boom-cha-cha*. You can see it in **Figure 1.3.** You can hear this on **Audio Track 4** as played by a hi-hat cymbal (triplets) against a four-on-the-floor kick drum.

Quarter Notes

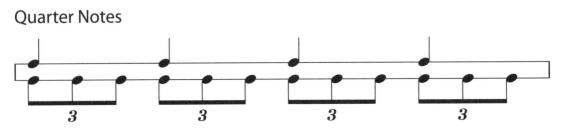

Triplet Eight Notes

Figure 1.3: The triplet rhythm shown against a quarter-note rhythm (slower tempo).

Audio Track 4: The feel of an accented triplet hi-hat.

Let's take a moment to look at and listen to the rest of the note durations in music. **Figure 1.4** shows the complete list of beat subdivisions from the quarter note through the 64th note. On **Audio Track 5** you hear a metronome click for each note duration for two measures (or eight beats each) back-to-back at the same bpm so you can hear how much faster the rhythm seems as the note duration gets smaller and smaller. Notice how the "1" stays accented.

Audio Track 5: A hi-hat sound playing the durations of rhythm, from quarter note through to 64th note. The quarter-note beats are accented through each subdivision.

Figure 1.4: The note durations of every value on the staff as they compare to each other and the span of one bar.

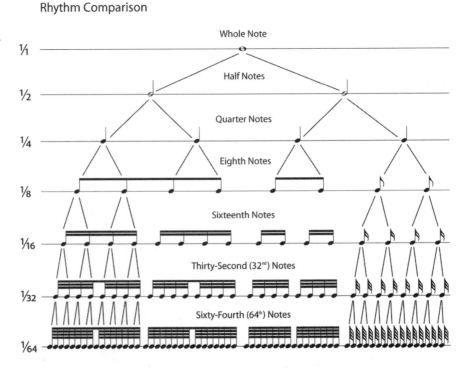

Coach's Corner: Peanut Butter Patterns?

We already know how to count the quarter notes and the eighth notes verbally as "1…2…3…4…" and "1…*and*…2…*and*…3…*and*…4…*and*…" respectively. Counting sixteenth notes, however, is a bit more complicated. Here, we use the verbal mnemonic "1-e-and-a, 2-e-and-a…," and so on. Another way of doing this is to quote the phrase "pea-nut-but-ter" where each phonetic sound represents a sixteenth note. If you hear a rhythm and you can say "peanut butter" along with it, you've found a sixteenth-note pattern!

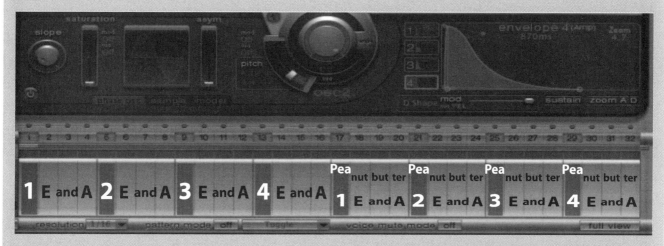

Figure CC1.1 shows how the sixteenth notes would be laid out if they were placed on the buttons of a standard drum sequencer along with the "peanut butter" mnemonic.

Coach's Corner: The Snap Test

A shortcut to hearing the difference between quarter and eighth notes is the snap test. Try to snap your fingers along with the beat. If it's very comfortable for your hand, odds are it's a quarter-note beat. If it's either too fast for you and you can just barely keep up or you need both hands to snap along, it's likely the eighth-note pattern. Even at really slow tempos, eighth notes can be hard to keep up with. Sixteenth notes are nearly impossible to try to snap along to.

At this point, you might be wondering if there are note values greater than the quarter note. The answer is, of course, yes. The two values are simple enough: the half note and the whole note, as seen in **Figure 1.5**. The half note plays as long as two quarter notes and the whole note plays as long as four quarter notes (or two half notes). Of course, two half notes also play as long as a single whole note.

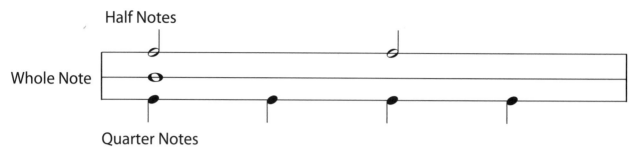

Half Notes

Whole Note

Quarter Notes

Figure 1.5: The quarter, half note and the whole note.If you listen to **Audio Track 6**, you'll hear a bass tone played over a simple house beat—the same one from Audio Track 3. Notice how the first two bass tones last a whole bar—four beats long. That tells you that these are whole notes. The second group of bass notes are in half notes—two play in the span of one bar. You can see the rhythm of Audio Track 6 written in **Figure 1.6**.

Audio Track 6: The standard house beat with bass tones that play for two measures as whole notes, then two measures as half notes.

Hi Hats
Bass Drum

Bass

Figure 1.6: The written rhythm of the standard house beat heard on **Audio Track 6**.

Let's continue this process of layering time divisions onto our simple rhythm. So far, we have heard whole and half notes with the bass, quarter notes on the kick, and upbeat eighth notes with the hi-hat. Now, lets add another layer—another hi-hat—playing sixteenth notes. Notice how it fills in the spaces between the hi-hats, which fills in the spaces between the kicks, which fill the time between the longer bass notes. This is the foundation of building rhythm—filling in the rhythm with different sounds playing at different time divisions to create layers of movement and interest. You can hear them on **Audio Track 7** and see them in **Figure 1.7**.

Audio Track 7: The standard house beat from Audio Track 6 with a bass line. At first the hi-hat plays eighth notes but when the phrase repeats, a sixteenth note hi-hat pattern is played.

Figure 1.7: The standard house beat with the bass from Audio Track 6. While the bass plays whole tones, the hi-hat plays eighth notes but when the bass plays half notes, a sixteenth note hi-hat pattern is played.

Lastly, lets also hear the two faster time divisions—the 32nd note and the 64th note. On **Audio Track 8**, you can hear this in the kick drum. We'll have it play as quarter notes at first in the standard house beat. You'll hear it accelerate as it plays eighth notes for one bar, then sixteenth notes for a bar, then 32nd notes, then 64th notes. Notice as it gets faster and faster, the tension you feel in the rhythm increases and how the individual kick hits get harder and harder to hear. At the 64th note level, the kick just sounds like a machine gun or a skipping CD. Also notice how the tension is released when the kick goes back to the quarter note afterwards.

Audio Track 8: The standard house beat with the half-note bass only and an accelerating kick drum pattern from quarter, to eighth, through 64th.

Rests and Accents

Each rhythmic subdivision also has an equivalent duration of silence, called a *rest*. The rest for each duration means that there is no sound for *that* designated duration. **Figure 1.8** shows the chart of rests on the staff, just above the chart of note durations on the staff so you can see how the two correlate.

Figure 1.8: The staff showing note and rest durations aligned vertically.

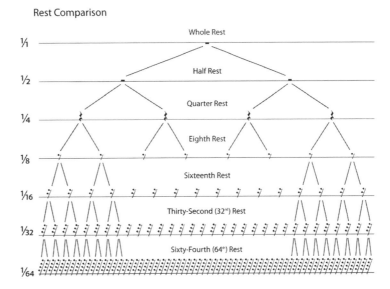

Note that the rest indicates silence. Silence does not necessarily just mean the space between notes. Rests are only where the note is *forced* to be silent, where normally it might try to play. Let's take a closer look at this in both the kick and the hi-hat pattern.

Figure 1.9 shows the standard house beat with the bass or kick drum only. Notice that on the top row there are no rests indicated as there is no *forced* silence—the kick hits each quarter note. Now, lets remove two of the kick drums—the second and fourth, as seen in the bottom row. Notice that in this case, we remove the two kick drums but we indicate two quarter-note rests in-between. That's because we need the person reading the chart (the kick player in this case) to recognize that the two quarter notes are to be played on the first and the third beat *only* whereas the second and fourth notes are to be silent. Also note that each kick only lasts for quarter note. If we wrote them as half notes as if we didn't need the rest, each kick would last twice as long—a half note instead of a quarter note.

Figure 1.9: The standard house beat with the kick drum only. The top staff shows all four quarter notes and the bottom staff shows kick two and four replaced with rests.

BD with No Rests

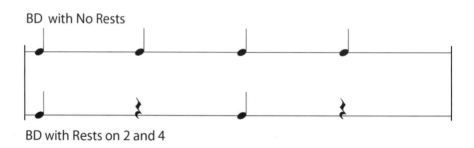

BD with Rests on 2 and 4

What do you think would happen if you did *not* enter the rest values? Couldn't it work the same way? The answer is no. Without the rests, you'd only see two quarter notes written, but you'd have no idea of which two they were. Should you play the first and second? The first and third? The third and fourth? Remember, all the written notes (and rests) have to equal four beats per measure in common 4/4 time.

If we only write two quarter notes, the reader might assume that we meant to only play two beats per measure and would then skip ahead to the next measure—two beats ahead of everyone else. That's just bad. The rests indicate that first there's a quarter note to be played, then a beat of silence, another quarter note to be played, then another beat of silence. All four indicators add up to four quarter-note/rest values totaling four beats per measure.

Coach's Corner: Why Care about Written Rhythms?

You might ask: "Why do I need to worry about this? I just produce my music in my DAW…" That may be true—if you're never going to work with someone else. Many people end up hiring talent to add a live feel to a digitally produced rhythm track—drummers, percussionists, and so on. While many of these players can add to your track by simply listening and playing along, others play best as music readers and need a printed score to keep up. Having your parts listed and written properly can save time, energy, and cash spent in the studio paying for an expensive player without having to explain every little detail.

Now that you have some experience in clapping rhythms, let's explore creating more depth and articulation to our rhythm with *accents*.

Articulation
This term refers to the way a note is played—either harder, softer, with more attack (staccato), or a softer intro (legato), and so on.

An accent is made when you emphasize a note more than the others. An accent is written with a small arrow that points to the right drawn on top of the note as shown in **Figure 1.10**. This emphasis is not hard, just a little louder.

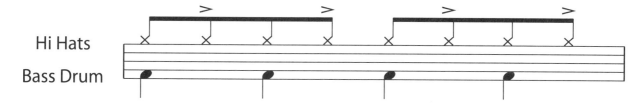

Hi Hats

Bass Drum

Figure 1.10: The standard house beat with an accent on the upbeat eighth note hi-hats.

Now play **Audio Track 9** and begin clapping the steady eighth-note rhythm. Notice that on the first bar, the eighth notes are flat. On the second bar, the second, fourth, sixth, and eighth beats play the accents on the upbeat eighth notes as written in Figure 1.10. This repeats a few times for you to hear it. Notice how the feeling of the rhythmic pattern has changed? By adding the accent, you allow the rhythm to take on a different level of meaning—the accented upbeat eighth notes suddenly become more "important" than the downbeat ones, drawing attention to themselves and giving the listener a stronger sense of the pulse of the beat.

Audio Track 9: Four bars of the standard house beat where the first and third bars have no accents while the second and fourth bars have the upbeat eighth notes accented. This four-bar pattern plays twice.

Worksheet 1.1: Building Your First Rhythm

This is the first of many worksheets within the book—exercises designed to get you to do one thing more than anything else and comfortable *using* the material in this book. Remember that this book of music theory is really music application; the theory is fine and is helpful in explaining a piece of music but at the end of the day, you get to do whatever you like. Additionally, this is designed to get you comfortable using your favorite DAW as not only a production tool but as a musical practice tool.

Be advised—we will *not* give you very many figures here. The idea is to do the exercise without the crutch of helper figures. You might just have to do it on your own, then compare to the audio provided and work until you get it right. It may be frustrating at times—but stick it out. As you overcome these little challenges, you'll "own" the knowledge and you'll never get it wrong again.

Coach's Corner: Homework to Home Run

Not surprisingly, many of the exercises we've assigned at Pyramind throughout the music theory, piano, and production classes grow up to be full-fledged songs—some of which have been signed by record labels! Trust us and follow along—you might just write a song out of this book!

We're going to assume that at this point, you have a basic understanding of your DAW and can at least get a drum part sequenced. We'll also assume that you understand basic quantizing of drums (aligning drum parts to the grid of a metronome in the DAW) so the parts you create are at least on the grid of the rhythm. If not, you'll likely want to use the audio tracks we've given you as a back rhythm to practice to while you learn how.

First, let's assign a function to the basic parts of the drums. The kick drum generally designates *the one*, the first beat of the pattern *and* the low frequency of the drum set—in short, it's the foundation of the rest of the rhythm. For now, let's place the kick drum on beats one and three, with quarter-note rests in between. Use your favorite DAW and drum sounds to do this worksheet.

The next part of the drum set creates the basic pulse of the pattern that sets it in motion. This part is called the *hi-hat* (or *high-hat*, or *hat*), and we've already used it a bit. Assign a pattern of eight eighth notes throughout the bar where there are exactly eight of them evenly spaced throughout the beat.

Notice how the feeling of movement has intensified. The next part of the drums is the *snare*. The snare creates what is called the *backbeat* by playing in the spaces where the kick drum is not playing. Place the snare drum on beats two and four.

You should compare your work to **Audio Track 10**. If yours doesn't sound like ours, check a few things:

☛ Make sure the tempo is set to 120 bpm on your sequencer.

☛ Make sure the kick is on beats 1 and 3, while the snare is on beats 2 and 4.

☛ Make sure the hi-hat has eight hits per measure—one for each eighth note. The accenting might be a bit different— play with it on your DAW to try and recreate the feel of Audio Track 10.

Congratulations! You have just created your first groove! OK, it's not the most amazing of beats, but it's the first step on a *long* road. Count your successes as they come and don't try to shoot for the moon yet…

 **Audio Track 10:** The result of Worksheet 1.1.

Coach's Corner: A Simple but Classic Beat

This particular beat—where the kick plays the first and third notes, and the snare plays the second and fourth beats—is often referred to as the 2-4 backbeat, as it denotes the snare playing on the second and the fourth beats of the measure. Michael Jackson's "Billie Jean" is one of the most classic versions of this, with No Doubt's "Hella Good" in a close second. But that's just my opinion…

Coach's Corner: Variations of the Three Drum Elements

Notice that up until now, we've been mostly working with the kick and the hi-hat drum. Many forms of music use the basic three elements of the drums—the kick, the snare, and the hi-hat—but others do not. Traditional reggae music, for example, often has no snare and relies exclusively on the hi-hat and kick. House can be similar in that a snare is not always necessary, but in hip hop the kick and snare often outweigh the hi-hat, and in rock and dubstep the snare is king. Start paying attention to what sounds are being used in the rhythms you enjoy as well as the positioning of those sounds within the beat.

Let's try a variation:

Simply move your kick drum on beat three to the *upbeat* after beat two—an eighth note earlier than the third quarter note. Notice how that simple change has changed the rhythmic expression of the groove. If you make other changes, you'll find that the expression continues to get more complex.

Try these alterations in your rhythm.

☛ Move the second kick drum to the *upbeat* after beat two. You might know this as the 2-*and*...

☛ Take your hi-hat and create an open hi-hat on the *upbeat* after beat four, closing it on beat one of the next measure. It should follow the extra kick you added. If you're not familiar with the sound of the open hi-hat, you'll likely hear a variation of the hi-hat on one of the adjacent MIDI keys playing your drum sounds. It sounds like the regular hat but is longer and has a "sizzle" sound. If you can't find anything, use a cymbal sound.

Compare your work to ours on **Audio Track 11.**

Audio Track 11: The 2-4 backbeat with alterations.

Grooves are usually created in one-, two-, four-, and eight-bar patterns. One way of keeping the rhythm fresh in a song is to create a few variations of the main rhythm, then change back and forth between them throughout the groove. For example, consider a straight rhythm for the verses while the slightly complex ones play in the chorus. In our example, try sequencing the straight 2-4 backbeat for four bars, then switch to the variation rhythm for another four, then back to the straight. You should notice that every four bars, the rhythm switches. Your listener will appreciate this as it helps them know when the energy of the song changes. It should sound like **Audio Track 12**.

Audio Track 12: The 2-4 backbeat with alterations after four measures. The first four measures are the straight 2-4 backbeat. The second four measures introduces an open hi-hat for slight variety. The third four has the shifted kick drum (no open hat) and the fourth has the shifted kick and the open hi-hat.

Now let's create a 2-bar groove. Our previous examples repeated the 1-bar groove four times, then switched. Here, the main rhythmic pattern will actually be two bars long—not just one bar. This differentiation gives the listener the sense that the rhythm is longer and keeps listener interest longer too. We will create even more motion and excitement by concentrating on the kick drum activity.

In your DAW, set your loop to match two bars worth of time. Then take a look at **Figure 1.11** and rebuild your drum part to match. Build it one instrument at a time, starting with the kick drum, as there is a good amount of complexity in this rhythm. Don't cheat and program it in with a pencil tool! *Read* the kick drum rhythm and then *play* the part in as you read it. Notice the changes between the first bar and the second. If it's too hard to do at a higher tempo, try at a real slow one such as 60 bpm.

Move on to the snare next. *Do not cheat* and listen to the audio to see if you've gotten it right—the idea is to test your ability to read rhythm and perform it, based on what you read! In this case, the snare stays the same throughout the pattern. This helps the listener feel grounded through the pattern: while the kick changes slightly, the snare stays the same.

Notice that the hi-hat stays the same here too, like the snare. With only the kick changing through the pattern, the rhythm has enough variety to make the pattern feel longer while keeping the pace strong and even in the stable snare and hat pattern.

Once all these parts are recorded, you can check your work against **Audio Track 13**.

Figure 1.11: A classic rock drum groove.

Audio Track 13: The groove created from Figure 1.11.

Coach's Corner: Rhythm Creation Checklist

You are, of course, as free as you like to create rhythms that you dig. Most people simply let the "feel" guide them, playing what they feel along to the metronome until they get it right. While doing this, start thinking about your beat in various ways: does it make you want to groove, or dance? Is there enough activity in the rhythm to make you dance? Is there too much activity? Are there more parts needed? Is the quarter-note feel strong enough? Where are the accents?

Answering all of these questions and more is an integral part of creating music and what separates the simple beats from the compelling ones. It's why Dr. Dre's beats are so strong, why Led Zeppelin is used as the drum benchmark for rock, and what makes tracks from DJs such as Jaytech and Kaskade so groovy. The rhythm, the pace, and the construction of the beat is what makes the pulse of the song "happen," but just as important as the notes are when to put in the rests. We often say at Pyramind - "It ain't the notes—it's the space between the notes—that makes you groovy…"

Swings, Shuffles, Dots, and Ties

Now that we have the basics of rhythm down, we can start to get a bit more fancy about the rhythms we create. Especially with today's DAWs that can automatically align a performance to the metronomic grid (known as *quantizing*), it's easy to create a straight up/down beat, where all the rhythms fall squarely on the metronomic grid. However, you can give your rhythm "life" by shifting each of the parts slightly off of the grid in musical ways during your songwriting and production phase.

> **Quantizing**
> Quantizing is the process of aligning the timing of a MIDI performance to a specific grid and to a specified rhythmic subdivision, such as eighth notes, sixteenth notes, and so on.

There's a problem with "straight" quantizing - while it results in rhythmic timing that's on the grid (and therefore on the beat) it can sound stiff and unmusical. Two functions, *shuffle* and/or *swing,* can make all the difference to quantized beats.

> **Shuffle Rhythm**
> A shuffle rhythm is when note durations of equal length are played with unequal durations.

In a shuffle beat, two eighth notes written equally are not played equally—one is held longer than the other. The result is a rhythmic feel that is "shuffled"—similar to the gait of someone with a limp. While this is sometimes not written in rhythmic terms, it is often indicated at the head of a piece with the term *shuffle* or *swing*. When written into the rhythm of the notes, you'll see it as a dotted eighth note. In **Figure 1.12**, you'll see a straight rhythm (with the shuffle implied) versus the dotted eighth note (the shuffle).

Figure 1.12: Two written versions of a shuffle rhythm—straight and dotted.

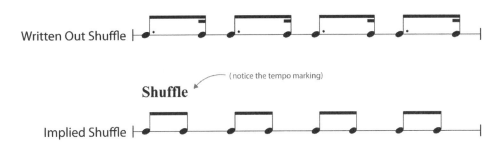

Written Out Shuffle

(notice the tempo marking)

Shuffle

Implied Shuffle

The dotted eighth or dotted quarter rhythm involves holding the first note (the dotted one) by 50% longer than usual and holding the second note 50% less than usual. For example, a dotted eighth note rhythm would have the first eighth note held for an eighth note and a sixteenth note while the note after, although written as a eighth note, would be held for only a sixteenth note. Therefore, the "weight" of the rhythm has been shuffled to give more priority to the first note and less to the second. The blues is known for using this sort of rhythm, as is jazz. You can hear this on **Audio Track 14**.

Audio Track 14: The blues shuffle beat played straight and then shuffled.

> **Swing Rhythm**
> Similar to the shuffle, swinging the beat involves changing the priority of the notes in a beat and adjusting the timing of the written notes to be a little lopsided. While a shuffle beat often involves the use of dotting a note to emphasize the weight of that note, swinging is subtle and often is not written at all. It is, however, extremely useful when producing beats with a DAW.

When you swing the beat, you first choose whether to swing it forward or backward. Swinging the beat forward tells the DAW to play the beat slightly early compared to the metronome grid while swinging backward tells the DAW to play the beat slightly later than the grid. One is useful for increasing the rhythmic energy (forward) and the other creates a laziness that decreases the rhythmic energy (backward). Genres that use the upbeat swing include bebop jazz, African, Latin music, and Latin-infused pop/ dance. Backbeat swing tends to be used in blues, rock, hip-hop, dub, and reggae music.

To add some swing to your beat, use the following steps:

☞ Revisit the beats you made earlier and call up the MIDI data you recorded.

☛ Highlight the notes of the beat (be sure to grab a whole bar's length—any more or less and you might get strange results).

☛ Choose "quantize" from within your DAW. The command will be in different places for different DAWs so consult your manual for specifics. You'll want to bring up the quantizing options—don't just quantize the notes without experimenting with different settings.

☛ Make sure you quantize the "note on" and nothing else.

☛ Make sure elements such as "swing" and "shuffle" are either not checked or set to "0" for now.

☛ Choose a beat subdivision to quantize the beat to. Choose the resolution that matches the smallest subdivision in your beat—quarter, eighth, or sixteenth if you have them. Hit "quantize."

At this point, your beat is hard-quantized to the grid and has no swing. It should sound tight but stiff—on the beat and perfectly lined up to the metronome, but with no feel. We call this an *up-and-down groove*.

☛ Now, activate the swing function and add a value of −20%. Sometimes, this will be a value box you type into and other times it'll be a slider you move.

☛ Requantize the beat. You should notice that the beat is now ahead of the metronome and has a bit of groove to it. Undo it and then redo it with +20% and notice the beat swinging later than the metronome. If you don't hear a big difference, *undo* the original quantizing and redo it with the swing.

☛ Play with the values and parameters until you find one that works for you.

Coach's Corner: Preset Possibilities

When working with swings and quantizes, there are *lots* of choices. Just about every DAW allows you to swing or shuffle the quantizing with several choices therein. When looking in your DAW, check to see if there are preset grooves. Both Avid's Pro Tools and Apple's Logic, for example, have loads and loads of preset swings—from the Akai collection, the Linn drum collection, the standard Logic eighth and sixteenth A-F settings—and the ability to extract a groove from both MIDI tracks and audio tracks. Yes, you can rip off the feel of your favorite drum loop and apply it to any MIDI performance and trick your friends into thinking you're the man. It's just too easy to fix a MIDI drum performance so there's no reason to accept anything less than a perfectly grooved beat these days.

Another way to add life to your rhythm is to break up a stiff rhythm by elongating notes. This is accomplished by taking a string of individual notes and *tying* some of them together to make a few notes sound like one. **Figure 1.13** shows a simple quarter-note rhythm with four unique quarter notes. The second version of the rhythm shows a tie (indicated by the arc below the notes—sometimes written above the notes, here represented by the dotted arc) where the last two quarter notes are tied together. Rhythmically, this is the same as a half note with one key exception—each of the tied quarter notes gets a certain emphasis while the note is held from the first note *through* the second note. You can hear this on **Audio Track 15** played as a bass tone.

Figure 1.13: A quarter-note rhythm where the first pattern has individual quarter notes and the second pattern has the first two as individuals with the second two tied together.

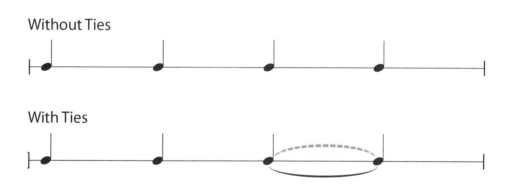

Audio Track 15: The sound of the untied and tied quarter notes from Figure 1.13.

Notice how the tied quarter note is still emphasized with a slight volume inflection even though the note started with the first one? Adding ties to rhythms allows you to play a phrase once with each note articulated then again with some notes tied together, creating a variation on the same melody and rhythm.

Figure 1.14 shows a variety of approaches to the bass line—some notes played individually and others tied—showing how a simple rhythmic melody can be changed through ties to sound like a different melody. **Audio Track 16** plays these melodies showing the emphasis on the tied notes while holding the length of the two tied notes together.

Figure 1.14: A variation of a bass melody—straight and with ties.

Audio Track 16: A variation of a melody showing the tied notes from Figure 1.14. Notice how on this synth, the tying of notes creates a difference in the sound: the tied notes blend into each other while the untied notes sound as though they were struck individually.

Time Signatures (a.k.a. meter)

Up until now, we've been working on the premise that all music has only four beats to a measure and that each of those beats represents a quarter note. While it is true for most music, it is not always the case. In fact, when we write music that has this four beats per measure with a quarter-note beat rhythmic structure, we call it *common time*—it's used that often.

> **Common Time**
> *Common time* refers to the rhythmic structure where there are four beats in a measure and each beat is worth a quarter note.

If you've ever glanced at the staff notation of piece of music, you may have noticed a symbol like this: 4/4, or 3/4 at the beginning to the left, as seen in Figure 1.15. This is called the *time signature*, or *meter*. Though it looks like a fraction written within the staff lines, it is more than that.

Figure 1.15: The written time signatures of 4/4 and 3/4 on the staff.

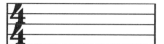   

> **Meter (a.k.a. time signature)**
> The numeric description of the rhythmic structure of a piece of music.

The top number tells you how many beats belong in a measure, and the bottom number tells you what type of note gets the beat (or count). For instance, the time signature 4/4 tells the musician that there are four beats to the measure, and the quarter note (hence the number four, being a symbol for a quarter) defines the beat. Another example could be 3/4. This says that there are three beats to the measure and that the quarter note defines the beat.

Coach's Corner: Common Time

Common time is just that—common. This means that it is the most popular meter around. If you love rock, hip-hop, dance, and pop, odds are, you already know what 4/4 time sounds like—you just nod your head down/up/down/up each measure and you can easily count along with a "1…2…3…4…"

Meters that are not 4/4—such as 7/8 (my favorite), 12/16, and so on, are often called "odd" meters. That too is a bit of a misnomer. 6/8, for example, which is often used in ballads, has two even numbers, although the meter is referred to as "odd." For now, let's just say that the term *odd* refers to a meter that's not common time and call it a day…

Figure 1.16 shows a variety of rhythms and time signatures, which can be heard in metronome form on **Audio Track 17**. We put a drum groove over each meter for a few bars so you can hear them in action. Try to count along with each. The best way to hear it is to count it out!

For something like 6/8 (which is very similar to 3/4—basically twice as fast), you'll count something like "1…2…3…2…2…3" or simply "1…2…3…4…5…6…" Your fingers will verify the eighth-note count when you do the snap test.

Others, such as 5/4, 7/8, and other true "odd" meters are harder at first—the usual balance of the bar count is off by a beat. Most people try to count along and find themselves expecting to hear that last eighth note—but it doesn't come—and they fall off the beat. Remember to *only* count the number in the meter. For example, don't try for an eighth beat in 7/8—only count to seven, then jump right back to one. It'll sound like this: "1…2…3…4…5…6…7…1…2…3…4…5…6…7…"

Rhythm 1

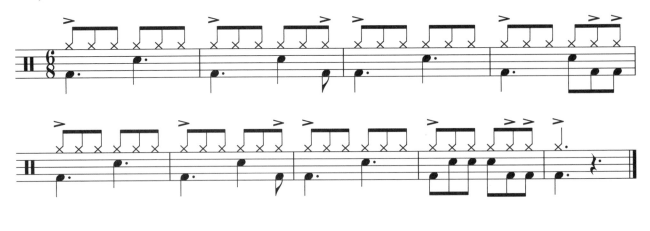

Rhythm 2

Rhythm 3

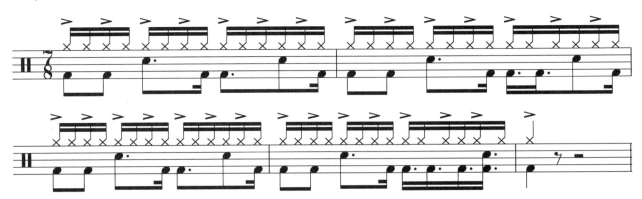

Figure 1.16: A variety of written meters with notated drum performances (kick, snare, hi-hat only) to show common applications of these meters.

Audio Track 17: A variety of drum performances (kick, snare, and hi-hat only) showcasing the meters from Figure 1.16.

Trying to determine the meter of a song by just listening is hard at first. We're very used to counting in fours, so hearing the repeat of the measure in a different number can be confusing. There are some easy-to-apply tricks to this but it will take some practicing. When listening to music that you think is in an odd meter, try these steps. They're not hard-and-fast rules, but they work most of the time.

☛ Find the "1." This is usually a kick drum and defines the downbeat that is the beginning of the measure, or the beginning of a loop.

☛ Find the next "1." It's going to sound just like the first "1" and you'll hear it come around again and again. When you do, you can define the bar as being the time from the first "1" to the next "1."

☛ Count how many beats there are from the first "1" to the next "1." It sounds easy, but you can often count this either too fast or too slow. Try to count at the middle of the pace—don't count to the fastest part (like a sixteenth-note hi-hat) and don't count to the slowest part (like the kick or snare only). You're looking for the "meat" of the beat—the pacing that makes you move. Try to feel it while counting it—it's easy to over-think this part.

☛ The number of beats you count is the top number of your meter. Once you know how many beats there are between the "1"s, you need to determine the lower number, or the value of the beat.

☛ Try the snap test from before—snap along with the meat of the beat. If it's comfortable, it's likely to be quarter notes. If it's too fast for you or you can just barely keep up, it's likely that the bottom number is an eighth note.

Close the book and listen again to Audio Track 17. For each beat, try these steps *without looking at the answers* in Figure 1.16. Did you get them right?

Chops Test

Welcome to your first chops test! The word *chops* in this case is used to measure your skills and acumen using the basic knowledge of rhythm that you've just read. You'll see a chops test at the end of every section of this book to keep you honest.

There's no one looking over your shoulder with these—they're merely benchmarks to see how well you've absorbed the material.

The idea is to test yourself; no multiple choice, no essays, just you looking at your chops and determining if they're up to speed. If you think not, go back and retry the pieces of this chapter again. It's likely you'll find a small nugget of wisdom that will help you put it all together. Once you do, retry this chops test before moving on.

If you nail it, well then, you're ready to move on to the next section.

Basic Chops

By now, you should be able to do the following:

☞ Recognize, by ear, the length of a played note as anywhere from a whole note to a 16th note.

☞ Visually recognize the length value of any *note* from a whole note to a 32nd to a 64th note.

☞ Visually recognize the length value of any *rest* from a whole note to a 64th note.

☞ Clap along with a simple written rhythm. Simple in this case means any written rhythm containing note or rest values no smaller than an eighth note.

☞ Recognize and count or clap along with a few simple meters by ear alone. Simple in this case means 4/4, 3/4, and possibly odd meters of 5/4, 7/4, and so on.

☞ Produce simple rhythms using a DAW (or sequencer of any type) with at least a 1-bar groove. Simple in this case means a rhythm containing note and rest values no smaller than an eighth note.

☞ Determine the proper quantization setting for that rhythm based on listening alone.

☞ Recognize where the "1" is in a set rhythm, assuming a simple meter is being used (see the previous "Time Signatures" subsection for simple meter definitions).

☞ Recognize and count or clap along with both the upbeats and the downbeats.

Advanced Chops

You might also be able to do the following:

☛ Recognize, by ear, the length of a played note as anywhere from a whole note to a 64th note.

☛ Be able to recognize the length value of any *note* from a whole note to a 64th note by listening only.

☛ Be able to recognize the length value of any *rest* from a whole note to a 64th note by listening only.

☛ Be able to clap along (or tap along on a surface) with a written rhythm. This includes rhythms containing up to 16th notes and rests.

☛ Be able to recognize and count or clap along with most meters by snap test or ear alone. These might include 6/4, 6/8, 7/8, 9/8, and so on, or might include complex meters where the meter changes from bar to bar (e.g., where the verses are 7/8 and the choruses are 6/4, etc.).

☛ Be able to produce 4/4 rhythms using a DAW (or sequencer of any type) with at least a 2-bar groove, containing up to 64th notes. Each bar will likely contain enough variety from the other as to make each bar unique to the other.

☛ Be able to determine the proper quantization setting for that rhythm based on listening alone.

☛ Be able to recognize where the "1" is in a set rhythm, no matter what meter is being used.

☛ Be able to produce complex metered rhythms using a DAW (or sequencer of any type) with at least a 4-bar groove, containing up to 64th notes. Each bar will likely contain enough variety from the other as to make each bar unique to the other.

☛ Be able to apply swing and quantization parameters to a rhythm to move the rhythm off the metronomic grid musically.

Section 2
The Major Scale—
Notes and Intervals

Building the Major Scale: The Notes and the Staff

RECAP

Rhythm is the pulse of music—the "groove" that makes us want to move our bodies to the sound. Rhythm is often a collection of instruments that play in sync—albeit in different rhythmic patterns and by using different time divisions. The time divisions of music are a whole note, half note, and quarter note down through a 64th note. Rests are forced silences in a rhythm and take the same time divisions as notes.

Rhythms can be varied to create unique feels by shuffling and swinging the feel to where the pace feels lopsided or uneven—even though written straight. Notes can be accented to provide greater emphasis as well. Rhythms are written in a way where the top number defines the number of beats per bar and the bottom number determines the duration of each beat. The combination is called the meter. 4/4 is called common time while other meters are often referred to as "odd" meters.

Remember that learning music is learning a new language—it comes in levels and you don't learn the whole thing at once! Having worked through the previous section, you should now understand the rhythm of the language—note and rest durations as well as meter basics (4/4 vs. 6/8, etc.)—and have a beginning understanding of how rhythm is performed using drums. Just like in any language, where and how you put the emphasis on your words (or your drums in this case) can change the meaning of the word or sentence.

In other languages we learn the letters, words, and usages before sentence structure, yet with music, we learn rhythmic sentence structure first, so we can learn the letters and words rhythmically. For us, the letters are called notes. The good news is that there are only 12 of them. In even better news, we're only going to start with seven of them: the C major scale, as shown in **Figure 2.1**.

MEMORIZE ME!
Figure 2.1: The notes of the C major scale, seen as letters on the piano and on the staff in the key of C.

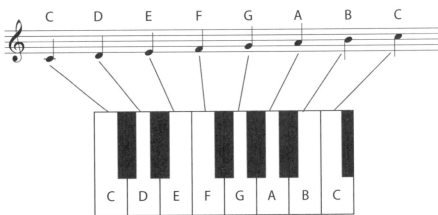

C Major Scale

Coach's Corner: Root Notes and Scale Degrees

This scale will never change in the key of C. Think of the key as the name of the lowest note in the scale, called the *root note*—C in this case. Each other note in the scale is just as important as the root, but it's the root that gives the scale its name. The position of each note on the scale is known as the *scale degree*. That is, C is the first position so it's the first scale degree, or the root note. D is the second so it's known as the second scale degree, and so on. The notes of C major and their scale degrees are as shown in **Figure 2.2**.

Scale Degree
The position of each note on any scale is known as its scale degree.

Figure 2.2: The notes of C major and their respective scale degrees.

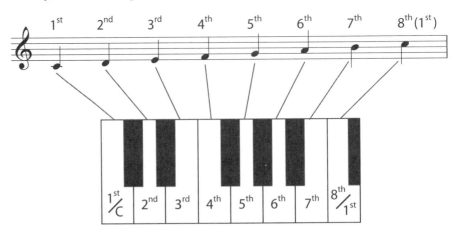

C Major Scale (in degrees)

For a while, we'll be working exclusively with the C major scale. It is the simplest version of the major scale as all of the notes are white keys on the piano and there are no alterations to the notes (as there will be later on). You can hear it on **Audio Track 18**.

MEMORIZE ME!
Audio Track 18: The C major scale played on the piano, up and down.

Coach's Corner: Tricks for Note Memorization

When looking at the staff (notation), there are some good mnemonic devices that people use to help them remember the note names and where they live on the staff. If you look at Figure 2.2 again, you'll notice that there are notes in-between the staff lines and others on the staff lines. There's a handy letter scheme we use to help early students identify each note. Two of the most popular are

FACE, which relates to the notes that live *in-between* the staff lines (F, A, C, E) as you move up the staff.

EGBDF, which relates to the notes that live *on* the staff lines (E, G, B, D, F). People usually remember this one as "Every Good Boy Does Fine." Don't like that one? Make your own!

Note that on Figure 2.2, the first note "C" is actually below this first staff line. When you see a note either below or above the staff line, there's a horizontal line drawn through it to indicate that this note would be ON the line if the staff had six lines (or more). Since we don't do that, the note below the staff with a line through it should be memorized as "C" which is lower in pitch than "E" which is the first note in the "EGBDF" moniker.

It's important to learn the C major scale in a few ways—on the piano, by the note names, scale degrees, and on the written staff. Before the music is written on the staff, a symbol is drawn at the beginning of each line. This symbol is called the treble or G clef, as seen in **Figure 2.3**. This symbol is called the G clef because the little curl at the end touches the G note line. The G clef is for notes that are within singing range (medium low to high). There are other clefs used in music (such as the bass clef which appeared in Figure 1.14) but for now, we will concentrate on the G clef—the one used for piano writing.

Figure 2.3: The symbol of the treble clef, or the G clef.

Take another close look at the piano image in Figure 2.2 (page 28) and find the note C. Now, find it on the piano in front of you. Notice that it has another white key directly to the left (B) and a black key just to the right, just "pushed in" a bit. Now, find the note F on the piano as well—see how it is laid out similarly to C.

You'll likely notice that there are only two places where this is the case—once at C (with B to the left) and once at F (with E to the left). You'll know which of these is C by the number of black keys to the right until the next "no black key in-between" location. At C, there are two black keys, then there's E and F (with no black key in-between them). At F, there are three black keys until B, where again, there's no black key between B and C. Use this clue to find C on the piano every time.

Coach's Corner: Seeing Notes in Color

It's a bit old school, but taking little pieces of tape and applying them to the keys with the note names is a good technique for learning and memorizing the notes and the names of the notes. At your local stationery store, you can buy colored circle-stickers that work really well for this.

One method is to group each collection of notes from C up through B with a single color. Start at the bottom of the piano with a dark color—this indicates that the notes are lower. Move up through the color wheel as you get brighter on the piano, changing colors at each C. So from the first C to the first B, use, say, brown, then at the second C use, say, blue through the second B, and so on. As we work on the piano, feel free to try each exercise in each color, or at least in a few different colors. You'll start to notice how each color group has a sound about it and you'll start to love the sounds in each group differently.

Another technique is to use a different color for each note. Start with the lowest C you can find on the piano, all the way to the left. Color that one, say, yellow. Then, color *each* C on the piano yellow. Move on to the next white key to the right of C, which is D. Use a different color—say, orange—to label D and all Ds. In this method, you'll begin to associate each note with a color and you'll be able to easily find all the "D"s, and so on, by simply finding that color.

Building Intervals

While you're labeling the keys and learning the notes of the piano, notice that the layout combination of notes repeats itself all the way up and down the keyboard (see "Seeing Notes in Color" for details). So if you look in the middle of the keyboard and find the note C, you've found what we call *middle C*. Crazy name, I know. If you go down one "level" to the C below it, you'll find that the sound is exactly the same, only lower by a "level." The same holds true up and down the piano. This relationship, where the note is the same only at higher and lower levels is called an *octave*.

> **Octave**
> Often called the "miracle of music," the octave is a note of the same name as another note but played at a higher (or lower) pitch. The musical sound is simply a higher or lower "copy" of the original note.

The major scale is the foundation of the vast majority of all music but its real power isn't in the notes, it's in the spaces *between* the notes. These spaces are called *intervals* and are the foundation of great melodies. You now know one interval—the octave. Well, for every note in the C major scale, there's a relationship between it and each other note in the scale and where there's a relationship, there's an interval.

> **Intervals**
> A musical interval is the distance between any two notes.

Coach's Corner: The More Things Change...

The distance between notes (the interval) is the foundation of one of the most important facets of music: *melody*. Great melodies stay with us forever but they're really just a series of notes—played at certain intervals apart—that are strung together in beautiful ways. When dealing with intervals and the major scale, it's important to note that the *interval* is the most important piece of the relationship—not the notes. If you were to play the same interval using different notes, the melody would be the same although the notes have changed.

In fact, at Pyramind, we always say that the notes will *always* change but the intervals *never* change. In other words, if two notes are a certain distance from each other, the sound of that distance will always be the same no matter what two notes you use to create the interval. Ask any singer who's had trouble reaching a high note—they'll turn around and ask to play the song in a lower key but they'll sing the exact same intervallic relationship. The key will have changed, but the melody remains.

Let's take a close look at the piano to dig deeper into the concept of intervals. As you can see from the staff lines in **Figure 2.4**, the first note in our major scale "alphabet" is C. The next note up is D, and the interval from C to D is called a whole step. From D to the next note E is another whole step. Note that this is not immediately evident on the staff but it is evident on the piano and that each of these steps has a black key in-between them. If you were to play from C to the black key in-between, it would be called a half step so if you skip the half step (or take two half-steps) you make a whole step.

You can hear this on **Audio Track 19**. Track 19 plays a whole step from C to D. Then you'll hear a half step from C to the note between C and D, then another half step up again to D. For now, let's call the note in-between C and D "C-and-a-half." It'll get a real name later.

C Major Scale (with whole/half step intervals)

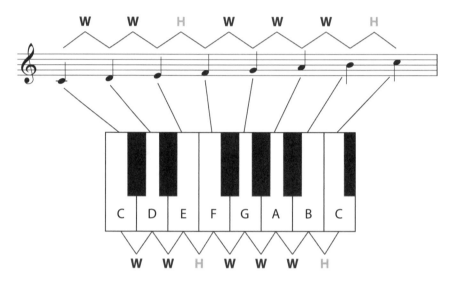

Audio Track 19: The note C, then D played straight, then with the note "C-and-a-half" in-between.

Listen for the quality of the whole step and the interval (distance) of a whole step. Right afterwards, you'll hear the note C played, then the black key in-between (C-and-a-half). Lastly, C-and-a-half then another half up to D, showing the other half step that makes the whole step from C to D. Note that not all half-step intervals require a black key. If we look at E and F, we'll notice that there's no black key between them. However, moving from E up to F is indeed only a half-step.

The black keys only notify us that a half step from a white key to a black key will get the name addition "and-a-half" to the note name. For example, C and D have a half step between the—temporarily called "C-and-a-half." However, E and F have no black key between them. We simply accept (for now) that there's no such thing as "E-and-a-half." We accept that E moves a half step up to F. The same holds true between B and C.

Half Step
The smallest melodic increment of Western music, the half step commonly refers to the distance between one note and the note directly up or down the piano from it.

Coach's Corner: Seeing Whole and Half Steps

It's much easier to see the whole and half steps on the piano as the black keys show up very clearly, but notice that when written on staff paper, there is almost no indication of two notes being a whole or half step apart. Sorry, you just have to memorize which notes are a whole step apart and which are half steps apart. After hearing it over and over enough times, your ear will be trained to recognize a half step from a whole step at any position on the piano… if you work at it, that is.

MEMORIZE ME!

C to D (whole step)
D to E (whole step)
E to F (half step)
F to G (whole step)
G to A (whole step)
A to B (whole step)
B to C (half step)

As you can see in Memorize Me! example, the C major scale and the intervals between the notes make a pattern.

In short form, we'd call it "whole, whole, half, whole, whole, whole, half," or "WWHWWWH." Try it in a rhythm—it's easy to remember! Check out **Audio Track 20** to hear it and commit it to memory. It's silly to hear it this way, but once you put the sound of the intervallic pattern in your ears, you'll never forget it!

 **Audio Track 20:** WWHWWWH spoken verbally with a quarter-note metronome.

Coach's Corner: The Need for Memorization

Regardless of how you memorize the major scale, you *need* to memorize the major scale and all of its intervals. All music can and will be built off of it. We joke at Pyramind about tattooing the major scale and WWHWWWH on the inside of one of your eyelids (or across your knuckles) so you always have a cheat— please don't try this at home—we are really just joking. Unless you're into that sort of thing…

Coach's Corner: The Sound of Solfège

You might recognize the major scale by ear if you play it on the piano. It's the foundation of a technique called solfège, which includes the standard: *do, re, mi, fa, sol, la, ti, do.* In this case, the notes of the major scale correlate to the names in solfège. Figure CC2.1 shows the major scale in intervals with the added row comparing the intervals and notes (key of C) to the names in solfège.

You can hear the major scale sung in solfège on **Audio Track 21**. If you want a bit of history and you're stuck babysitting the neighbors' 4-year-old (ugh!), watch The Sound of Music. Solfège plays a big part in the movie's soundtrack. Plus, it'll be sure to put the youngster to sleep! And maybe you too…

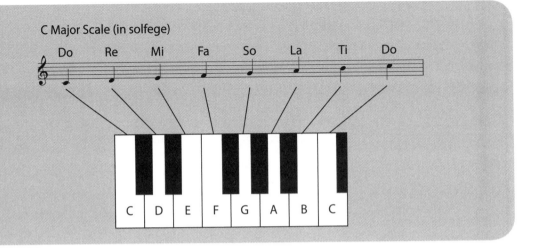

Figure CC2.1: The notes of the major scale (key of C) along with the intervals and the names of solfège.

Audio Track 21: C major scale sung in solfège.

We stated earlier that the intervals between the notes never change and that the intervals are the foundation of great melodies. So far, we've only seen the C major scale as written in terms of whole or half steps from one note to the next. But what are the intervals between *all* of the notes? Is there an interval larger than a whole step? Smaller than a half step?

The short answers are yes and no. While there are intervals larger than a whole step, the half step is the smallest interval we have in Western music. Unlike note durations, there's no 1/8th step or 1/4th step (however, in many forms of other cultural music, there are as many as 21 steps between notes!). The major scale has seven notes in it, eight if you include the octave C above the first note. **Figure 2.5** shows the piano and staff notation of the C major scale in intervals from C to each other note on the scale. Notice that each interval is marked with either an "M" for major or a "P" for perfect. Each two note interval from the root to the second note is defined according to figure 2.5 as either major or perfect. There will be other names later as we dig deeper.

MEMORIZE ME!

Figure 2.5abc: The piano and staff notation of the C major scale in intervals from C to each other note on the scale as well as a chart of the note name, the interval name, and the number of half steps. Note the empty columns on 2.5c; we'll fill those in soon…a

A.

C Major Scale (ascending with intervals)

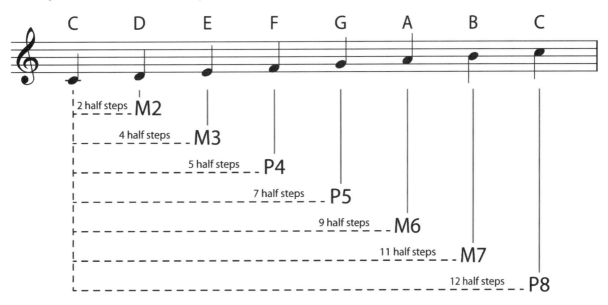

B.

C Major Scale (with intervals)

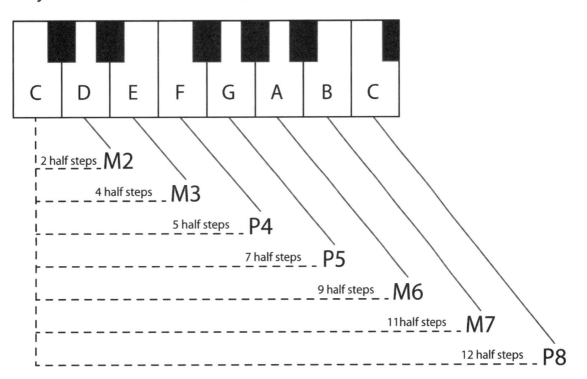

C.

C Major Interverals

	Intervals	Emotion (Melodic)	Emotion (Harmonic)
C	Unison 0 half steps		
D	M2 2 half steps		
E	M3 4 half steps		
F	P4 5 half steps		
G	P5 7 half steps		
A	M6 9 half steps		
B	M7 11 half steps		
C	P8 12 half steps		

Coach's Corner: The Happy Scale

Notice that the intervals in the major scale either have the name *major* (M) or *perfect* (P). Yes, the major scale is pretty damned happy and, as such, is probably deserving of such shiny happy names as major and perfect. It's not that it is better than the other scales, it's just always happy—like a Disney after-school special on TV. Later on, we'll dig into the dark side but until then, it's all Jedi, no Vader.

Every interval has an emotion attached to it, that is, it elicits a certain emotional response from us. Although each of us will have slightly different responses to each interval, many of us will have similar responses to each interval. Knowing this emotional relationship of intervals is a key ingredient in creating great melodies!

If we look at each interval of the major scale, just the two notes being looked at are likely to be a melody you might already know. Listen to **Audio Track 22** and try to identify a song that you know that has each interval in it. On the track, you'll hear each interval played in order from C to C, C to D, then C to E, and so on.

We've listed a few songs in **Figure 2.6** as well as highlighting the section of the melody that has this particular interval in it. Try to study the sound of these melodies and how they show the interval in question. The next section will dig deeper into this important concept—using intervals to create melodies.

Audio Track 22: The intervals of the major scale played as half notes.

Figure 2.6: A list of songs that contain each interval as a defining piece of the melody.

Ascending Melodic Intervals

Intervals	Songs
M2 2 half steps	Row, Row, Row Your Boat (Row, row, ***row your*** boat) Maria and the Children (***Do, a*** deer, a female deer)
M3 4 half steps	When the Saints Go Marching In (***Oh when*** the saints) Kumbaya (***Kum-ba-***ya)
P4 5 half steps	Here Comes the Bride (***Here comes*** the bride) Amazing Grace (***A-maz-***i-ng grace)
P5 7 half steps	Twinkle, Twinkle Little Star (Twin-***kle, twin-***kle little star) Star Wars (John Williams: Dum-dum-dum (intro notes then...) **Daa - Daa**)
M6 9 half steps	NBC Jingle (***N-B-***C) Jingle Bells (***Da-shing*** through the snow)
M7 11 half steps	Immigrant Song (Led Zepplin: The first to the third note of the first vocal line) Take on Me (A-Ha: ***Take on*** me, Take me on)
P8 12 half steps	Over the Rainbow (The Wizard of Oz: ***Some-where***) A Christmas Song (***Chest-nuts***)

WORKSHEET 2.1: Attaching Emotion to Intervals, #1

An exercise we often do with students has to do with absorbing the sound of every interval and assigning it a feeling. The feeling you assign can be anything you feel—there's no right or wrong answer, only the *first* thought that comes to mind. This exercise helps do two things at once: memorize the sound of an interval and begin to develop a language of internal emotion.

Here's how it goes:

☛ Play the series of intervals as listed earlier in Figure 2.5 and heard on Audio Track 22. Note that Audio Track 22 plays the intervals melodically. That is, one note at a time. Fill in the blanks yourself for the column labeled "melodic" by playing the two notes together.

☛ Write down the *first* feeling that comes to mind. Give yourself only five seconds to write an answer down. Any longer and you're thinking, rather than *feeling*. Have your answer written down *before* you hear the next interval on the CD. There's not a lot of time here so work fast. The faster the better as the answer will be more in line with your gut reaction. If the CD is too fast, use your piano and play it for yourself. Be sure to set a timer for :10 so you don't pontificate forever.

☛ *Do not filter*. This is very important. Filtering in this case means *not* writing down the *first* feeling that comes to mind because it sounds silly. This is absolutely against the point. The point is to be in touch with the feelings that certain sounds create within you instinctively so that you can call on them trying to create those feelings in others. There is no wrong answer—except the one that you choose *instead* of the first one!

Use the chart in Figure 2.5c to fill in the blanks with your own terms, or create your own and keep it posted near your piano somewhere. Remember—do not filter. Write down the *first* word that comes to mind—happy, sad, chocolate, laundry, funk-delio-shus… whatever. The associations you make now will stay with you *and* will help train your ear to hearing the interval successfully each time.

When the intervals we hear are played note-to-note we call them melodic intervals and when they are played together as a single note, we call them harmonic intervals. The underlying principle here is that melody (melodic) is a string of notes one-at-a-time while harmony (harmonic) is a duo (or more) of notes played at once. Go back and play the two notes together now (harmonic) and fill in the blanks. You might want to give yourself some time so your melodic responses don't color your harmonic ones.

Coach's Corner: Notes and Emotional Responses

Knowing the emotional relationship between notes can help you create great melodies. Looking for the sound of something regal or heroic? Try a perfect fifth. Looking for something not quite right or sickly sappy sweet? Try the major seventh. After going through this exercise, you'll have your own set of "rules" regarding intervals to use when writing music. You can use the same rules to support the emotion your looking for. Feel free to add to this chart as your experience grows—it's likely that your interpretation of the intervals now will be different over time.

WORKSHEET 2.2: Piano Technique Introduction, Intervals

The best way to put music theory into practice is to use and learn the piano or keyboard. Once you have decoded the mystery of the white and black keys and some basic theory, you'll be able to find notes, intervals, and scales with ease. This will make your songwriting and production process more fun *and* faster! The piano is one of the first instruments people learn and for good reason—our software and hardware tools are often modeled off the piano keys and DAW software instruments primarily listen to MIDI as input trigger information (which tend to come from a piano keyboard). After all, the piano *is* called the "mother of all instruments" for a reason.

To understand finger placement and patterning of notes and scales, we assign numbers to our fingers. Thumbs are always "1" and fan out to the pinky or fifth finger ("5") as described in **Figure 2.7**.

Figure 2.7: Finger number diagram for the piano.

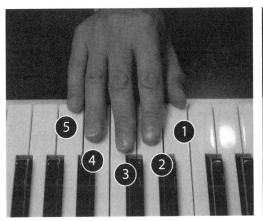 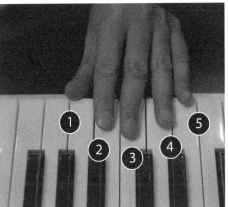

You should try to sit at the piano with good posture—present and upright. Try to find a good seat, bench, or chair for your keyboard or piano. Also adjust the height of the stand if you are using a keyboard so the hand and wrist are level.

The shape that your hand makes is the shape your hand will take when placed on the keyboard. Try not to be too rounded that the finger tips are curved in—you want the pad of the fingers to be comfortably placed on the keys while the hand maintains this round shape, as seen in **Figure 2.8**. Hold an orange or a baseball or softball (depending on the size of your hand) or any similar round object to help condition your hand to the curved position of piano playing.

Figure 2.8: Detail of the curvature of the hand with multiple views, preparing for the piano.

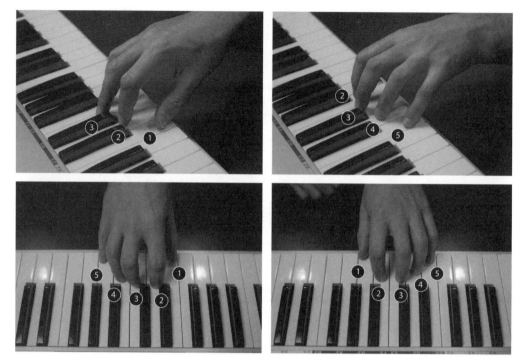

Try to keep your wrists, shoulders, and elbows relaxed. If the wrist, shoulder, or elbow is too tight, you will become tired faster and more prone to tendonitis—that's bad. Take breaks and keep checking in with your body as you practice. Shake out your hands and wrists to loosen the muscles that you are building by working on these exercises. If you're doing it right, it'll hurt a bit at first but your hand will get stronger with time and you'll be able to play for longer and longer stretches of time—just like any workout.

A good way to begin your workout is by warming up. As a starting point, find all the As, then Bs, then Cs, and so on, up and down the octaves while playing them with different fingers. Start with the left hand pinky and move through the fingers to your thumb. Repeat with the right hand, beginning with the thumb. For example, for the left hand (LH), start with the pinky on the lowest C, then use the ring finger for the next highest C, then middle on the next one and so on. Go up five octaves, then go back down backward, ending on the low C with the pinky. Do the same for the right hand (RH), starting with the thumb and ending with the pinky five octaves higher, then come back down the same way.

Once that's done, we can begin our full warm-up and practice routine by playing the C major scale in a single octave range. First, play the "space" notes in the treble clef (FACE) then play all the "line" notes in the treble clef (EGBDF). Make sure you know where middle C is!

Next, position your hand over the keys, where the thumb is starting with middle C, as seen in **Figure 2.9**. Practice playing the first five notes *only* (from C to G), ascending and descending a few times with each hand. Be sure to use the *next* finger to play the next note. IE, on the RH, start with the thumb on C, then the pointer on D, middle on E, and so on. For the LH, start with C on the pinky, then D with the ring finger, E with the middle, and so on.

To make it interesting, I usually suggest that you fire up your DAW (if you have one) and loop a simple beat at a modest tempo. A good starting place is 60 bpm—one key per second. As you get better, practice faster and faster but *always* keep the beat. You can call it quits on this exercise (or speed up the tempo) when you can play it perfectly three times in a row.

Figure 2.9: Proper finger position over middle C, leading with the thumb.

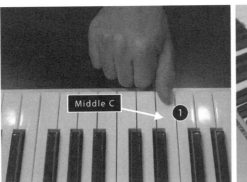 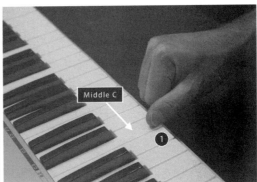

DVD Callout: Music Theory and Piano: 5-Finger Technique

Work these keys first with the left and right hands separately and then with the two hands together. Focus on proper hand position, posture, and evenness of tone and strength. That means, try not to slam the note with your thumb if the pinky can't play it as loud. Repeat three times in each hand before trying together.

You may notice one hand is stronger than the other. Work more on the weaker hand—instead of three times, try doubling up to six times before moving on. This is likely to be your left hand if you're a righty and vice versa. Keep in mind that the left hand leads with the pinky while the right hand leads with the thumb. Doing this 5-note practice will help train your brain to work different fingers on different hands while keeping the rhythm constant—a great technique to develop for the future.

Once you have the technique of the first five notes (C, D, E, F, G), let's work on extending this the rest of the way to a complete octave—from C to C. Since there are only five fingers on each hand, there's going to have to be a time at which you move your hand up the keyboard and you'll need to cross your fingers over too. Each hand has a different place where it makes sense to switch over and you'll see it in the pattern shown below and in **Figure 2.10**.

☞ **Right hand (RH):** CDEFGABC 123-12345

☞ **Left hand (LH):** CDEFGABC 54321-321

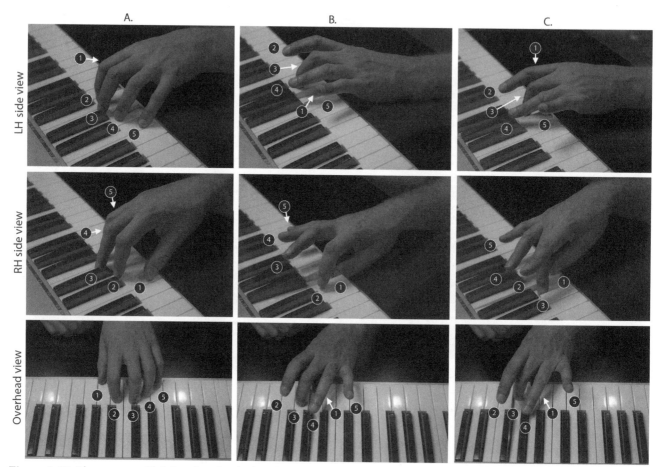

Figure 2.10: The pattern of left-hand and right-hand techniques for crossing fingers: a) base; b) cross over; and c) landing position. Note the numeric assignment to each finger.

DVD Callout: Music Theory and Piano: Full C Major Scale

Just as before, try playing to a rhythm or a metronome to develop some feel in your fingers while you're also developing your speed and accuracy. Feel free to use either the rhythms from Section 1 or a favorite from your library of loops. Whatever it is, it should be simple enough to avoid confusion with the exercise and fast enough to play along and feel like "real" music.

What's important more than anything else is to *keep practicing*! We suggest as much time as possible, but at minimum, do an hour per night. You'll be *amazed* at how fast you'll progress this way!

Coach's Corner: Staying with It

We see lots of students fall off the practice schedule early. Keep in mind that this is hard—you're learning a new language *and* developing new muscles and at first, they're going to hurt. Like going to the gym for the first time in a while, the first few visits are hard, and it's easy to stop going. For those that stick it out, though, await all the spoils. It's the same with the piano. Stick with it and you'll get "in shape" fast, which will increase your musical confidence, give you more enjoyment and will make your productions better—faster.

Once you're comfortable running up and down the octave with the C major scale, you can start practicing playing and hearing intervals. One of the simplest exercises is to play the intervals sequentially, from C up to the octave C. In this exercise, simply "lock" the position of your RH with the thumb over C. With each subsequent finger, play the next interval.

Play C, then D with your index finger (#2). Move up through the scale, from C to E with finger 3, C to F with finger 4, and C to G with finger 5. Once you go to play C then A, you can "jump" to it with the pinky. Be sure to end with the octave C played with the pinky. You can add to this exercise by moving up through the scale by playing from C to D, then from D up to the next C. Next, play C to E, then E up to the next C and so on until you hit all the intervals.

DVD Callout: Music Theory and Piano: Dyads

It is vital that you get this basic foundation down well before going too much further. Mind you, you don't have to be a genius nor Mozart at this stage. Just successfully playing the C major scale up and down a few times well along with a metronome is plenty.

Interval Inversions

Sometimes, melodies play in linear fashion—from one note to the next on the scale to the next, and so on, but other times, you'll jump around the scale playing any old note before and after any other old note. In playing the interval exercise, you may start to hear how melodies can be created with larger jumps in notes. That's when you know you're getting good with the C major scale!

You might also have noticed that as you played your exercises from C up to the next C octave through the intervals, the intervals from C to the next note didn't really sound the same as the intervals from the second note up to the next C octave. For example, the sound from C to D is different than from D to the octave C. In fact, if we take a close look at these two intervals, we find ourselves in unfamiliar territory.

Take a look at **Figure 2.11**. Shown here in the piano and the staff, you can see that the first interval, from C to E is a major third (noted with a capital "M"), or two whole steps. You should remember this from Figure 2.4. However, from E up to the octave of C, is four steps, or eight half-steps. From our work earlier with the major scale, you should know that there is no interval in the major scale that actually has eight half-steps. That should tell you that this interval is not a major (or perfect, for that matter) interval. In this case, the interval is called "minor" and is denoted by a lowercase "m". More on minors later…

Figure 2.11: Intervallic relationship between C and E then E up to the next C. Note that the "M" denotes a Major interval whereas the "m" (lower case) denotes a minor interval. These will be explained in more detail later in the book.

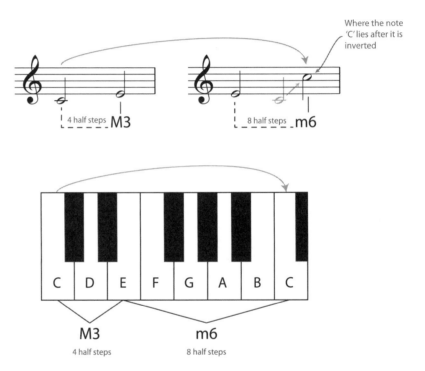

What we're discussing is known as an intervallic inversion, or the "opposite" of the distance between two notes—C to E, and then E to the octave C in this case. It's the opposite, because it goes "up" to the octave above, not back down to the root. For example, the interval C to E is one interval, but its inversion is from E *up* to the octave C—its opposite, or inversion.

Intervallic inversions
The inversion of any interval is the remaining distance between the second note of an existing interval and the next octave *up* of the first note.

In the above example, the interval is a major third—from C up to E (two whole steps). The inversion, or opposite, is from E up to the next C. From E up to C is four whole steps, or eight half-steps.

There is no interval on the major scale with four whole steps. *However,* there is an interval with four whole then a half step and another with three whole and a half step, so our 4-step interval must live right in-between. This in-between interval must be some sort of fifth "plus" or sixth "minus." For now, let's call it a *sixth minus.* That is, it's one half-step below the major sixth.

Let's take a moment to discuss the naming of the inversions as we're about to be introduced to some new terms.

There are five main terms that we use in music to describe intervals—major, perfect (we've seen both already in the major scale), minor, diminished, and augmented. There are some funny rules around these names so let's just define them so you can memorize them (see Memorize Me! on the left). Yes, there is more memorization. Sorry.

Notice that only the second, third, sixth, and seventh can be either major or minor, while only the fourth can be augmented and the fifth can be diminished. Each of these qualities are opposites—major and minor can be thought of as "happy" versus "sad" as can perfect (happy) and diminished/augmented (sad). You can think of the minor as the opposite of the major and the augmented/diminished as alternatives to the perfect fourth and perfect fifth of the scale. Note, however, that if you tried to augment the fifth, you'd have a minor sixth and if you tried to diminish the fourth, you'd have a major third, so we just don't try. For now.

When written as abbreviations, you'll often see the interval of a major written with a capital M and the minor written as the lower case m, or with a minus sign (−). This is shown in **Figure 2.12** where a few intervals are written in letter-form as either major (M) or minor (m). But, what about the perfects? What's the inversion of something perfect? Something flawed? Broken? No—they're perfect! The perfect fifth is the inversion of the perfect fourth and vice versa.

The inversions of intervals always have a few interesting characteristics.

☞ The *Rule of 9*. Every interval on the major scale and its inversion *must* add to the number 9. For example, the major second and its inversion—the minor seventh—add to 9 (2 + 7 = 9).

☞ The perfect fourth and its inversion the perfect fifth also add to 9 (4 + 5 = 9), and so on. Notice that each perfect interval is still perfect in its inverted form. Maybe that's why it's perfect…

- The quality of the inversions usually flip—if the first is major, then the second is minor. This is an example of music behaving like a mirror—the "image in the mirror" of one interval is the exact opposite (major becomes minor in the interval, etc.). We'll see this mirror-like behavior a few times throughout the book.

- The inversion of the diminished is the augmented and vice versa. Consider the diminished fifth. Its inversion is the augmented fourth. Notice that they are exactly the same as each other on the piano, but by calling one the diminished fifth and the other the augmented fourth, we keep the Rule of 9 intact.

C Major Scale (descending with intervals and their inversions)

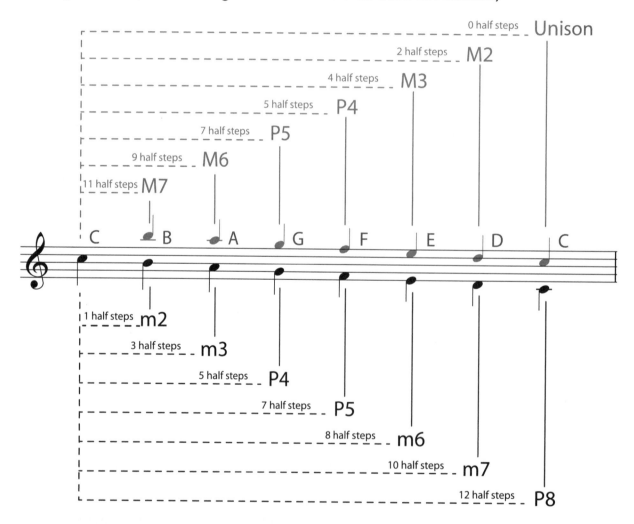

Figure 2.12: The intervals and inversions of the C major scale written in letter form as either major (M) or minor (m and/or −) or perfect (P).

Coach's Corner: Memorize, Just Memorize—For Now

There are a lot of funny rules in music regarding names of notes and chords (called *nomenclature*). We'll discuss them in more depth as we progress through the book, especially when we get to *enharmonic equivalents*. For now, just memorize the rules as they are given to you—it'll take way too long to dig into side-explanations at this stage. Just like learning English, there are lots of funny rules that change all the time, like—"i before e, except after c" except when it's "neither," "weird," "height," and so on…

WORSHEET 2.3: Melodic Intervals and Inversions

Let's finish off our work on the major scale and its intervals with some piano work on the intervals and their inversions.

This one is pretty simple and will help get you comfortable with the concept of intervallic inversions in the C major scale. Also, it'll help you hear the other intervals *not* naturally found in the C major scale—the inversions.

☛ First, warm up by doing your standard C major scale exercises.

☛ Begin your interval exercise by playing C to D, then D up to C octave. Do this to a metronome at first, where you play C with the first beat, D with the second, D again with the third, and the octave with the fourth.

☛ Move to the next interval, C to E and play it the same way—using all four beats of the metronome.

☛ Continue this through the scale, up and down—three times until you're done.

☛ Run up the scale *and* use your intervals. With C to D, then D to C, nothing changes. For C to E, play C-D-E, then E to C (octave) and back down. This helps tie scale work to interval work and starts the process of melodic work.

☛ Do this where each note is either two beats long, or in half notes. If you're playing it in half notes, play C to D over two beats, D to E over another two, E to C octave in another two beats, and finally, C down to C below. Run this up and down three times perfectly with each hand, then both hands together before stopping. Shorten the note-length as you get better from half notes to quarters, then to eighths as you get really fast.

☛ As another advanced alternative to this, try moving up the scale in the LH and down the scale in the RH—and vice versa.

You can see and hear these exercises on **Figure 2.13** and on **Audio Track 23**.

WorkSheet: Melodic Intervals and Inversions

Advanced

Figure 2.13: Staff notation of the interval piano exercises.

Audio Track 23: A piano playing all the versions of the exercise listed for intervals and inversions. The first stanza is played three times—at 80 bpm, 100 bpm, and at 120 bpm—for you to practice along with. The second and third stanzas do the same.

Harmonic Intervals (Dyads)

When working with the major scale, the first way we use it is with melodic intervals, or in scale form. We do this by practicing the scale in sequence and by mixing it up too, as you've seen with intervallic inversions. There are times when we might want a more complex sound than just one note at a time. After all, you can't write a sentence with only one-letter words!

When we play two notes together, we call it a dyad, also known as a harmonic interval.

> **Dyad**
> Two notes played together.

With seven notes to choose from in the C major scale, it's easy to see that the range of creative expression gets larger as you add notes together. Let's take a look at some of the dyads possible using the notes of the C major scale.

The first dyad, C and C (the *same* C, *not* the octave) is known as the unison—two of the same note played at once. This is physically impossible on the piano (at least in standard tuning) but on guitar and other instruments, it's very common. Note that each of the other dyads shown in **Figure 2.14** takes the same name as the interval that makes it. For example, the second dyad, C-D, is a major second harmonic interval dyad, the same as the interval C to D when played as a melodic interval (also a major second).

C Major Dyads (harmonic intervals)

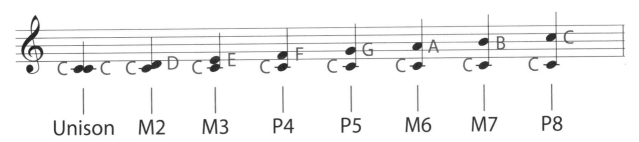

Figure 2.14: A collection of dyads in the C major scale from C to each step in the scale, shown in letter, piano, and staff form.

Figure 2.14 only shows the dyads with the lower note being the root—C in this case. Most of the time, we think of dyads as only being from the root note to the next note, but in fact, you can create dyads with any two notes of the major scale. That is, the note C doesn't even have to be involved at all! Take a look at

Figure 2.15. You'll see a collection of C major dyads that are all of similar intervals.

Similar Intervals

Figure 2.15: A series of dyads in C major where each collection of dyads are the same intervals as each other (major second, major third, etc.).

Major 2nd

Major 3rd

Perfect 4th

Perfect 5th

Major 6th

Notice that there are a few of these dyads that are major second dyads but only one where the two notes are C-D. This is further example of the interval being consistent while the notes are changing. The different major second intervals (the one's that aren't C-D) do make the sound of that interval higher or lower in comparison to C-D but the major second quality stays the same for all of them.

Just as with note inversions, dyads can be inverted too. In the case of the dyad C-D, the interval is still a major second so the inversion is still a minor seventh, D to octave-C in this case. The same rules apply here too, including the Rule of 9 and the "mirror effect," where the first dyad interval is major but the inversion is minor, and so on, as shown in **Figure 2.16**.

Figure 2.16: A chart of the dyads and their inversions in the key of C

Intervals and their Inversions

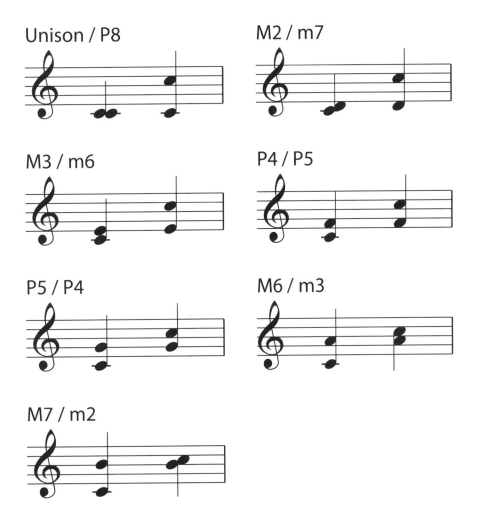

WORKSHEET 2.4: Attaching Emotion to Intervals, #2

Remember earlier on Figure 2.5c where you wrote down the emotion that was attached to the melodic interval? When we did the test earlier, we first heard one note, then the next, creating the interval. Now, we'll do the same test only we'll play the dyad—two notes together. Write down your answers again with *fresh ears*! That means, try not to think about the answers you already have—try to listen to these dyads freshly and write the *first* thought that comes to mind. Remember, if you have to take more than five or ten seconds, you're thinking and not feeling. Use **Audio Track 24** as your dyad guide.

Audio Track 24: A collection of harmonic dyads played through C major that match the emotional chart intervals on Figure 2.5. Use the right half of Figure 2.5 in this case to fill in the harmonic dyads (two notes played together). Compare this to the answers you put on the left column of Figure 2.5. Are they the same or similar? Or do you experience the dyad interval (harmonic) differently than the note-to-note (melodic) interval? When the interval stays the same but the notes move, do you have a different feeling? If so, how different? My guess is that the harmonic interval feels the same—or at least similar to—the melodic intervals.

Here are a few techniques for practicing the dyads in the C major scale.

☛   As a warm-up, play the C major scale with the RH and then with the LH separately ascending and descending. To get really loose, play it up and down two octaves.

☛   Now, play the C major scale up and down in dyads using the third interval only. Use fingers 5 and 3 in the LH and fingers 1 and 3 in the RH. This means that you first play C-E using thumb and middle finger, then D-F, E-G, and so on, using the same two fingers.

☛   As an advanced alternative to this, use the alternating finger technique. In the LH, play the first dyad (C-E) with fingers 5 and 3, then move up to the next dyad (D-F) using fingers 4 and 2. Continue this until you run out of fingers, then slide your hand upward starting over with finger 5. In the RH, play the first dyad (C-E) with fingers 1 and 3, then move up to the next dyad (D-F) using fingers 2 and 4. Continue this until you run out of fingers, then slide your hand upward starting over with finger 1.

☛   Be sure to focus on a solid, rounded hand position with both hands. Working on controlling the thumb and pinky will help you develop a solid piano hand shape and technique.

Chops Test—Piano Technique Introduction

OK, now it's time to test yourself. Do not attempt this part of the book until you've been practicing for a week or so. Give yourself ample time to get going with the C major scale and get some confidence before attempting this.

This Chops Test is really there to see how far you progress on your own with your practicing. We leave it to you to figure out these exercises—it wouldn't be a good test if we gave you all of the answers. Once you think you're comfortable with the C major scale, take the test. If there's a bunch you can't do, go practice that stuff for another week, then try again.

Everything in the following Chops is useful and will prepare you for later sections.

Let's see what you can do…

Basic Chops

By now, you should be able to do the following:

☛ Identify all the As, Bs, Cs, and so on, across the piano.

☛ Identify all the notes of the C major scale at any octave on the keyboard.

☛ Play only the notes *on* the staff lines, by sight-reading. Have a friend test you here by writing random notes on the staff lines for a few bars and see if you get them right. If no one's around to help, do a few on your own then shuffle the pages to keep it fresh.

☛ Play only the notes *in-between* the staff lines (the spaces between the staff lines) by sight-reading. Use a similar test here too.

☛ Play the first five notes *properly* from C to G, leading with the thumb on the RH and the pinky on the LH.

☛ Play the C major scale through to the octave *properly* paying attention to the crossing over points (one hand at a time up and down).

☛ Play the C major scale in intervals from C to the octave C each hand, one at a time.

☛ Identify each of the intervals and their inversions in both hands up and down the octave.

☛ Be able to play various dyads (melodically and harmonically) with C as the root. Have a friend test you by calling out random intervals from C and then play the interval. Verify your work and reference Worksheet 2.1 to see if your description of the intervals still holds true.

Advanced Chops

By now you *may* be able to do the following:

☞ Play a C major scale with your hands together (one octave).

☞ Play a C major scale with your hands together (two or more octaves). Spend more time on mastering this—with your hands separately before trying together.

☞ Play a C major scale for one or two octaves in contrary motion (LH up and RH down)—notice that the crossover fingers are the same here, but the hands are moving in opposite directions on the keyboard, making this a challenging exercise.

☞ Play the scale—with your hands separately or hands together—with the hip-hop, rock, or house beat from the previous section. Start by playing each note of the scale as a half note and then increase the value, every quarter note, eighth, and then sixteenth note.

☞ Play intervals from C to the octave C in two hands, up two octaves.

☞ Play the intervals and their inversions throughout the C major scale in both hands together and opposite.

☞ Be able to play various dyads (melodically or harmonically) with any note of the C major scale as the root. Have a friend test you by calling out random intervals *and* the starting note and then play the interval. For example, if your friend calls "D perfect fifth," you will find D then find the perfect fifth interval above it. Verify your work and reference Worksheet 2.1 and Worksheet 2.4 to see if your description of the intervals still holds true. These both also refer to image 2.5c.

Section 3
The Major Scale— Triads

Introduction to Triads

RECAP

The major scale is the most important scale in music as it is the foundation of all harmony and melody. It is built out of a collection of whole-step and half-step intervals and it's the relationship between the notes (the intervals) that makes it so important. The pattern of these intervals is WWHWWWH. The root note relationship to each other note in the major scale is called either major or perfect. The opposite, or inversion, of that interval is either called minor, augmented (fourth), or diminished (fifth).

The distance between the notes of the scale are called intervals and their opposites are called inversions. When two notes are played together, it's called a dyad or harmonic interval, and like notes, dyads have inversions too. The same rule of note inversions applies to dyad inversions—the Rule of 9 and the "mirror effect" of the opposite quality (major to minor, etc.).

At this point, we should know the C major scale fairly well. We'll move onto other keys in a later section, but for now, we're going to stay in C. We've already seen two relationships: note-to-note intervals (melodic intervals) and two-notes-at-a-time, or dyads (harmonic intervals). What happens if we add a third note?

Before we do, let's start imposing a few rules. We'll break them soon enough…

When adding a third note to a dyad, we call the resulting three-note group a *triad* (creative, I know). Each note in a triad should be a third away from the note before it. Keep in mind that you can't just throw any three notes together and call it a triad. More likely, a random combination of three notes might be thought of as a "chord cluster" but not necessarily a proper triad. There are rules to creating triads and, of course, there are exceptions to these rules.

There are five main types or qualities of triads—four out of five names should be familiar to you at this time. They are the same names as the intervals and their inversions, with a new one added for good measure: major, minor, diminished, augmented, and suspended (the new guy). We don't have perfect triads in case you were wondering…

Coach's Corner: You're Suspended!

Technically, the suspended is not a triad but is rather something of an in-between chord. It's neither happy nor sad—just suspended waiting to go somewhere. For now, let's just call it a triad and we'll discuss its uniqueness later.

The Major Triad

The major triad is recognized for its obvious "happy" sound. Here are some of the characteristics that tell you a triad is major:

☞ The major triad is built using the first, third, and fifth scale degree of the major scale from any given root note. That means that in the key of C, a C major chord is built using C-E-G as the primary notes, shown as a collection of thirds in **Figure 3.1** and heard on **Audio Track 25.** The first interval in the triad—C-E—is a major third (two steps). This first interval usually determines the name and quality of the triad.

☞ The second interval in the triad—E-G—is a minor third (one-and-a-half steps). Even though this interval is minor, the triad is considered major as the first interval is major.

☞ The first and last note of a triad are a perfect fifth apart.

Figure 3.1: The C major triad as seen on the staff, along with intervallic relationships.

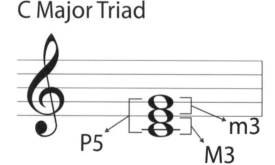

Audio Track 25: The C major triad played twice on the piano.

The Minor Triad

The minor triad is recognized by its obvious "sad" or "serious" sound.

☛ The minor triad is built using the first, third and fifth scale degree of the major scale *but the third is flattened a half step from the major triad*. More on this later, but when we lower a note by a half step from its original form, we call it *flat (written with a symbol that looks like a lower-case "b")*. That means that in the key of C, a C minor chord is built using C-E♭-G as the primary notes. The middle note, E♭, would be the same as "E-minus-a-half." You can see it in **Figure 3.2** and hear it on **Audio Track 26**.

☛ The first interval in the triad—C-E♭—is a minor third (three half-steps). This first interval usually determines the name and quality of the triad.

☛ The second interval in the triad—E♭-G—is a major third (two whole-steps). Even though this interval is major, the triad is considered minor as the first interval is minor.

☛ The first and last note of a triad are a perfect fifth apart.

Figure 3.2: The C minor triad as seen on the staff, along with intervallic relationships.

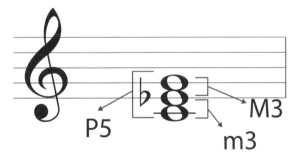

C Minor Triad

Audio Track 26: The C minor triad played twice on the piano.

The Diminished Triad

The diminished triad is recognized by its "tense," "nervous," or "anticipated" sound.

☛ The diminished triad is built using the first, third and fifth scale degree of the major scale *but the third and the fifth are flattened a half step from the major triad*. That means that in the key of C, a C diminished chord is built using C-E♭-G♭ as the primary notes. You can see it **Figure 3.3** and hear it on **Audio Track 27**.

☞ The first interval in the triad—C-E♭—is a minor third (three half-steps). This first interval usually determines the name and quality of the triad. Since the first interval is minor, we *could* call the triad minor, but the flattened fifth (diminished fifth interval) takes precedence and makes the triad diminished.

☞ The second interval in the triad—E♭-G♭—is a also a minor third (three half-steps).

☞ The first and last note of a triad are a diminished fifth apart, hence the triad name. Remember that the perfect fifth is called diminished when it is flattened by a half step.

Figure 3.3: The C diminished triad as seen on the staff, along with intervallic relationships.

C Diminished Triad

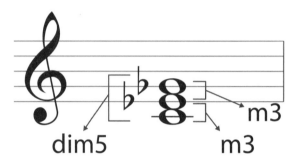

Audio Track 27: The C diminished triad played twice on the piano.

The Augmented Triad

The augmented triad is recognized by its "otherworldly" or "outer spacey" sound.

☞ The augmented triad is built using the first, third and fifth scale degree of the major scale *but the fifth is sharpened a half step from the major triad*. More on this later, but when we raise a note by a half step from its original form, we call it *sharp* (written with a symbol that looks like the number sign #). So in the key of C, a C augmented chord is built using C-E-G♯ as the primary notes. In this case, the G♯ is the same as "G-and-a-half." You can see it in **Figure 3.4** and hear it on **Audio Track 28**.

☞ The first interval in the triad—C-E—is a major third (two whole-steps). This first interval usually determines the name and quality of the triad. As the first interval is major, we *could* call this a major triad but in this case, the sharp fifth note gets precedence over the first major interval, thus the triad is called augmented (it has an augmented fifth).

☛ The second interval in the triad—E-G♯—is also a major third (two whole-steps).

☛ The first and last note of a triad are an augmented fifth apart. Remember that the perfect fifth is called augmented when it is sharpened by a half step.

Figure 3.4: The C augmented triad as seen on the staff, along with intervallic relationships.

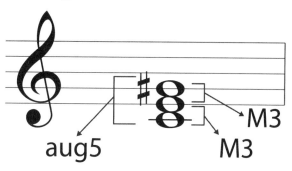

Audio Track 28: The C augmented triad played twice on the piano.

The Suspended Triad (two forms)

Each of the two suspended triads is considered to be emotionally neutral—not really happy and not really sad—as there's no third to tell us major (happy) or minor (sad). Since the third is temporarily held, or suspended, the emotion of the suspended triads isn't really shown until the third is no longer held—at that time, the feeling is then shown as either happy or sad.

☛ The suspended triad is built using the first and fifth scale degree of the major scale *but the third is temporarily suspended as either the second or fourth scale degree.* The second or the fourth that "holds" the third is either the major second or perfect fourth found naturally in the major scale. That means that in the key of C, a C suspended second chord is built using C-D-G as the primary notes. A suspended fourth chord is built using C-F-G as the primary notes. You can see them **Figure 3.5** (suspended second) and **Figure 3.6** (suspended fourth). You can hear the suspended second (sus2) on **Audio Track 29** and the suspended fourth (sus4) on **Audio Track 30**.

☞ The suspended chord always suspends the third and no other note.

☞ The suspended triad usually resolves to the third from the suspension: the suspended note (the second or the fourth, depending on the suspension) becomes the third and the chord is said to have resolved. See the Coach's Corner "Suspended Chord Classics" on suspended triads for more on this.

☞ The first interval in the suspended second triad—C-D—is a major second (one whole-step). This first interval determines the name and quality of the suspension. The first interval in the suspended fourth triad—C-F—is a perfect fourth (five half-steps). This other first interval also determines the name and quality of the suspension.

☞ The second interval in the suspended second triad—D-G—is a perfect fourth (five half-steps) while the second interval in the suspended fourth triad—F-G—is a major second. Notice that the suspended second and the suspended fourth have opposite "mirror-like" intervallic relationships.

☞ The first and last note of the triad are a perfect fifth apart.

Figure 3.5: The C suspended second triad as seen on the staff, along with intervallic relationships.

C Sus2 Triad

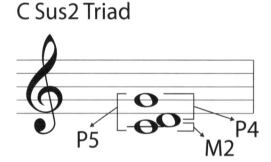

Audio Track 29: The C suspended second triad played twice on the piano.

Figure 3.6: The C suspended fourth triad as seen on the staff, along with intervallic relationships.

C Sus4 Triad

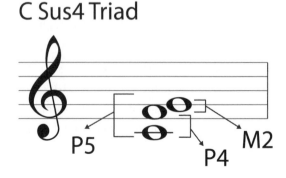

Audio Track 30: The C suspended fourth triad played twice on the piano.

The following list summarizes the intervallic relationships within each triad:

- ☞ Major triad: M3 + m3

- ☞ Minor triad: m3 + M3

- ☞ Diminished: m3+ m3

- ☞ Augmented: M3 + M3

- ☞ Suspended: M2 + P4 or P4 + M2

Coach's Corner: Suspended Chord Classics

It should be noted that the suspended chords don't *have* to resolve to a major triad—they often resolve to a minor triad. As long as the third is what is suspended and then played as the release, it can be either a major or a minor triad.

Take the case of the classic rock standard "Pinball Wizard" by The Who. The first two chords in the song are the sus4 which resolves to the major triad—that is, the first triad (in the key of C as an example) would be C-F-G and the suspension of the third, E, is held in the F for a moment. The second chord is C major, where the F "falls" to the E, resolving as a major triad. This is one example.

Another classic is the song "Cold as Ice" by Foreigner. In this song, the first triad is also a sus4 but here, it resolves to a minor triad. In the case of C major, it would be C sus4 (C-F-G) resolving to C minor (C-E♭-G).

Another classic is the song "Cold as Ice" by Foreigner. In this song, the first triad is also a sus4 but here, it resolves to a minor triad. In the case of C major, it would be C sus4 (C-F-G) resolving to C minor (C-Eb-G). If neither of these classics floats your boat, try something more recent. Check out Pyramind graduate Dheeraj Sareen's track "Saudade Yerba Buena" on Beatport.com to hear how he used the sus4 triad and the minor resolution in this ambient tech-house track:

http://www.beatport.com/release/saudade-yerba-buena/269792

Worksheet 3.1: Attaching Emotion to Intervals #3

Remember earlier where you wrote down the emotion that was attached to an interval? Then we did it again for dyads? Yup! We're gonna do it again for triads.

Coach's Corner: Add Emotion with Triads

Just as we did with intervals and dyads, performing the exercise of putting emotion to sound still works. As we go through the triads, start applying your own emotional character to the triads. The descriptors used earlier are a good starting place but as always, *your* name and *your* association is what counts. How it makes *you* feel is likely similar to how it'll make your audience feel too.

In this case, we'll replay the triads that you heard on Audio Tracks 25 to 30 back to back on **Audio Track 31**—all as C triads. This will help you compare the five triad types as they will all be some version of a C triad. As usual, write down the *first* feeling that pops into your head.

Audio Track 31: The five varieties of triads played over C.

Figure 3.7 should be familiar to you—it's a chart of the five-triad types with a column for you to fill in the emotional states of each triad. This goes along with Audio Track 31. For the "suspended" row, simply write the emotion of each triad next to each other—the sus4 being first, then the sus2.

Triads

Triads	Emotion
Major	
Minor	
Diminished	
Augmented	
Suspended	

Figure 3.7: The chart of emotional triads with a blank column for you to fill in your emotional response to the triad.

When listening to Audio Track 31, ask yourself these questions. How did each chord make you feel? Did you hear the differences in the two suspended chords? What about the others? Was one happier than another? Meaner? Orang-er (this is entered for comic relief *and* to illustrate the point that the emotion you attach to the chord is yours to be whatever you like).

Coach's Corner: Suspended Triads—An Old, Old Classic

The suspended triads are a technique used in old church music from the sixteenth and seventeenth centuries, usually as a concluding moment. If you play a sus4, sus2, then a major triad and sing the word "amen" over them, you'll instantly get the point.

Harmonizing the C Major Scale

RECAP

The major scale is built from the intervallic relationship WWHWWWH. Two notes played in sequence are called melodic intervals while two notes played together are called harmonic intervals, or dyads. Three notes played together are called triads. Triads are built from stacked third intervals in five ways. The five main types of triads are major, minor, diminished, augmented, and suspended (second and fourth). Each is built using intervals of thirds, but the first interval is what mostly determines the quality of the triad. Only in the suspended triad are the thirds not present—temporarily. The suspended triad usually resolves by changing the middle note from a second or a fourth to a third. This resolution can either be to a major third or a minor third.

We already know the intervallic relationship between the notes and the dyads of C major and we know that they follow a pattern. The first pattern, laid out melodically, is WWHWWWH. The results in terms of intervals from the root are:

- ☛ Unison
- ☛ Major second
- ☛ Major third
- ☛ Perfect fourth
- ☛ Perfect fifth
- ☛ Major sixth
- ☛ Major seventh
- ☛ Octave

But what happens if we play the same scale where each scale degree is played in triads?

The good news is that the WWHWWWH pattern doesn't change—the bad news is that the pattern of triads is a whole new pattern to memorize. No, this won't stop happening—there will be more memorization, sorry.

Let's do a little exercise that will help you see how we build the triads of the C major scale. Write down your answers on a notepad and we'll compare afterwards to see how well you did.

☞   The first step in building any collection of triads in any key is to first spell the scale of the key. By spell, I mean literally laying out the notes note-by-note. Spelling the word "scale" would look like this: "S-C-A-L-E." In the key of C major, it looks like this: "C-D-E-F-G-A-B-C."

☞   Once the scale is spelled, we can go about using these notes (and *only* these notes) to build the triads. It is important to know that *only* these notes can be used to build the triads. Did I mention that only these notes can be used? I meant that *only* these notes can be used… for now.

☞   The easiest way to build the triads is to spell them like you're playing "leapfrog." Simply take the first, third, and fifth notes in the scale (skipping the second and fourth), then put them together for your first triad. In our case, we will use C-E-G as shown in **Figure 3.8**.

☞   For the second triad, move up a note from C to D and do it again. In this case, the triad is D-F-A. Notice, for this triad, only the even scale degrees are used—second, fourth, and sixth. Do you know the quality of the triad? (Hint: Count the steps and write down the intervals, then refer to the definitions of the five triads given earlier.)

☞   Continue this process until you've gotten them all. If you run out of notes, continue writing the scale above the C octave until you've written it twice. There should be enough notes for you to work with. **Figure 3.9** shows you what it would look like as you tried to create the last triad before the octave, starting with B. Notice in figure 3.9, we use the word "Diatonic" which indicates that these notes are exclusively for the "C" Major scale.

Diatonic
Refers to a scale of notes and dyads and chords exclusively related to those notes.

Figure 3.8: The C major scale laid out with the scale degrees 1, 3, and 5 showcasing the leapfrog technique of building the first triad.

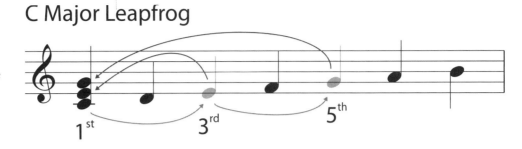

C Major Leapfrog

1st   3rd   5th

Figure 3.9: The C major scale laid out and written *twice* with the final B triad using the scale degrees 7, 9, and 11 to showcase the leapfrog technique of building triads.

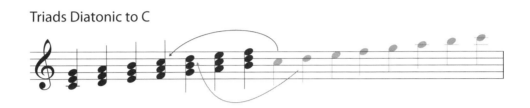

Triads Diatonic to C

Coach's Corner: Over the Octave

As notes are written above an octave, they continue the numbering system. In other words, in Figure 3.9 where we wrote the scale twice to accommodate for B, the notes starting with the C octave would be called 8 (C), 9 (D), 10 (E), 11 (F), and so on. So the B-D-F triad created wouldn't consist of the 7-2-4 of the scale. It would consist of the 7-9-11 of the scale. More on this later when we discuss extended chords.

Did you get the same notes in each triad on your notepad as we did? You should have the following list as the triads and their quality:

- ☞ C major: C-E-G

- ☞ D minor: D-F-A

- ☞ E minor: E-G-B

- ☞ F major: F-A-C

- ☞ G major: G-B-D

- ☞ A minor: A-C-E

- ☞ B diminished: B-D-F

- ☞ C major (again)

If not, go back and try it again. Once you've been able to successfully create the triads of the C major scale, compare the qualities you assigned to them. Take another look at the intervals to make sure you've counted the steps correctly, then, using the definitions of the triads, rename them until you get it right. Listen to them on **Audio Track 32** to start familiarizing yourself with their sounds.

Audio Track 32: The triads of the C major scale so you can hear them back-to-back.

Coach's Corner: Momentary Tension

Notice that the suspended triads did not make it into the final sequence of triads, nor did the augmented. Again, the suspended triad only holds tension for a moment before releasing it to either a major or a minor triad. As a rule, the suspended triad is not a part of this scale. The augmented didn't make it because it does not exist in the major scale either.

There are many ways to write the triads of the major scale beyond the standard words we are using here. One of the most common is the use of roman numerals. Each triad is given a roman numeral based on both its scale degree and its quality. If, for example, we look at the third triad in the sequence, we come to E minor. As E is the third scale degree in the C major scale *and* the triad is a minor one, we would use the Roman numeral "iii" as a shorthand for the third triad—minor in the C major scale. Notice the difference between the capital and lowercase Roman numerals? See Coach's Corner "Roman and Nashville Notation" for more details. **Figure 3.10** shows the C major scale with its Roman numeral analysis.

Figure 3.10: C major triads with their Roman numeral analysis.

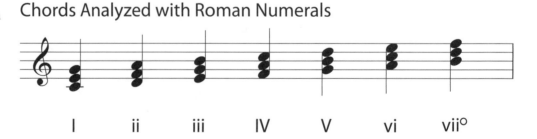

Chords Analyzed with Roman Numerals

I   ii   iii   IV   V   vi   vii°

Coach's Corner: Romans and Nashville Notation

The lower-case writing of the triad is shorthand for the minor quality. Major triads are written using capital letters—F major, for example, is written as "IV," or the fourth triad, which is major. While this is a common tradition, it is not always used. For example, some folks write the triads as capitals regardless of their quality. These folks write E minor as "III," not "iii." At Pyramind, we tend to use the lower case/upper case standard to help you learn the quality of the triads at the same time as learning the scale degrees.

The practice of replacing the actual chord names with the Roman numerals (or even Western numbers) is called *Nashville notation*. It comes from the desire to often change keys of a song mid-rehearsal or recording. For convenience, the players simply learn the relationships of the chords and then they can play those relationships in any requested key. Yet another validation of "the notes change but the relationships stay the same."

While capitalization is not a standard convention, it is helpful when learning the triads and their quality in the major scale. Other conventions include capitalizing the letter name instead of the Roman numerals. If a triad is major we would capitalize the name only. The first triad being C major would be written as "C" only. The second triad being D minor would be written as "d." Other conventions include the use of "+" and "−" for augmented and minor.

This process continues onward until we reach the final triad—the seventh or diminished triad. We would certainly use the lower case letter to describe the diminished triad (it does consist of two minor intervals after all) with the addition of a symbol similar to the degree symbol, "vii°." So in the case of C major, the seventh triad is b diminished (also written as "dim"), or "b°." **Figure 3.11** shows the C major scale triads as written in a few versions of shorthand, including a combination of the Roman numerals and the symbols.

Figure 3.11: The triads of the C major scale as written in the various shorthands.

Chord Nomenclature

As a point of interest, you should notice that the triads of C major (really, *any* major scale) follow the pattern MmmMMmd, which is similar to the rhythmic pattern we established earlier. Remember listening to the WWHWWWH against the two beats? It's on Audio Track 20 if you don't remember. Did you wonder why we did that? Seemed silly at the time, no? Well now, listen to **Audio Track 33**—it plays the same pattern of MmmMMmd against the same eighth-note beat and then it plays the triad sequence against the same beat.

Audio Track 33: The verbal MmmMMmd played over triads instead of the scale notes of C major.

Worksheet 3.2: Dyad and Triad Piano Techniques

Let's remember that what we've done so far is known as "harmonizing the scale." This refers to taking a scale—any scale—and creating dyad and triad harmony from each scale degree. You've already done this with dyads when you played each scale degree along with the root note through the scale. Do you remember this? It was C-D, then C-E, C-F, and so on. Well now, we'll do it with triads.

> **Harmonizing a Scale**
> The process of establishing the triads for a major scale is called "harmonizing the scale."

Here are a few techniques to practicing the triads in the C major scale.

☛ As a warm-up, play the C major scale with the RH and then with the LH separately ascending and descending. To get really loose, play it up and down two octaves.

☛ Then play the C major scale up and down in dyads using the third interval only. Use fingers 5 and 3 in the LH and fingers 1 and 3 in the RH.

☛ As an advanced alternative to this, use the alternating finger technique. In the LH, play the first dyad (C-E) with fingers 5 and 3, then move up to the next dyad (D-F) using fingers 4 and 2.

☛ Continue this until you run out of fingers, then slide your hand upward starting over with finger 5. In the RH, play the first dyad (C-E) with fingers 1 and 3, then move up to the next dyad (D-F) using fingers 2 and 4.

☞ Continue this until you run out of fingers, then slide your hand upward starting over with finger 1.

☞ Be sure to focus on a solid, rounded hand position with both hands. Working on controlling the thumb and pinky will help you develop a solid piano hand shape and technique.

Now, let's start the triad work.

☞ First, establish each hand as a triad over C major in both the LH and the RH. For the LH, place your fingers as 5-3-1 over C-E-G. For the RH, its fingers 1-3-5 over C-E-G in the octave above. For extra comfort, feel free to play these as either one or two octaves apart between the two hands.

☞ One at a time, in rhythm with a metronome, play each triad of the C major scale with the LH, the RH, then both hands together. Start in whole notes (four counts per triad), then half notes (two counts per triad), up through eighth notes.

☞ As an advanced alternative to this, play along with your favorite beat from the previous section, then accelerate your playing as above—whole notes, half notes, through eighth notes. If you're *really* good, you can play through sixteenth notes! Be sure to play it *well*—here, speed is secondary to accuracy.

☞ Another version of this exercise involves playing each hand differently. In the LH, play the triad all at once and the RH as an arpeggio. This means that you "spell" the triad note-by-note in the RH so the C major chord would be played C then E then G in the RH (melodically) while the LH plays C-E-G at the same time (harmonically). Move upward through the scale in rhythm as before. Switch the hands after a while and do the arpeggio in the LH and the triad all at once in the RH.

☞ Yet another alternative is to play the triads using the above techniques while playing "leapfrog." With both hands (or separately at first), play the triads in this order—C major, E minor, D minor, F major, E minor, G major, F major, A minor, G major, B diminished, A minor, C major, B diminished, D minor and ending on C major. Play this up and down the scale. You can do this in harmonic triad form (all three notes together) or in melodic triad form (arpeggios or one note at a time).

Coach's Corner: Sounds Familiar

As you play through this triad exercise, you might recognize a song in there. If you're not familiar with the old Bill Withers soul classic "Lean on Me," search for it online and check out the first four chords. The first four triads sure seem familiar, don't they? I Major, ii minor, iii minor, and IV Major then the same chords going down. Once you listen to the song, you'll be happy to know that you already know how to play most of it—just play the first four triads upward, holding the last one for a half note, then descend downward. It looks like **Figure CC3.1** and sounds like **Audio Track 34**.

Lean on Me

Figure CC3.1: The staff and piano roll in the style of "Lean on Me" in C major (notice that the root of each chord is doubtled, i.e., it is repeated above each triad).

Audio Track 34: A piano playing in the style of Bill Withers' "Lean on Me" in C major.

DVD Callout: C Major—Music Theory and Piano: Triads

Triad Cadences

RECAP

The major scale consists of notes derived from the intervals WWHWWWH. From these notes, we can build a triad—a harmonic sound whereby three notes are played together, all spaced apart by a third interval. There are five main triads: major, minor, diminished, augmented, and suspended. The suspended triad can be created by suspending the third downward to the second or upward to the fourth scale degree temporarily.. The tension is resolved by playing the third afterward. The major scale consists of a list of triads that always follow this pattern: MmmMMmd. This is known as the harmonized major scale.

Now that we know what the seven triads of the C major scale are, a pretty obvious question comes to mind—how do we use them? In the piano worksheet on triads, you've gone through various exercises using the scales and dyads as a means of getting comfortable playing the piano. However, harmonizing the scale is just that—creating harmony.

Harmony
The use of multiple pitches played simultaneously to create a pleasing sound.

Coach's Corner: The Basic Framework

We're at the point in the book where the elephant in the room needs to be uncovered—songwriting. The whole point of playing the piano is to write songs and to produce music, right? So *how* does one do that? There are as many strategies on songwriting and production as there are songwriters and producers, so we won't try to list them all here. What we will do, however, is to create a simple framework for songwriting and production and let you fill in the blanks. After all, you wouldn't want us coming to your studio to tell you what to write, would you?

Coach's Corner: Three Key Components

At Pyramind, we say that most good songs have at least three primary components—rhythm, harmony, and melody. It's not a new concept by any means but it's so important that we refer to them as the "first holy trinity" of music. We started the book with rhythm, worked through the C major scale (the most basic foundation of melody), and are now starting to work through the harmonic portion of the C major scale—triads. Note that the C major scale only produces one group of sounds—there are dozens more to contend with but at this early stage, it is the most important to learn as it will set us up for the rest.

One of the best ways to start the process of songwriting and creating harmony is to use triads to move around on the keyboard. There are seven triads in the major scale which you can use to build a harmony track around the sound of the scale, and for us, for now, the sound is the C major scale. There are several ways to combine these seven triads and there are no real rules as to when or how to combine them. There are, however, a few traditional ways to combine them, and these are called cadences.

> **Cadence**
> A cadence is a two-chord progression that usually concludes a larger musical phrase.

There are four common cadences used in songwriting, all of which have origins in the church music of Europe. Think of these as "template phrases"—templates of triad progressions that can plug in anywhere toward the end of a musical paragraph. They are equivalent to phrases such as "…happily ever after" or "…or so he thought." The idea is that they are commonly used conclusion phrases that present a particular feeling at that conclusion.

Authentic Cadence

One of the most important cadences is the authentic cadence. In the authentic cadence, the two triads used are C major and G major, or the I and the V of the scale. Technically, the authentic cadence involves playing the V *then* the I. We'll be referring to this cadence a lot as it is considered the strongest cadence in all of music. **Figure 3.12** shows the authentic cadence in the key of C major, which you can hear in **Audio Track 35**.

Figure 3.12: The V-I authentic cadence.

Authentic Cadence

Audio Track 35: The V-I cadence as played on the piano.

Half Cadence

The half cadence is effectively the opposite of the authentic cadence—it's I played up into V and since it doesn't end on I, it is considered weaker than the authentic cadence. In fact, the half cadence can be *any* triad played into V. For example, a half cadence could be the I-V or the ii-V. **Figure 3.13** shows a few varieties of the half cadence and you can hear them in **Audio Track 36**.

Figure 3.13: Most of the versions of the half cadence: I-V, IV-V, ii-V, iii-V and vi-V.

Half Cadence

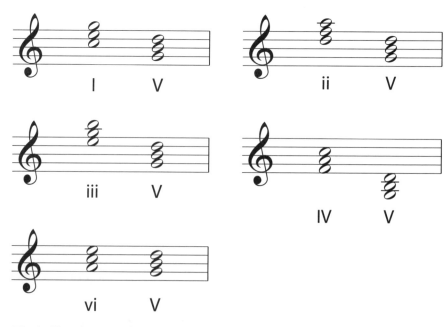

Audio Track 36: The half cadences of Figure 3.13.

Plagal Cadence

The plagal cadence is another strong cadence—from the IV to the I. Ending on the I is what makes it strong. You might know it as the "amen" cadence, as it is traditionally used as a conclusion to church music. It often comes after an authentic cadence as a second conclusion. You can see it in **Figure 3.14** and hear it on **Audio Track 37**.

Figure 3.14: The IV-I plagal cadence.

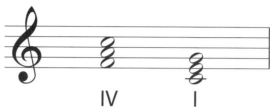

Audio Track 37: The IV-I plagal cadence as played on the piano.

Deceptive Cadence

The deceptive cadence involves moving from the V to any other triad, other than the I. In this case, several might exist such as V-vi, V-ii, or V-IV, and so on. You can see them in **Figure 3.15** and hear them on **Audio Track 38**.

Figure 3.15: Several deceptive cadences: V-ii, V-iii, V-IV, and V-vi.

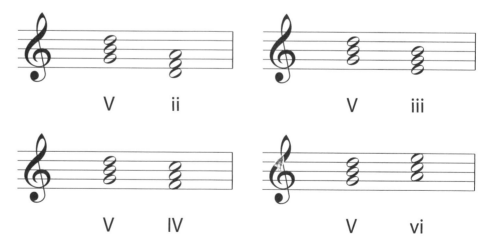

Audio Track 38: The series of deceptive cadences of Figure 3.15 played on the piano.

Coach's Corner: Tradition and Beyond

Just because these triad cadences are the traditional ones, it doesn't mean they're the *only* ones we can use. These are just the ones that are traditional. Mind you, this tradition is almost 600 years old and it's safe to say that the vast majority of the music written over that period is pretty good!

The following is a pretty good summation of these cadences and what they do in emotional terms. We use the terms *tension* and *release* (calm) as shorthand for the two most basic states of emotion—sad (tension) and happy (release).

- ☛ Authentic: first chord = tension, second chord = calm

- ☛ Half: first chord = calm, second chord = tension

- ☛ Plagal: first chord = calm, second chord = calm

- ☛ Deceptive: first chord = tension, second chord = tension

Worksheet 3.3: Cadences in Action

The four basic cadences in the previous section are traditionally meant to conclude pieces of music, and are included here only as guidelines for composition. They're not really songs or song structures, merely phrases or pieces of sentences. Writing songs usually involves working with cadences, but as these cadences get strung together they start to become progressions or larger musical phrases.

Chord Progression
A series of harmonic chords played sequentially with the intention of creating a specific emotional phrase.

We'll start our work with cadences and progressions by stringing together some of the cadences to make the most popular (by far) progression in Western music—the classic I-IV-V-IV (a.k.a. the *1-4-5*, here shown with the common move back to 4). It's used in *all* forms of music—pop, rock, dance, hip-hop, soul, boogie, disco, reggae, ska, polka, punk—literally *all* genres have some representation within the I-IV-V-IV.

In the case of the I-IV-V-IV, we are effectively joining together an inverted plagal cadence I-IV then a half cadence (IV-V, ending on V), then a deceptive cadence (V-IV, moving away from V but *not* to the I), and when we repeat the phrase you hear a plagal cadence down to I (IV-I). You can repeat this as often as you like. Remember that normally, cadences are *conclusions* not progressions. We're only showing you how you can easily string together two-chord structures to create progressions and, thus, songs.

You can see this in **Figure 3.16** and hear it on **Audio Track 39**. In fact, Audio Track 39 does this a few ways—you'll first just hear the triad progressions against a metronome, then you'll hear it in "real life," as a few variations of the 1-4-5 using different and relatively unrelated genres.

Figure 3.16: The I-IV-V-IV progression written on the staff and the piano roll.

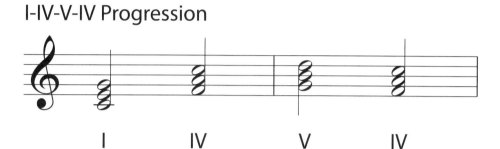

I-IV-V-IV Progression

I   IV   V   IV

Audio Track 39: The I-IV-V-IV progression using the piano.

Now that you know the I-IV-V-IV progression, let's play it on the piano.

☛ Begin with one hand only. You can start with the LH as it often plays the harmony (chord) while the RH plays the scales (melody) or with triads in the RH as the LH will only play the bass (root) notes. Over time, practice both so you develop triad skills with both hands. We'll start with the LH technique for now…

☛ Position your LH over the C major triad using fingers 5-3-1 to cover C-E-G. This should be starting to feel familiar to you by now.

☛ Slowly, "jump" your hand upward to the IV triad using the same fingers 5-3-1 to cover F-A-C. You'll notice that your hand literally "leaps" into position and maintains mostly the same hand position. This will get hard to hold if you are too tense so be sure to keep loose! Practice makes these muscles stronger so keep doing it and it'll stop hurting over time. Don't do this with the metronome yet—we want you familiar with the size of the jumps first before introducing pacing.

☛ Keep your hand close to the keys as you move. Use the geography of the white keys and the black key groups to move into the correct position. Be sure to land accurately—it's much better than speed at this point.

☛ Now, jump to the V using the same fingers 5-3-1 to cover G-B-D. Notice that your hand still holds the same position and that the only real difference is the position on the piano bed.

☛ Jump back to the IV with the same fingers.

☛ Lastly, jump back to I, holding the same fingering.

☛ Get to know the distance of a fourth versus a fifth from the root as you practice the triads. Your work with intervals should have prepared you to do this effectively. Try this with hands separated and then hands together. Once you think you have the hang of the chords and the positioning (with one or both hands), turn on the metronome.

☛ Choose a tempo that's *slow* to start with and remember that neatness counts. Play with the click at your intro tempo (start with 60 bpm and move up in 5 bpm increments until you feel the burn) and start by jumping every whole note, then every half note, then quarter note, and so on. Remember to keep the metronome set until you can comfortably perform this three times perfectly!

☛ Keep doing this until you feel fluid enough to play along with your favorite rhythm from Section 1.

☛ As an advanced alternative to this, vary the structure of the rhythm of the triads. Try improvising the movement between chords while playing along with the various beats from the rhythm chapter, for example, playing the I as a half note and the IV-V-IV as quarter notes, and so on. In this way you can play with the rhythmic phrasing of the 1-4-5 so the pacing isn't so stiff.

☛ As another alternative to this exercise, allow yourself to mix up the chord order as you play also—try a I-V-I-IV or a IV-IV-I-V, and so on. Feel free to spell the chords up and/ or down to add some new variation to the playing.

Coach's Corner: Cadences, Progressions, and Songs

While this exercise may seem musically boring to you, keep in mind that we are still near the beginning of the process. After all, we're still in C major and we're only playing triads. By varying the rhythm and the order of the cadences, you'll start getting the hang of how these cadences can be put together to make progressions, and how those progressions become songs.

Of course, knowing and varying the 1-4-5 in different ways to string them together differently is great but it doesn't cover the reach of working with cadences. In the next section, we'll start using these cadences and others—along with other triads to start building our first songs.

Chops Test: Dyads, Triads, and Cadences

OK, now it's time to test yourself. Do not attempt this part of the book until you've been practicing for a few weeks or so. Give yourself ample time to become familiar with the dyads and triads of the C major scale and achieve some confidence before attempting the following.

That said, this Chops Test is a useful way to gauge how far you've come on your own with your practicing. Once you think you're comfortable with the dyads and triads of C major scale, take the test. If there's a bunch you can't do, go back and practice that stuff for another week, then try again.

Let's see what you can do...

Basic Chops

By now, you should be able to do the following:

☛ Play the C major scale up and down in one or two octaves with both hands separate and together.

☛ Play all of the dyads in C major starting at C and working up the scale in each hand separately and together.

☛ Play all of the triads in C major up and down the scale with hands separate and together.

☛ Play each of the cadences in C major to a metronome at a quarter-note pace.

☛ Play the I-IV-V-IV progression in C major with both hands at a half-note pace.

Advanced Chops

By now you *may* be able to do the following:

☛ Play the C major scale in leapfrog fashion up and down the scale in two octaves with hands together moving upward and downward.

☛ Play the C major scale in leapfrog fashion up and down the scale in two octaves with hands in opposite directions moving upward and downward.

☛ Play the C major scale in dyads using the proper positioning from the five-finger technique only.

☛ Play the cadences of C major in order at an eighth-note pace.

☛ Play all the triads in C major in order at an eighth-note pace.

☛ Play the C major scale in triads in leapfrog fashion along with a metronome at a quarter-note pace.

Section 4
Songwriting

RECAP

The C major scale consists of notes starting from C and moving upward in the intervallic pattern of WWHWWWH. Combining two notes together creates dyads—harmonic dyads when played at the same time and melodic dyads when played in sequence. Three notes together are known as triads. There are five types of triads: major, minor, diminished, augmented, and suspended (fourth and second). Only the major, minor, and diminished triads appear naturally within the C major scale. There are four types of two-chord groupings called cadences that traditionally conclude musical phrases. By arranging, rearranging and stringing together cadences, we can begin to create musical phrases or progressions.

Getting Started

We've gone through music theory this way to help you work with and understand three things:

- To teach you about rhythm. Rhythm and the note/rest durations never change so getting the basics under your belt should have been pretty easy. *Using* rhythm is a whole other matter as every style and genre of music has its own rhythmic interpretation and creation—that can take years to master and is well outside of the scope of this book. Variations of those interpretations are what push those styles forward and keep the art fresh.

- To teach you about the basics of music theory (C major scale, intervals, and triads so far). We've spent a *lot* of time on C major, which is the easiest scale to learn. It's not necessarily the most popular or the most expressive, but it does make the theory easy to get into. Once you have these basics down, we can start leaving this scale and getting into more expressive ranges of emotion and tonality, which is where the *"real"* music lives.

- To get you to play the piano. Knowing the theory is useless without the application. The piano is the mother of all instruments and as such, it should always be the first one people learn. With the piano under your fingertips, you can step into any studio anywhere and play the MIDI keyboard and execute your ideas—or the ideas that hopefully someone is paying you to execute!

By this time, you should have a solid understanding of these concepts and skills. That is, you should have passed all of the basic chops tests before progressing forward. If you haven't, take a day, a week, or a month to get yourself to this point. Without this knowledge or these skills under your belt, moving forward will just confuse you and make things worse. We're not kidding—please go back and get it right before pressing onward or at least proceed at your own risk of frustration. You have been warned.

Assuming that you've got the basics of rhythm, the C major scale, the intervals of the C major scale, the dyads and triads of the C major scale, the five types of triads, *and* the four types of cadences under your belt, then you're ready to start building songs.

One of the hardest parts of songwriting is starting out. What comes first in a tune? The beat? The harmony? The melody? The lyrics? While everyone's got their own method, a popular starting place (at least with dance and hip-hop producers) is the beat.

When creating the beat, ask yourself: What style of music am I creating? Certain genres of music make the beat creation easier than others. The blues usually has a simple shuffle beat, reggae has a kick-heavy and snare-light beat, while certain dance genres almost always have the four on the floor as the starting beat. Since there are too many styles and genres to cover in this book, we'll use a few basic beats as backdrops for songwriting with triads. We leave it to you to build rhythms for yourself based on the genres you like but for the purposes of using chords and harmony to build songs, we'll start with some pre-fabricated rhythms.

Worksheet 4.1: Building Your First Song—Rhythm

In Section 1, we had you follow along to written notation and clap along. We also had you read rhythms and see them laid out across three instruments: the kick drum, snare, and the hi-hat. Now, we'll test your memory of rhythm and reading rhythms and we'll apply that knowledge to your skills as a producer.

I suggest choosing one of the following exercises only as a starting point. Pick the one that's closest to your preferred genre before moving onward. You can always go back and do the others, but for now let's assume we're starting one song with only one rhythm. Build that one, then go back and build another in a different genre. See how well they compare to each other afterwards!

Exercise #1: Hip-Hop

Figure 4.1 shows one of the rhythms as written on the staff that we'll use as a backdrop. Take a few moments to build it yourself at a tempo that you like. This first one is a hip-hop beat and would probably play well between 65 and 85 bpm. Build it in your favorite DAW, *then* compare it to the beat heard on **Audio Track 40**. The patterns should be exactly the same but the sounds and tempo might be different. The one on the audio track is at 75 bpm. What tempo did you choose?

Figure 4.1: The staff notation of the hip-hop beat for triad rhythm background.

 **Audio Track 40:** The hip-hop beat at 75 bpm.

Exercise #2: Pop/House

One of the rhythms (as written on the staff) that we'll use as a backdrop is shown in **Figure 4.2**. Take a few moments to build it yourself at a tempo that you like. This one is a pop/house beat and would probably play well between 120 and 130 bpm. Build it in your favorite DAW and then compare it to the beat heard on **Audio Track 41**. The patterns should be exactly the same but the sounds and tempo might be different. The one on the audio track is at 128 bpm. What tempo did you choose?

Figure 4.2: The staff notation of the pop/house beat for triad rhythm background.

Audio Track 41: The pop/house beat at 128 bpm.

Exercise #3: Rock

Figure 4.3 shows another of the rhythms as written on the staff that we'll use as a backdrop. Take a few moments to build it yourself at a tempo that you like. This one is a rock beat and would probably play well between 95 and 115 bpm. Build it in your favorite DAW and then compare it to the beat heard on **Audio Track 42**. The patterns should be exactly the same but the sounds and tempo might be different. The one on the audio track is at 105 bpm. What tempo did you choose?

Figure 4.3: The staff notation of the rock beat for triad rhythm background.

Audio Track 42: The rock beat at 105 bpm.

Once you've executed the beat of your choosing (do all three, or build your own if you're feeling adventurous!), we can begin to build a song over these rhythms using the triads of the C major scale.

Coach's Corner: In C

Keep in mind that during this songwriting exercise, we're only going to have so much expressive territory available. The C major scale is one of the happier scales in music and if you're looking to build something more moody, this one won't be it. However, the exercise is still valid—the triads we choose now will be revisited later in other keys and other modes, and you'll see how the cadences never change but the triads always change. You might have heard something like that before related to intervals.

If you've practiced the I-IV-V-IV (a.k.a. 1-4-5) progression from Worksheet 3.3, you already know what to do here. Play your 1-4-5 over the beat you chose from the previous exercise, hitting each triad on the whole note. Now, listen carefully to the rhythm you've chosen and target one of the three drum elements in your mind—the kick, snare, or hi-hat. Try to play the triads in a rhythm either with, or in-between, a particular instrument of the drums. For instance, play your chords every time the kick hits, every time the snare hits, or along with every hi-hat, depending on which rhythmic part you choose to follow. This will help you play piano rhythmically *and* show you how the same chords can make different songs by playing rhythmically with different elements of the rhythm.

Note that for hi-hats, you can play every other hit to keep your triads in quarter-note rhythm if the hats play eighth notes.

Next, try adding some variation by playing when the kick *doesn't* hit or when the snare *doesn't* hit. Be careful here—with the snare drum, it might play in quarter-note rhythms with the occasional eighth note. Try to pick the simpler rhythm of the two (likely quarter notes) and play in-between the snares at the quarter-note resolution. You can also vary the rhythm or the chords by playing some with the kick and others in-between the kicks. These sorts of variations will instantly help take the straight I-IV-V progression and make it more musical. **Audio Track 43** is an example of playing with the first beat only. Use the beat you created and practice playing more rhythmically interesting varieties of the 1-4-5 over it.

Audio Track 43: A piano playing a I-IV-V progression in time with the kick: hip-hop version, house version, and then rock version.

DVD Callout: The I-IV-V and Rhythm Tracking Parts 1, 2 & 3

Coach's Corner: Bass and Space

Remember the previous expression "It ain't the notes, it's the space between the notes…" It means that the playing of the note (or chord) is important, but being able to leave room for the other instruments is an equally important part of composition. After all, if everyone played at the same time, the music would be a big wall of sound with no variation and no groove to dance in.

Bass players know this instinctively. In fact, the bass is incorrectly considered by some to be a simple instrument. In fact, it is quite complex to master, as it needs to hold the "first holy trinity" of the song together—the rhythm, the harmony, and the melody. Great bass players can find the rhythm of the drum and often play with the rhythm of the kick drum pattern *and* play rhythmically with the drums. While they're doing that, they also play their note based on the piano chords, but they also hold melody and often vary from the set harmony to create little melodies in support of the other players. They truly are the heart of the song and are usually the hub of the band.

Now, let's move beyond the 1-4-5.

We'll vary the triads a bit here and start stringing together other cadences and triads into different progressions. We're still going to use the triads from C major, but we'll be choosing them randomly and we'll allow for you to improvise a bunch as well.

To start with, let's go through four variations where the ending chord is a different triad, just so you can hear the variety created by changing just one triad in the sequence. We'll end with the ii, then the iii, vi, and lastly the vii°. See them all in **Figure 4.4** and hear them in **Audio Track 44**.

Figure 4.4: Variations of the I-IV-V cadence with other chords added.

I-IV-V-? Progression

Audio Track 44: Variations of the I-IV-V cadence with other chords added at the end. Notice how similar the vii and the V are to each other.

For the record, you can put the triads of the C major scale together in pretty much any combination you like. The cadences are the "traditional" way to go about it, but there's nothing stopping you from building any combination you like. As you play with the triads, you'll likely stumble on combinations that may also remind you of songs you know—this is a really good sign as it means you're starting to hear the sounds of the triads and you're able to compare the sounds and the intervals of the triads against the sounds in your head.

Listed below are some popular four-triad progressions that you should know. You'll also hear them in **Audio Track 45**. They're played here with the three beats we created, but you should start working with them against the beats on your own. Remember to speed them up and slow them down to fit your tastes. We'll revisit these progressions later in a variety of ways so you can see how the triads change, but the progressions never change. This should sound familiar at this point.

- I ii iii IV
- I ii V I
- vi ii V I
- I iii IV V
- I iii vi IV
- vi V IV ii

Audio Track 45: The previous progressions played over the beats provided in Exercises 1, 2, and 3.

Notice that all of the progressions, except the last one, contain the I triad and many of them start or end with the I. Did you notice that the last progression feels different from the others? A bit unsettled perhaps?

Many progressions don't contain the I at all. Take a look at the following list of triad progressions and recognize that none of these have the I in them anywhere. They should sound decidedly different than the triad progressions above, and they are. Some would argue that they're in a whole different key.

And they're right.

More on that to come… But first, listen to these progressions on **Audio Track 46**.

- vi V IV ii
- iii IV vi V
- ii iii IV V
- ii IV vi V

Audio Track 46: The above progressions played over the beats provided in the Exercises 1, 2, and 3.

Play along with your favorite beat using one or all of the progressions listed above—both the progressions with and without the I. Remember to keep the movement in rhythm with the beat at the pace you feel comfortable with. Start with whole or half notes at first then move to quarter notes as you get faster. As before with the 1-4-5, feel free to vary the rhythm too. Play some chords longer and others shorter and you'll find that when you play the simple triads over a real beat, they start to feel like songs.

Coach's Corner: No Pain, No Gain

One thing you might be finding here is that your hands and forearms are starting to hurt. You might also find it difficult to jump around so much between triads that are "far away," such as the ii and the vii. There are two reasons for this. One is that your muscles are not used to doing this sort of work, and you're using new muscles as well. Keep using them and they'll get stronger.

The second reason is that you're doing this the hard way. Yes, we are forcing you to do things the hard way so that you can appreciate the difference once we show you the easy way. The easy way is easy on your hands, but hard on your brain, so getting things down pat now will help. A lot.

Coach's Corner: The Payoff

At about this time in the Pyramind curriculum students are asked to play with triads and attempt songwriting for the first time. Several months later in the Advanced Producing and Arranging class we hear the results of this first exercise; exercises with music theory often lead to immediate applications of music theory, a.k.a. songs.

Yes, oftentimes, a student's first attempts at working with triads produce a real piece of music. That's because it's just not that hard to write a song when you have a few chords working for you. Never mind that these songs are all in the key of C and are somewhat similar to each other—they are real songs and they *work*. We're betting that right about now, you're likely to be writing your first pieces too.

Triads and Inversions

RECAP

The C major scale is made out of notes and their intervals follow the pattern WWHWWWH. When using these notes in sequences of thirds and played together, the result is a triad. There are five types of triads, major, minor, diminished, augmented, and suspended (second and fourth). The major scale harmonized as triads creates the pattern MmmMMmd. Playing some of these triads next to each other creates cadences, and stringing cadences together created triad progressions. These progressions and the variations of their rhythm comprise the underlying principle behind writing songs.

When you were playing the triad progressions in the last section, did you feel uncomfortable moving around so much on the keyboard? Was it difficult to keep up with the rhythm because of all of the moving up and down the keyboard? Did the triads sound stiff and boring? Odds are, all of the above.

One reason for this is that playing triads in root form—where the lowest note is always the 1, the second note up is always the third and the highest note is always the fifth—is boring, as well as hard to accomplish because you have to move up and down the keyboard so quickly. There are solutions, luckily, and the main one is already familiar to you: inversions.

As a reminder for yourself, feel free to revisit the section on interval inversions. You should know by now that "flipping" the notes of an interval around creates different sounds and different intervals—even though the same notes are involved. Triads are no different, except here, we have three notes to flip around, and the iterations get a little more complex.

There are three types of triads when it comes to inversions—root form (spelled 1-3-5—what we've been working with this whole time), first inversion (spelled 3-5 then the 1 above), and the second inversion (5, 1 above, then the next 3 above that). You can see the C major triad in all three inversions in **Figure 4.5** and hear them in **Audio Track 47**. Notice that Audio Tracks 47 through 52 will be played an octave lower than usual so it's easy to hear the inversions as they get high in pitch.

Figure 4.5: Three versions of the C major triad.

C Major Inversions

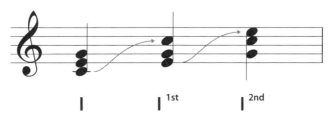

Audio Track 47: Three triad spellings of the C major triad.

There are a few things to note about major triads and their inversions:

☞ Only the root inversion has the 3 notes of the triad separated by *only* thirds.

☞ The first inversion triad starts with a *minor* third interval (between the third and the fifth scale degrees) but ends with a fourth interval (between the fifth and the first above).

☞ The second inversion triad starts with a fourth interval (between the fifth and the first above) and then has a *major* third between the first and the third notes of the triad.

Now let's look at the other two types of triads found in the major scale—the minor and the diminished and their inversions. We'll start with the minor triad—D minor in this case. **Figure 4.6** and **Audio Track 48** show the inversions of the ii in C major—D minor.

Figure 4.6: Root, first, and second inversions of the D minor triad.

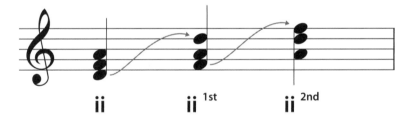

Audio Track 48: Three triad spellings of the D minor triad.

There are a few things to note about minor triads and their inversions:

☞ Only the root inversion has the three notes of the triad separated by *only* thirds.

☞ The first inversion triad starts with a *major* third interval (between the flat third and the fifth scale degrees) but ends with a fourth interval (between the fifth and the first above).

☛ The second inversion triad starts with a fourth interval (between the fifth and the first above) and then has a *minor* third between the first and the flat third notes of the triad.

Coach's Corner: Flat Inversions

Note that in the minor triad inversions, the third is described as *flat* between the first and the third above. Remember that a minor triad consists of a minor third interval (root note to the flattened third) and a major third interval above that (from the flattened third to the fifth scale degree). It's common to refer to the minor third as a *flat third*, as it's flattened compared to the major triad. In the case of the D minor triad, the flattened third is F. Since the D *major* triad has an F# (D-F#-A), we refer to the F in D minor as the flattened third—a half step lower (flat) than its major triad counterpart. You can interchange the terms flat third and minor third at times when referring to triads.

If we continue this process up the C major scale and its triads, we'll next come to E minor—the iii. The rules for minor triads are still the same and **Figure 4.7** and **Audio Track 49** shows the results of the inversions of E minor. In this case, the E minor chord—E-G-B—is inverted to become G-B-E (octave) as the first inversion, and B-E (octave)- G above as the second inversion. The point is that inverting minor, diminished, augmented, or suspended chords works the same way as major chords.

Figure 4.7: The inversions of E minor.

E Minor Inversions

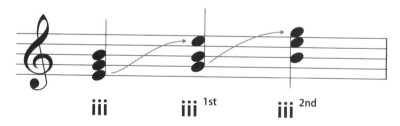

iii   iii ¹ˢᵗ   iii ²ⁿᵈ

Audio Track 49: Three triad spellings of the E minor triad.

Next, we come to F major, the IV. The rules for major triads still apply here and would also apply for the V—G major. **Figure 4.8** and **Audio Track 50** shows the two triads and their inversions.

Figure 4.8: The inversions of F major and G major.

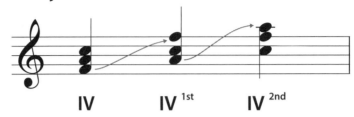

Figure 4.9: The A minor triad and its inversions.

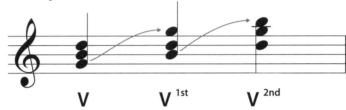

Audio Track 50: Three triad spellings of the F and G major triads.

Next is A minor, which holds to the same rules as D and E minor, and is seen and heard in **Figure 4.9** and **Audio Track 51**.

Figure 4.9: The A minor triad and its inversions.

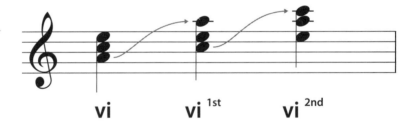

Audio Track 51: Three triad spellings of the A minor triad.

Lastly, is B diminished, seen and heard in **Figure 4.10** and **Audio Track 52**.

Figure 4.10: B diminished and its triad inversions.

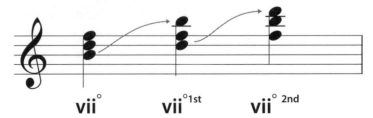

Audio Track 52: Three triad spellings of the B diminished triad.

There are a few things to note about diminished triads and their inversions:

☞ Only the root inversion has the three notes of the triad separated by *only* thirds.

☞ The first inversion triad starts with a *minor* third interval (between the flattened third and the flattened fifth scale degrees) but ends with a *sharpened* (or *augmented*) fourth interval (between the flattened fifth and the first above).

☞ The second inversion triad starts with a *sharpened* (or augmented) fourth interval (between the fifth and the first above) and then has a *minor* third between the first and the flattened third scale degrees of the triad.

Coach's Corner: Shortcuts Are Great, But...

When looking at the triads and their inversions, there are a few shortcuts to figuring out the inversion. Remember that triads are built by stacking thirds on top of each other and playing them together. Also remember that triad *inversions* aren't all thirds—there's a fourth interval too. In the case of any first inversion, you'll notice that the fourth interval, or "gap," is at the top of the written triad, between the middle note and the top note. This is a good indication that the triad is not only inverted, but is the first inversion. If the "gap" is at the bottom of the written triad - between the lower note (fifth) and the middle note (first), the indication is that the triad is not only inverted but is the second inversion.

Remember that these shortcuts are only a small piece of understanding the nature of triads and their inversions. Yet the ability to recognize the triads by name and simply know their name—no matter the spelling—is important and extremely useful. For example, the triad F-A-C is always going to be F major, whether it's F-A-C or A-C-F, or C-F-A. Recognizing that the collection of notes is what defines the triad helps keep you from mistaking the F triad as some sort of A "something" triad (A-C-F) or C "something" triad (C-F-A). After all, if the triad C-F-A were to be a version of a C "something" triad, you wouldn't have stacked thirds. The only conclusion you can draw is that both A-C-F and C-F-A are some form of the "mother" triad F-A-C, only in an inverted form.

Think of it this way. The word C-A-T is simple and can only mean one thing. Rearranging the letters to A-C-T has a whole different meaning. With music, it is different. The triad C-A-T would have the same meaning if it were spelled A-C-T or T-A-C. The sound would change but the triad meaning remains. This is a big difference between the language of music and spoken/written language.

Using triad inversions isn't just an exercise—it has a real purpose. Part of the work we do as songwriters and producers with triads and inversions is to create harmony through movement between triads in triad progressions. We know that we can string chords of a key together to make progressions and thus, songs but how do we create richer textures with these chords? We've already determined that all-root inversion progressions lose their flavor—quickly. The solution is to trick the ear into thinking that large spans of triad "jumps" aren't as large to our ears as they really are. In other words, make big triad jumps seem small and feel small to our fingers and ears. This concept is known as *voice leading*.

Voice Leading
The process of writing chord progressions while keeping the relationship between successive notes of those chords simplified and keeping with the proper quality of the chords themselves.

Coach's Corner: The Fingertip Choir

The point of inverting the triads isn't just to make it easier to play on the piano—that's a side benefit. The real point is to make it easier to move note-to-note *within* the progression of triads. The history of inversions comes from the church where composers (often monks or priests) would have to write music to accommodate church choirs.

Imagine each of your fingers as a member of this choir. By moving triads around in root inversion, each finger (voice) has to make large jumps in the notes played, which can stretch their capabilities (and vocal cords). By inverting the triads, you can make large triad jumps without moving your fingers (voices) very much. This allows each voice in the choir to stay within its musical range (baritones stay low while sopranos stay high, etc.) Another side-benefit to triad inversions is that the chords sound more complex and rich, making the music much more pleasing and dynamic to listen to—even if the chord progressions are quite simple.

With voice leading, the idea is that each finger (often referred to as each *voice*) leads the next note played by that finger (voice) in a gentle, melodic motion. Let's see a simple voice leading exercise in play.

Figure 4.11 shows a simple I-IV-V-I triad progression, all played in root position, both on staff and in Roman numeral form. Notice that each triad keeps its spelling (1, 3, 5) and the whole spelling moves up from the I to the IV, then up again to the V, then down all the way to the I. As you recall, this is more difficult to play on the piano and sounds very boring.

Figure 4.11: I-IV-V-I progression in C major—root inversion—both in staff and Roman numeral form.

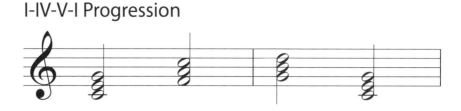

Now, let's zoom into the I-IV movement and use some voice leading. **Figure 4.12** shows the progression where the I is in root position and the IV is in second inversion (C-F-A). **Audio Track 53** plays the same progression in root inversion, then with voice leading. Did it sound different? How?

Figure 4.12: I-IV in root to second inversion spelling.

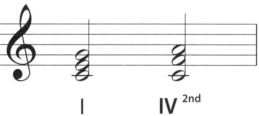

Audio Track 53: The I-IV played in root inversion, then with voice leading as seen in Figure 4.12.

One of the rules of voice leading is based on the *common tone*—keeping notes the same if they are common to both chords. Notice in the case of the I-IV that C-E-G moves to F-A-C. Also notice that C is common between them. Where there is a common tone, the note remains.

In this case, the C would be played with the same finger (or voice) and the other notes would be played with the other fingers (voices). Moving simply (that is—to the next closest note) it's easy to tell that E would move a simple half step to F while G would move a whole tone to A. This is the only solution where each finger, or voice, gets to move a small distance.

Continuing this for the full I-IV-V progression, we can move to the next cadence: IV-V. As we spelled the F major triad in second inversion, we are left with the triad C-F-A and now need to go to G major, or G-B-D. What is the most efficient way to do this? Notice that there are *no* common tones between the IV F major and the V G major.

Looking at it note-by-note and starting at the bottom with the C, where is the most logical place to move that note to in G major? C-G? That's a fifth up and big jump in voicing and for your fingers. You could also move it to D making C-D—that's only a major second interval. Much better.

You'd then have to choose the next note in C major (F in this case) and figure out where *it* goes. Since D is now taken, you only have G or B left. Which is closer to F? B is an augmented fourth away—an unpleasant sounding interval for sure and a big jump as well. Therefore, you'd likely choose to move F to G as it too is only a major second away.

Lastly, what about the A? We've figured out that the C goes to D, the F goes to G, so then the A must go to B, only a half step away. That works! All notes have moved minimally from IV F (second inversion) to the next triad V G major (also second inversion). In this case, the C moved to D, the F moved to G and the A moved to B, yielding the V G major triad as D-G-B.

If you're wondering "how did I go from F major to G major using common tone voice leading—where there are *no* common tones?" the answer is simple—*keep the same inversion*. In the case above, where F major (second inversion) needs to move to G major and they share no common tones, we simply keep the second inversion and move to G major directly from F major, keeping the G major in the second inversion.

You can see the note-by-note progression in **Figure 4.13** and hear it on **Audio Track 54**.

Figure 4.13: F major (second inversion) to G major (second inversion).

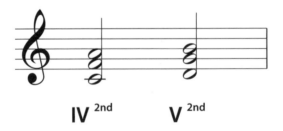

IV $^{\mathbf{2nd}}$ V $^{\mathbf{2nd}}$

Audio Track 54: The piano playing the voice leading of IV F major to V G major.

OK—we've figured out how to move from C root inversion to F second inversion and then G second inversion. To round out the progression, we'd now have to move from G major second inversion to the I (C major) again. Let's keep the voicing we have and simply add the last triad.

We left off with G major second inversion as D-G-B, but now need to go to some form of C-E-G. Using the same logic—keeping the note-to-note jumps small—how can we "solve" this movement? Let's play it out and see what happens:

☛ We start by searching for the common tones. In this case, D-G-B going to C-E-G has the tone G in common. We'll start by keeping the same G in the same pitch and then determine how to move the other two voices.

☛ Since we're left with D-B needing to go to C-E, it's a simple matter of process of elimination.

☛ Let's assume that we want to try taking D and dropping it to C. That leaves B needing to go to G. That's too big a jump.

☛ Instead, let's take B and raise it a half step to C. That leaves D moving up a whole step to E. Much better!

☛ Result? G goes to G, D goes to E, and B goes to C. No movement is larger than a whole step.

Again, the goals are to keep the voice movement to a minimum, to keep the common tone where possible and to maintain the correct notes of the triads.

Figure 4.14 shows the result of the I-IV-V-I triad progression using the voice leading we just performed. **Audio Track 55** plays it for you. Bear in mind, there isn't always only one solution to these progressions using voice leading. However, once you choose the first triad and its inversions, the remaining triads tend to solve themselves. Much like in the previous example where one tactic led to a "dead end," a second tactic will likely present itself as the best option.

Figure 4.14: I-IV-V-I in C major solved in staff and letter version through voice leading.

I-IV-V-I with Voice Leading

Audio Track 55: The I-IV-V-I progression played in inversions with voice leading.

Coach's Corner: Poor Spelling? No Problem!

While it is unusual in a written language to see a word spelled differently and keep its meaning, that's exactly what we do with music. For example, taking the word KALE and respelling it like LAKE would completely change the meaning of the word. However, in music, by writing our triads with voice leading, we've actually kept the meaning of the word intact, only with different letters in different positions.

Let's take another look at the C major I-IV-V-I progression through voice leading. **Figure 4.15** shows a few ways to play the progression, starting with the C major in root position, which we've already seen, then in first inversion then in second inversion. As we change the starting position of the first triad the other triads change their inversion and position as well. Play them all over a metronome, then over your favorite beat. Which one sounds best to you? Compare yours to ours heard on **Audio Track 56**.

Figure 4.15: Three versions of I-IV-V-I progressions—starting in root, then first, then second inversion.

I-IV-V-I with Voice Leading

Audio Track 56: The piano playing the I-IV-V-I progressions from Figure 4.15.

Triad Substitutions

So far, we've been using the triads of C major in a variety of ways—in cadence form (two triads back and forth), as a string of cadences that become progressions, and as inversions with voice leading to create smooth transitions between the triads. If you look closely enough, you'll find that many of the triads have sounds and notes in common—so much so that we can effectively use triads as substitutes for each other.

For example, let's look at C major (C-E-G). If you break the triad into its dyad partners, you end up with C-E and E-G. Each of these dyads is shared among other triads in the scale, which is the basis of substitutions. A minor is one of them (A-C-E shares C-E) and E minor is the other (E-G-B shares E-G). To this end, whenever you see a C major in a triad progression, you can substitute either A minor or E minor. By substituting the C major at times, you can take a simple chord progression and keep it interesting to the listener. If we expect C, then get A, something unexpected happens tricking the listener into thinking there's been a big emotional shift, when there has only been a small shift! Keep in mind that this technique works well when the substitution is used sparingly. Otherwise, if we don't hear the original chord enough, it's hard to tell that it has been substituted.

Coach's Corner: Triad Substitutions

Triad substitutions work a bit like a thesaurus—you can choose several words that have similar meaning with different inflections. "Elated" and "overjoyed," for example, represent two varieties of the emotional state "happy," but each has a slightly different meaning. Using triad substitutions is similar to this. The "meaning" of A minor is different from E minor, but both can represent a substitution for C major as they have shared dyads within them.

This, however, is only a metaphorical explanation for *why* substitutions can work. It can be argued that A minor is an opposite emotional state (sad, minor) to C major (happy, major) and as such, is not a true substitution. Try to remember that music is its *own* language and as such, has its own rules. The rules of English won't always apply. After all, the rules of English don't apply to Mandarin, do they?

Let's revisit our friend the I-IV-V-I progression to show how this works.

Figure 4.16 shows the I-IV-V-I progression where the first "round" of triads plays C major. Then in the second round we substitute the first C major with A minor. You can hear the two back to back in **Audio Track 57**.

Figure 4.16: A I-IV-V-I triad progression played once then with the first C major triad substituted with A minor.

I-IV-V-I with Voice Leading

I   IV   V   I

vi-IV-V-I with Voice Leading

vi   IV   V   I

Audio Track 57: I-IV-V-I then vi-IV-V-I.

The advantage to the substitution in this case is to redirect the listener to hear the progression twice but with a twist. As the listener enters the progression the second time, the substitute gives them the sense that they're listening to a whole different progression. It is different, of course, but since A minor and C major are only off from each other by one note (A instead of G), it's nearly the same phrase. **Figure 4.17** shows a list of triad substitutions in C major. Note that these triads are subs in any major scale, not just C.

Figure 4.17: A list of triad substitutions for the triads of C major.

Chord Substitutions

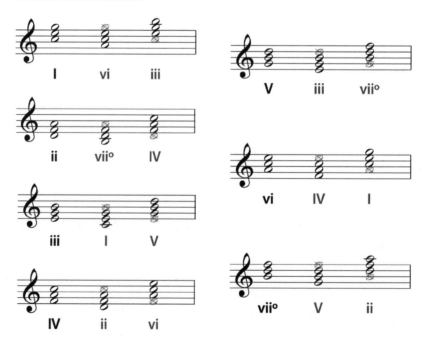

Triads and Inversions

Worksheet 4.2: Using Inversions to Play Triad Progressions

Remember these triad progressions from earlier?

- ☞ I-ii-iii-IV
- ☞ I-IV-V-I
- ☞ I-ii-V-I
- ☞ vi-ii-V-I
- ☞ I-iii-IV-V
- ☞ I-iii-vi-IV
- ☞ vi-V-IV-ii

Take some time to play them again—in root inversion *only* then with proper voice leading. If you're really good, you'll try each one four times—once in all root, once starting in root but with voice leading, once with voice leading starting in the first inversion, and lastly in second inversion with voice leading. We'll bet that there's one that you like best—can you identify which one and *why*?

Coach's Corner: Favorite Inversions

As you go through each of these progressions with good voice leading, you should find that playing them all in root inversion is harder and sounds very stiff. A typical question that pops up here is, "how do I know which inversion to start with?" It's a good question and there's a good answer—whichever one you like the best! Try to isolate the feeling of each inversion and, as before, attach an emotion to it.

As you get more familiar and comfortable with inversions, you'll find that there's a note in the inversion that resonates best with you at the time. If it's the root note, then likely the root inversion will work best; the first inversion is good if the third is your most attractive note; and the second inversion if it's the fifth. Oftentimes, it's the lowest note of the inversion that draws the strongest attention and will determine which inversion works best for you in the moment. This decision does have a lasting impact though—it usually sets the stage for the first note of a melody line and the voices of each triad that follow.

Determining the inversion that's best to start with when writing songs is usually a function of the *feeling* of the inversion itself. Consider the root inversion of C major (C-E-G) for a moment. Notice that when you play it, the triad is easily identified as major *and* is easily identified as C by the lowest note. Its sound is strong and grounded. It's a good place to start a song if you want to lead off with a basic sound.

Next, consider the first inversion (E-G-C). As the lowest note is actually the third of the triad, and the first interval we hear from the bottom note up is a minor third, the sound is at first a bit confusing. However, the root on top does clearly identify the triad as C. In fact, with the root note on top, the weight of the triad is in the upper sound and can give the triad an uplifting feeling. This is a good place to start if you want your song to start feeling upbeat with a bit of the sadness in the lower notes.

Lastly, the second inversion triad (G-C-E) is somewhere in-between. With the fifth in the bottom, the triad is grounded—the fifth is a very strong note after all. With the major third in the upper note, the interval at the top is a major one, so there's a strong note of happiness above. Use this one to project strength in the first chord.

Now, if we look at something like A minor (A-C-E), the same concepts still apply. The root inversion triad is grounded and easily identifiable while the first inversion feels unstable similarly to the major triad C major. However, with the root being a minor third and the first interval as a major sixth, confusion still defines the triad. The second inversion triad similarly feels grounded with the fifth in the bottom but as the top note is the minor third, the feeling is not uplifting but rather sadness.

Of course, these descriptions are just opinions—a group of interpretations. Just as before, you should try to identify these triads emotionally on your own and make your own choices as the triad inversion to start with. Play each of the triads of the C major scale in each inversion and identify all of them with your own emotional descriptors.

Create a chart on paper for each of the three inversions for each chord of the C major scale in a similar fashion to the chart of intervals and their emotions. It should look like **Figure 4.18**. Now, play each triad in each inversion and let the sound hang for a bit. Write down the feeling that each inversion gives you. Keep these in mind when starting a song—which inversion gives the right feeling to start your song?

Figure 4.18: A chart of the C major triads and their inversions, tracking the varying emotional states of the triads.

Triads and Inversion Emotions

Chords	Emotion		
	Root Inversion	1st Inversion	2nd Inversion
C maj			
D min			
E min			
F maj			
G maj			
A min			
B dim			

Now, let's look at the piano and play some triad progressions using voice leading. You can use *any* triad progression you like—the list of progressions above is a great start—so feel free to create your own. The majority of the steps listed below will be the same except for the finger positions of course, but the overall sentiment should remain. Let's look at doing this with one of the progressions from our list: the vi-ii-V-I.

☞ As a warm-up, play the progression above (vi-ii-V-I) in root inversion over a metronome. Use the standard whole, half, and quarter note rhythmic pacing to keep it moving fast enough.

☞ Keep the metronome playing and then vary the first chord to an inverted form. It's likely as you start out that you will need to chart your inversions on paper first prior to just playing them—inverting triads "on the fly" might be out of your reach at this time.

☞ Chart out several voice leading examples where the first chord (vi) plays in all three inversions and vary your choices at each step until you feel that you've exhausted the possibilities. Remember to keep your voice changes to a minimum and make it easy.

☞ Play each of the triad progressions with inversions until you feel you have one that feels right and is manageable in your fingers. Which voices did you choose for the starting ones and the ending ones?

☞ Switch the metronome for the beat and play along. Remember to vary your speed and your rhythm as you get more comfortable and if possible, record your practices. I bet you find a few songs in there that you either already know, or will start to write!

☞ Start to play progressions twice with the first one as written and the second with some triad substitutions. Feel free to vary which chord gets subs—and with what sub. For example, sub the first chord one time, then sub the second chord the second time, and so on. The list of combinations becomes very large and you'll see just how many songs are available to you using only the C major scale and only this one progression!

DVD Callout: I-IV-V Rhythm Practice, Part 5

At this point, I'd like to ask you to take a moment and breathe. You are now just about halfway through this book and although we've only covered the C major scale, we've actually covered a tremendous amount of music theory and application. You should pat yourself on the back and feel very good about your progress. If you have kept up with your playing and your practicing, you should be ready for what amounts to a mid-term exam! I know you just *love* those!

If you can do the Basic Chops Test you get a score somewhere between a C– and a B+. If you can't even do this bit, you get a D. That's a good indication that you need to go back and try again—seriously this time. It's like a diet—if you cheat on it, the results are in the scale. Get it? Scale? [groan]

If you can do the Basic Chops Test, then try the advanced stuff. Just trying gets you a B+, even if you can't do it well. Nailing it gets you an A and a gold star! It also means that you're practicing well and progressing well. Remember that there's no finish line—only your progress and the betterment of your music. You should know by now if that's actually getting better. It always does. Always.

If you're practicing, that is.

Chops Test—The C Major Scale, Intervals, Dyads, Triads, Inversions, and Voice Leading

Basic Chops

By now, you should be able to do the following:

☛ Play the C major scale with both hands—separate and together—up and down the octave to a metronome. You should be able to do so while switching your fingering correctly—after the thumb in the LH and after middle finger in the RH as follows:

Right hand (RH): CDEFGABC 123–12345

Left hand (LH): CDEFGABC 54321–321

☛ Play the C major scale in intervals, from C to D, then C to E, and so on, up to C (the octave C) up and down in both hands—separately and together.

☛ Play and recognize the melodic intervals and their inversions in both hands—separate or together—from C to D then from D to C octave up and down the octave range.

☛ Play the harmonic intervals of C major in both hands—separately and together—up and down the octave.

☛ Play and identify all of the notes in all of the triads in C major in root inversion in both hands up and down the octave—separately and together.

☛ Play each triad in C major using all three inversions in both hands up and down the octave—separately and together.

☛ Play and recognize all triads and all of their inversions of the C major scale in any octave when seen written on the staff and as notes on a piano.

☛ Write and play any progression of triads within the C major scale using proper voice leading and avoiding large intervallic jumps in voicing. You should be able to do this in both hands—separately and together.

Advanced Chops

You may also be able to do the following:

☛ Play the C major scale with both hands—separate and together—up and down the octave to a metronome. You should be able to do a variety of versions of this, including the "leapfrog" arpeggio where you play C then E then D then F, and so on.

☛ Play the C major scale as above in opposite, where the RH moves upward and the LH moves downward using the leapfrog technique *and* vice versa.

☛ Play any harmonic interval with eyes closed and properly choose the interval *by ear*. The same is true for the interval inversion—*by ear*. You might need a friend to help you with this part to keep it honest.

☛ Play a series of leapfrog melodic intervals throughout the C major scale—C-E, then D-F, then E-G, and so on. You should be able to do this in both hands, up and down the scale, using similar and contrary motion—that is, play the C-E dyad in the RH while playing the C-A downward dyad in the LH and vice versa.

☛ You should be able to do this using alternating fingers—5-3 for C-E in the LH and 1-3 in the RH, then 4-2 for the LH and 2-4 in the RH, and vice versa.

☛ Play and identify all of the triads of the C major scale and their inversions *by ear*—that is, you should be able to recognize any given triad's inversion simply by listening.

☛ Play and leapfrog the triad substitutions of the C major scale—up and down the piano—with similar and contrary motion, hands separately and together. For example, you can play C major, then A minor in the LH while playing C major, then E minor in the RH. The next triads should be B diminished, then G major in the LH, and D diminished then F major in the RH, and so on.

☛ You should be able to do the same using all three inversion types—up and down the piano using hands separately and hands together.

☛ Write and play any progression of triads within the C major scale using proper voice leading and avoiding large intervallic jumps in voicing. You should be able to do this in both hands—separately and together *and* without having the triads written out for you. So if you were somehow just told the triad names *only*, you should be able to play between them without hesitation and while using proper voice leading.

☛ Write and play any progression of triads within the C major scale using proper voice leading and avoiding large intervallic jumps in voicing. With the LH, play the triad and with the RH, play the triad as an arpeggio, and vice versa. Additionally, you should be able to play a simple melody in the RH while holding the triad in the LH.

Go ahead and take this test. Did you pass? Are you *sure*? Remember that if you cheat, the only one who loses is you.

I know you rocked it, right? Well since you did, give yourself a big clap on the back and get ready to move out of C major land. Or, as Cypher told Neo before he took the red pill in my favorite movie *The Matrix*, "Buckle up, Dorothy, 'cause Kansas is going bye-bye…"

Section 5
Beyond C Major—The Chromatic Scale

RECAP

The major scale consists of interval relationships in the pattern WWHWWWH. By playing three of these notes at a time in stacked third intervals, we get a chord known as a triad. The major scale harmonized in triads makes the pattern MmmMMmd. Triads can be inverted in ways where each of the three notes can be the lowest of the triad (or the root). Using inversions helps chord progressions sound smooth while keeping the note-to-note distances short and easy to manage. This process is called *voice leading*.

Even though we've spent all of this time working with C major alone, you should stop and take a moment to realize that you've actually covered a tremendous amount of material. Everything you've done so far is foundational, setting the stage for the rest of our work with music theory.

To repeat—everything you've covered so far is the foundation of all of music theory. It's that important. That's why we spent half of the book on the C major scale. We can forever use it as a guide and a gauge for how well we know our stuff. Everything from here on is compared to C major, which we *know* you all have well-memorized…

Now that we have this foundation, we can leave C major and begin delving into other keys, tones, moods, and sounds. Our first stop in this new adventure involves every single note on the piano. Once we leave C major we need to introduce something new—the black keys.

Remember in the very beginning when we defined intervals as the spaces between notes? Remember that there were two places on the keyboard where there was a half-step between two adjacent white notes? For those who don't remember, they live between E and F as well as B and C. While those two half steps are on the white keys, the rest of the half steps are not—they live on the black keys.

We get to the black keys by altering each of the notes of the C major scale by either raising the note slightly (sharp, or "♯") or lowering the note slightly (flat, or "♭") to the very next note. Therefore, each note is sharpened or flattened by a half step. This is what we were calling a note such as "D-and-a-half" (D♯ or D sharp) and "D-minus-a-half" (D♭ or D flat). When these altered notes show up in a key where they don't belong, they are called *accidentals*. All of the notes in Western music—the C major scale *and* its accidentals—are called the *chromatic scale*, as seen in **Figure 5.1** and heard in **Audio Track 58**.

Accidentals
A note is said to be an accidental if it is played as a sharp or flat note in a given key when it is not regularly played as sharp or flat.

Coach's Corner: Sharps and Flats

Every note can be either sharp or flat depending on the situation. However, it should be noted that generally, if any note is sharp in a particular scale, there won't be a flat note as well. Notes are either sharp or flat within a particular scale; very rarely are they mixed within a scale.

Chromatic Scale

Figure 5.1: The chromatic scale in sharps (increasing) and flats (decreasing). Note that the sharps on the way up sound the same as the flats on the way down.

Audio Track 58: The C chromatic scale.

The chromatic scale is the collection of all possible notes in Western music, which means that you can't make any harmonic or melodic music with any notes that don't belong to this scale using standard instruments. That's the good news. The bad news is that the notes in the chromatic scale don't always come with the same names all the time. An altered note always has two names but only *one* fits a particular circumstance at any one time. When the same pitch carries two names, the two notes are called *enharmonic equivalents*.

Enharmonic Equivalent
Notes are enharmonic equivalents when the written sharp of one note, or pitch, sounds the same as the written flat of another.

Remember that notes that are sharp are raised in pitch and notes that are flat are lowered in pitch. If we look at the note A, for example, and we raise it, the result is A♯. At the same time, let's look at the note B. If we lower it, the result is B♭. Take a look at the piano in **Figure 5.2**. Notice that A♯ and B♭ are the same key on the piano! Try it on your piano—do they sound the same? They should. This means that A♯ and B♭ are enharmonic equivalents of each other.

Figure 5.2: Enharmonic equivalents on the piano—an A♯ equals a B♭.

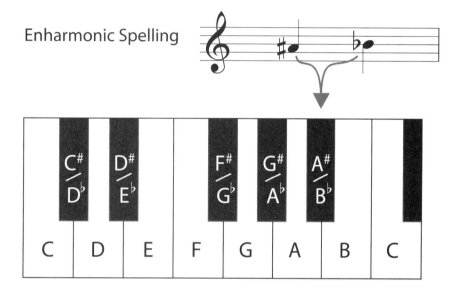

Enharmonic Spelling

Coach's Corner: Two Names, Same Sound

It's important to know that two note names can describe the same sound, much like a letter can have two sounds. It's similar to the letter "E" and knowing that it has two sounds—"eh" and "eee." Only in this case, it's the *sound* that has two names!

Note that in this example, A♯ and B♭ each land on black keys, whereas the *un*-altered notes live on white keys. If that were always the case, it would be easy to determine the sharps and flats—they'd only be on the black keys. Ready for some more bad news? Sharps and flats don't always land on black keys.

Take a look at the note E in **Figure 5.3**. If you notice on the piano, raising E to E♯ doesn't get you to a black key—it gets you to the white key F. So is E♯ = F? By association, does F♭ = E? The answer is yes. Sharps and flats don't always land on the black keys but they are *always* slightly raised or lowered versions of the "regular" note. If you look at the note B instead, you will see similar results. Raising B to B♯ is the enharmonic equivalent of C. Lowering C to C♭ is the enharmonic equivalent of B.

Figure 5.3: A sharp (or flat) may not fall on a black key, as seen on the piano and the staff—E/F and B/C.

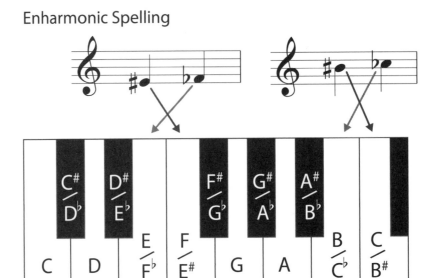

Enharmonic Spelling

Coach's Corner: Some Sharp versus Flat Clarification

One of the most common mistakes that many make early on in their learning of music theory is confusing the concept of sharp and flat keys with the white and black keys. A note is sharp or flat if it has been raised or lowered from its C major equivalent. However, it doesn't work the other way around. While some of the white keys can be sharp or flat if the note has been raised or lowered (E/F and B/C most commonly), the black keys are *always* sharp or flat. In other words, there are no black keys that *aren't* called sharp or flat. We will later discuss nomenclature (naming) but for now, just remember that the sharp or flat term means raised or lowered—*not necessarily* black or white.

Worksheet 5.1: The Chromatic Scale

The following are some piano exercises using the chromatic scale. The goal here is to learn the chromatic scale fingering in each hand separately at first. It's rare that the chromatic scale is employed in its entirety in a piece of music (except as a short-burst flurry of notes), so being able to play it with one hand is enough for now.

We'll start by doing a *trill* exercise—one where you play a few notes together quickly—with the effort focused on finger flexibility.

☛   Either after your C major scale warm-up or as an alternative warm-up, play the chromatic scale with each hand separately.

☛ With the RH, play the chromatic scale octave from C3 to C4, ascending. This is the octave from middle C to the C above it. The finger technique used here is this: 1-3-1-3-1-2-3-1-3-1-3-1-2. That means you will alternate the thumb and middle finger where you lead with C on the thumb, then C♯ on the middle finger—the first 1-3. You'll move your hand to the right to play D with the thumb again, then D♯ with the middle finger again—the second 1-3. At E, you'll introduce the index finger where the thumb leads with E, the index plays the F and the middle finger plays the accidental F♯ again—the next 1-2-3. Notice how the thumb always plays the white keys and the middle always plays the black keys.

☛ As an advanced alternative to this, continue this from the lowest note on your keyboard through the highest note.

☛ With the LH, play the chromatic scale upward using the 5-3 5-3 5-4-3 technique. This means you lead with the pinky on C, play the C♯ with the middle finger and move your hand upward—the first 5-3. Continue this until you reach E, where you'll play with the pinky on E, the ring finger on F and the middle finger on F♯—the first 5-4-3.

☛ As an advanced alternative to this, play from the lowest note on the keyboard through the highest note on the keyboard.

☛ When playing the scale downward, simply switch the fingering technique between hands. The RH plays the 5-3, 5-3, 5-4-3 technique and the LH plays the 1-3, 1-3, 1-2-3 technique.

☛ As an advanced alternative, play both hands ascending and descending together.

☛ As another advanced alternative, play both hands ascending and descending in opposite directions. Challenging!

The Circle of Fifths

OK, so now that we know what the chromatic scale is *and* what to call the black keys, we can start moving into other major scales. We don't just randomly move through the notes of the C major scale and make them major all at once—there is a trick to it that involves building major scales by adding only one sharp or flat to the scale at a time. It's called the *circle of fifths* and short of the C major scale, it's one of the most important pieces of knowledge in music.

The Circle of Fifths
A circular representation of the major scales of music in order of increasing sharps.

Do you remember the fifth scale degree of C? You should—it's G. If C is the first note on the circle of fifths, G is the second. This is the beginning of the pattern that defines the circle. It's a progression of notes built in fifths starting from C. Once we know that G is the first "stop" along the circle, we'd then look to the G major scale to determine its fifth scale degree and so on. **Figure 5.4** shows the circle of fifths in its most basic form—as a series of notes that are fifths *higher* than the note before. Later on, we'll see what happens when we move to a fifth lower. (We know, the circle is incomplete. Don't worry, we'll fill the rest in later).

Figure 5.4: Half the circle of fifths—clockwise in order of increasing sharps (no flats yet).

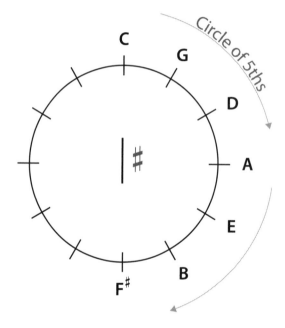

When we start with C major, we already know that there are no accidentals in the key. However, if we were to take a look at the next step in the circle of fifths, G, and begin to make a major scale out of it, we'll see something interesting—a single sharp note in the key, occurring naturally.

Let's build the G major scale and see that sharp. Remember that the C major scale is built from the interval progression WWHWWWH. Well, if we use that interval progression but start with G instead of C, we end up with the G major scale, shown in **Figure 5.5**. Here's how we build it:

☛   G is the starting point since it's the root note of the key G major.

☛ Using WWHWWWH, we simply add the intervals from G up. The first one is a W or whole step from G, yielding A.

☛ From A, we add another W or whole step, yielding B.

☛ From B, we add the H or half step, yielding C.

☛ From C, we add the W to yield D.

☛ From D we add another W to yield E.

☛ From E, we add the last W to yield F♯, the first and only accidental in the scale. Note that F♯ is the seventh scale degree and is the "new" sharp in the circle of fifths.

☛ From F♯, we add the other H to yield G again as the octave.

☛ The resulting scale is GABCDEF♯G. The first fifth in the circle of fifths has one sharp.

Figure 5.5: The G major scale with intervals shown.

G Major Scale (with whole/half step intervals)

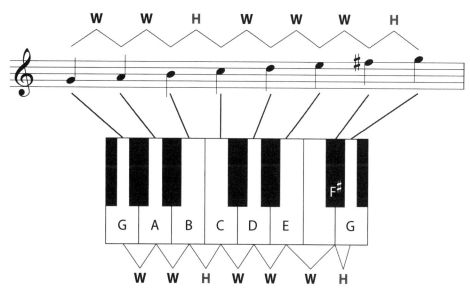

Notice that our first sharp (F♯) lies near the end of the scale. This is the reason that G is next in the circle—it's the first key with a sharp—one sharp exactly. If we look at G and study its fifth—D—we'll see that its scale has two sharps—exactly. As we continue through the circle of fifths, we'll find that each of the subsequent fifths introduces a new sharp to the scale, as shown in **Figure 5.6**. We'll play them all from within one octave on **Audio Track 59**. Try to follow along on your piano to see if you can instinctively find the correct sharp as you play!

MEMORIZE ME!
Figure 5.6: The major scales of
each step of the circle of fifths.

All Major Scales in the Circle of 5ths

Audio Track 59: Each of the major sharp scales.

When dealing with the circle of fifths and each new major scale, it's a good idea to memorize the following rules:

☛ As we progress through the circle of fifths, each step introduces a new sharp from the one before it.

☛ As each sharp is introduced the sharp note from the scale before it remains. So, in the key of D major, we retain the F♯ that was created in G major.

☛ The new sharp is always at the seventh scale degree.

Let's continue our look at the circle of fifths and build the next scale note-by-note to see how the "rules" work. We've seen G major so let's take it further. For this example, we'll look at the second scale in the circle, D major.

☛ D is the starting point, as it's the root note of the key D major and the second position on the circle of fifths.

☛ Using WWHWWWH, we simply add the intervals from D up. The first one is a W or whole step from D, yielding E. Remember not to play D and think "W." The note is the note and the "W" is the whole *step* up to E.

☛ From E, we add another W or whole step yielding F♯. Note that F♯ was first introduced in G—one position lower on the circle of fifths—but it remains here in D major.

☛ From F♯, we add an H or half step, yielding G.

☛ From G, we add the W to yield A.

☛ From A we add another W to yield B.

☛ From B, we add the last W to yield C♯, the second and last accidental in the scale. Note that C♯ is the seventh scale degree and is the "new" sharp in the circle of fifths—just like F♯ was in the key of G.

☛ From C♯, we add the other H to yield D again as the octave.

☛ The resulting scale is DEF♯GABC♯D. The second fifth in the circle of fifths has two sharps.

Coach's Corner:

When you look at the staff of a song, you'll often find collections of sharps at the beginning of the very first measure of the song written without actual notes—just sharps written in the spaces and on the lines as if they were notes. By looking at these, you can instantly tell what the key of the song is. For example, **Figure CC5.1** shows two sharps, F♯ and C♯, written in a particular order from left to right. As there are two sharps, you should know that the key is the second position on the circle of fifths, or D major.

Figure CC5.2 shows A major, the next scale in the circle of fifths. Also notice the order—F♯, C♯, *then* G♯ from left to right. Remember that the first sharp, F♯, is the sharp that appears in the major scale at the first position on the circle of fifths—G major. As this is the first sharp in the circle (and it will be in every next scale in on the circle), F♯ is always written first. Next comes C♯, introduced in D major, and now G♯ which is introduced in this particular key (A major). In fact, the sharps are always written in the order that they appear in the circle of fifths.

Figure CC5.1: The key signature of D major on the staff.

Key Signature of D Major

Figure CC5.2: The key signature of A major on the staff.

Key Signature of A Major

MEMORIZE ME!
Figure 5.7: The staff of all sharp keys of the circle of fifths.

All Major Key Signatures With Sharps

Figure 5.7: shows all of the sharp key signatures as written on the staff in increasing order of sharps as determined by the circle of fifths.

Earlier, we made note that the circle of fifths wasn't complete. That's because if we continue down the path of sharps, we get stranger and stranger keys. C♯ (the key a fifth up from F♯) isn't that bad, but it does have notes like B♯—enharmonic equivalent of C—which is really confusing for most folks. Worse, a fifth up from that is G♯, which has eight sharps in a scale that only has seven notes. How does that happen? The answer is double sharps... fun stuff. Instead of dealing with that, let's just skip to flats.

The Circle of Fourths

The circle of fifths is really only one side of the musical equation (literally, you only saw one half of the circle). Did you notice that all the scales have only sharps? How about the flats? When do they show up? As long as you move in fifths upward through the circle, the answer is: they don't. So how do the flats show up in other major scales?

The answer lies in the analysis of the fifth itself. Remember from early on where we looked at note inversions and we uncovered the Rule of 9? Well what is the note inversion of the fifth?

… (insert pause to see if you actually remember…)

Right—the perfect fourth! Applying that to the circle of fifths, you'd recognize that a fifth down in the circle is the same as a circle of fourths up! (Of course, you knew that already… didn't you?)

Let's look at this idea another way.

From C up to the next fifth yields G. But what if we move C down to the lower fifth? It yields F. Guess what? F is a fourth up from C. So moving up in fourths is the same as moving down in fifths—the results are the same. **Figure 5.8** shows the circle of fourths with all keys and their associated sharps and flats (Again, the circle is incomplete, but don't worry.)

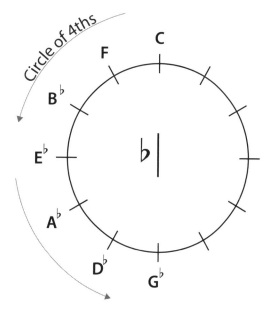

When dealing with the circle of fourths (a.k.a. the circle of fifths down) and each new major scale, it's a good idea to take a look at some rules.

☛   Each step through the circle of fourths introduces a new flat.

☛   As each flat is introduced, that flat persists in all future scales on the circle.

MEMORIZE ME!
Figure 5.8: Half the circle of the fourths—flats only, in clockwise motion.

☞   The new flat is always found at the fourth scale degree.

Now let's take a look at the first flat key—F major as the first stop on the circle of fifths down, or fourths *up*—and see how the flat keys are built.

☞   F is the starting point since it's the root note of the key F major.

☞   Using WWHWWWH, we simply add the intervals from F up. The first one is a W or whole step from F, yielding G. Again, remember that the W is the step up from F to G—not F itself.

☞   From G, we add another W or whole step yielding A.

☞   From A we add the H or half step, yielding B♭. Notice that B♭ is the first flat of the key and it's the fourth scale degree.

☞   From B♭, we add the W to yield C.

☞   From C we add another W to yield D.

☞   From D, we add the last W to yield E.

☞   From E, we add the other H to yield F again as the octave.

☞   The resulting scale is F G A B♭ C D E F. The first key in the circle of fourths has one flat (**Figure 5.9**).

F Major Scale (with whole/half step intervals)

Figure 5.9: The F major scale with intervals shown.

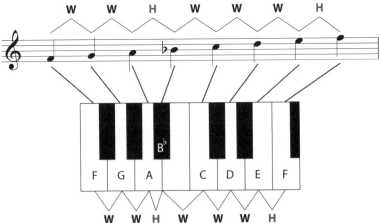

Figure 5.10 shows all the scales following the circle of fourths. You can hear them on **Audio Track 60**. See if you can play along and naturally find all the correct flats! All of the flat key signatures are written on the staff in increasing order of flats as determined by the circle of fourths in **Figure 5.11**.

Audio Track 60: The major scales of the circle of fourths.

MEMORIZE ME!
Figure 5.10: The major flat scales of each step of the circle of fourths.

All Major Scales in the Circle of 4ths

C Major   (no flats)

F Major   (1 flat)

B♭ Major   (2 flats)

E♭ Major   (3 flats)

A♭ Major   (4 flats)

D♭ Major   (5 flats)

G♭ Major   (6 flats)

All Major Key Signatures with Flats

Coach's Corner: Staff Flats and Sharps

The rules for writing the staff in flats are the same for writing the staff in sharps. At the beginning of a song, the accidentals required are written in order of how they appear throughout the circle of fourths. If you see three flats, you should know that you are on the fourth position of the circle of fourths: E♭. Remember that C is the first stop, then F, then B♭, then E♭.

Earlier, we made note that the circle of fourths wasn't complete. That's because if we continue down the path of flats, we get stranger and stranger keys. C♭ (the key a fourth up from G♭) isn't too bad, but a fourth up from that is F♭ (a.k.a. E), which has eight flats in a scale that only has seven notes. How does that happen? The answer is double flats... fun stuff. And since we skipped over how to deal with this problem before, let's skip it here also.

Each time we showed a circle (whether it be the circle of fourths or fifths) only half of it was filled in. Let's now complete those circles. In **Figure 5.12**, you'll see the circle of fifths and fourths combined. You'll notice that from C, if we follow the circle clockwise the progression of the circle of fifths appears. If we go backwards, counterclockwise, the progression from the circle of fourths shows up (also known as the circle of fifths down), both progressions joining at the bottom of our completed circle with the keys F♯/G♭.

Figure 5.12: The entire circle of fifths.

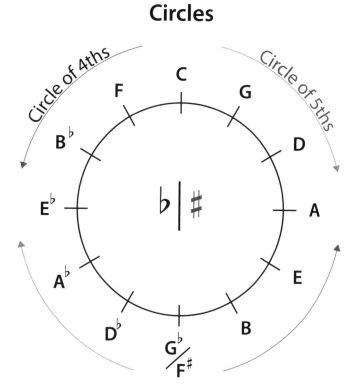

Why are both F♯ and G♭ together at the bottom you ask? It's because those scales are enharmonically equivalent. Let's go to the piano and play the G♭ major scale. Now play the F♯ major scale. Notice something? You just played the same scale twice. That's because if notes can be enharmonically equivalent and scales are made up of notes, scales can be enharmonically equivalent as well.

Let's go one step further. Earlier, when covering the circle of fifths, we said C♯ wasn't that bad, but G♯ had eight sharps in a scale of seven notes. We can deal with that by having double sharps, but musicians are lazy and don't want to deal with those especially when we can use enharmonically equivalent scales. G♯ has eight sharps, but what if we used G♯'s enharmonic equivalent, A♭? It only has four flats and is much easier to deal with. And if we continue along our completed circle of fifths, where G♯ would have been we find A♭. Ah, the solutions!

Let's quickly go the other way. When covering the circle of fourths, we didn't want to deal with the scale F♭; it has eight flats—one of which is a double flat—and it's just a mess. If we use F♭'s enharmonically equivalent scale E, we only have four sharps to deal with. E is much nicer, much easier to deal with in this case.

The Circle of Fifths/ Fourths and Triads.

At this point, we now know the major scale in the key of C and we know the major scale in both the circle of fifths and fourth but we should take a moment to also discuss how triads are handled across other keys. The good news? We already know how to do this. The bad news is that there's a bit of memorization involved. Lets take a look at the first stop on the circle of fifths and harmonize the scale in triads – G major.

Remember that all major scales are built using the intervallic relationship WWHWWWH. Also remember that by using that major scale, we can build a series of triads that follow the pattern MmmMMmd.

Remember that we can only use the notes of G major to build the triads of G major. In the key of G, the first triad is G major (G-B-D). The second triad is A minor (A-C-E). So far, it looks very much like the C major scale. However, when we get to the third scale degree – B – things will change a bit.

When we build B minor – the third triad – we can to only use the notes of the G major scale. Remember that in C major, the quality of the B triad was diminished (B-D-F). Well in G major, we don't have F natural, we have F♯. The resulting chord is then B minor (B-D-F♯). This should make sense since we know that the third triad in all major scales is a minor triad (MmmMMmd).

The fourth scale degree – C – yields a major triad (C-E-G) but look at what happens at the fifth scale degree – D. The triad is major, as we'd expect, but look at the notes - D-F♯-A – and recognize that the F is now sharpened. Remember that the quality of the D triad in C major was D minor (D-F-A) but much like the B chord, we don't have F natural. We must use only the notes of the G major scale and since the quality of F in this scale is F♯, every time we see F we need to use F♯ instead.

The sixth scale degree – E – yields an expected minor triad (E-G-B) but on the seventh scale degree, we find ourselves at F♯. Much like in C major, the quality of the seventh scale degree triad is diminished and in the key of G major, that's F♯ diminished (F♯- A- C). Figure 5.15 shows the triads of G major as the harmonized scale.

The Triads of G major

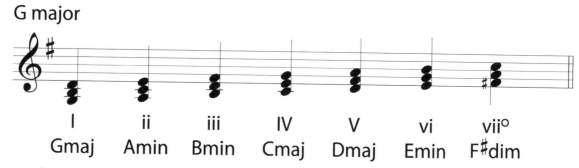

Figure 5.15: The scale of G major harmonized in triads.

This process is repeated for all of the major scales – whether the circle of fifths (sharps) or the circle of fourths (flats). Each scale has a series of triads that follow the pattern MmmMMmd – without fail.

The good news is that if you remember MmmMMmd, you can easily build the triads for any major scale. The bad news is that you need to know how many sharps (or flats) belong to that particular scale in order to build them correctly. Want some more good news? If you know WWHWWWH you can correctly build any major scale and its associated triads - without fail.

Take a moment to see how well (or poorly) you can build major scales using the patterns WWHWWWH and MmmMMmd. Try this:

☞ While we're on the circle of fifth, progress to the next scale – D major.

☞ Starting with the note D, build the major scale using the pattern WWHWWWH. This has already been done for you but try it by hand to test yourself. You can use pencil/staff paper, regular paper or just hit the piano. Double check your work and see if you get it right!

☞ Now, using only those notes, build your first triad – D major. Did you get it right? It should be D-F♯-A. Remember that the F♯ from G major stays with us in the D major scale.

☞ Continue onward through the scale degrees and build your triads. You should have results that follow the triad quality pattern MmmMMmd. Are you right? You can check yourself on figure 5.16 which not only shows the key of D major in scales, but all of the major scales and their triads.

Major Triads in All Keys

Figure 5.16: The major keys, harmonized in triads.

Worksheet 5.2: The Circle of Fifths/Fourths

Just to recap, at this point in our journey, we've really only covered two scales—the major scale and the chromatic scale. The work we just did on the circle of fifths and fourths is nothing more than other major scales with different starts and ends beyond C—all of which follow the pattern WWHWWWH. Along with moving the starting note in these scales comes new sharps and flats that belong to each scale. Learning how to play the major scale, the dyads and triads of the scale in other keys than C is a huge part of songwriting.

If you've ever worked with singers, you know that they have a range of keys where they're most comfortable. You might compose a song in one key, only to find that some of the notes of the singer's part fall above or below their comfortable range. If the song is already sequenced using MIDI, it's no big deal to simply transpose the parts. However, if you're still songwriting, they'll likely ask you to just play it in a different key.

And since you've been practicing, this'll be easy for you… right?

Well if you haven't, here's what you'll need to do:

☛ Play root notes around the circle of fifths, and then other way in the circle of fourths. By playing each of the notes that lead through the circles, you can become familiar with both the notes of each circle and the sound of the fifth and fourth intervals.

☛ As an advanced version of this, keep all of the notes in one octave. For example, **Figure 5.13** shows the circle of fifths as it increases continually versus keeping it within on octave. Knowing the circles in the octave range is handy for songwriting and voice leading.

5ths Ascending vs. Within One Octave

Figure 5.13: The circle of fifths written upward on the staff versus within one octave (to five positions only).

☛ Begin each practice session in the key of C and play the five-finger-only exercise up and down the scale. Try this with each hand separately, then together.

☛ Move through each circle, fifths first, and continue playing the five-finger technique in each key. Remember that each "new" sharp starts on the seventh scale degree, which you won't play using the five-finger technique, so if you only play the first five notes of G major, you won't get to F♯. You'll start to see some of the sharps in the key of D—two steps into the circle of fifths.

☛ After going through the circle of fifths, move to the circle of fourths and do the same, as seen in **Figure 5.14**.

4ths Ascending vs. Within One Ocatve

Figure 5.14: The circle of fourths written upward on the staff versus within one octave (to five positions only).

☛ As an advanced version of this, use your proper technique to step through the entire scale, starting and ending on the root.

☛ As another advanced version of this, play each scale in leapfrog position—the 1, then 3, then 2, then 4, and so on, starting and ending on the root note.

☛ Dyads: After the scale workout, try applying the previous dyad workouts to the circles. In one example, you could play from the root through the intervals—say, G-A, then G-B, then G-C, and so on.

☛ Dyads: As an advanced version of this, you could play the dyads with one hand simultaneously in leapfrog fashion where you'd play G-B, then A-C, then B-D, and so on.

☛ Triads: With your hands separate, play the triads of each scale as you flow through the circle of fifths first, then fourths—in root inversion. Be mindful of the sharps and flats in the particular scale you're playing in to ensure you get it right! Remember your MmmMMmd order, and cycle through each scale three times perfectly before moving to the next scale.

☛ Triads: As an alteration of this, try spelling the root inversions—1-3-5—on each triad through the scale. Move upward and downward through the scale this way until you've played all the triads. Do this three times perfectly before moving to the next scale.

☛ Triads: As an advanced version of this, play the triads in root inversion, then first, then second inversion, back to first then back to root inversion on each triad. Then, move to the next triad and do all three inversions as well in the same order.

☛ Triads: As yet another advanced version of this, play simple cadences in each of the keys as you cycle through the circle of fifths and fourths: choose a few progressions (I-IV-V-IV, or vi-ii-V-I, etc.) and play them through each key. Try to choose some progressions that when added, play each triad in the scale at least once.

DVD Callout: The Circle of Fifths and Fourths— A Musical Exercise

Successfully playing the major scales up and down a few times well along with a metronome is plenty to tackle at this stage. It can be difficult to wrap your head around the various keys and where and when to play the sharps and flats. We often suggest practicing at the first step in each circle for a while—G and F, along with C. Once you've gotten them down well, move to the next step—D and Bb. Play *all* of the variations listed on Worksheet 5.1 in each key. You'll get very good, very fast if you work it for an hour every night.

Odds are, the amount of exercises we've given at this time starts to add up to more than an hour per night. If so, start splitting your exercises into daily groups, for example, play one group on Monday, Wednesday, and Friday, and a different set of exercises on Tuesday and Thursday. Maybe one group is all scales and the other group is all dyad/triad work. Another variety is to work on the circle of fifths on M/W/F while working on the circle of fourths on T/Th. Mix it up, but practice it all during the week. Much like going to the gym, you work muscle groups every other visit. Same here—we're conditioning the whole musical body— not just the scales or triads!

The Relative Minor

Earlier in the section on triads, we saw a collection of triad substitutions—where one triad could be subbed for another based on common (but not exact) tones. The most common of these is known as the relative minor. This is where a major triad is subbed with a minor triad and vice versa. Specifically, the major triad is subbed with a minor triad that is exactly a minor third lower (three half-steps). For example, the relative minor of C major is A minor. Conversely, C major is called the relative major to A minor.

In the case of C major to A minor, the substitution is based on two common tones—C and E. C major triad is spelled C-E-G (root inversion) while A minor is spelled A-C-E (also root inversion). Thus, the C and E are common to both triads and they are close enough to each other to act as subs for each other. Also notice that A minor is the triad based on the sixth scale degree of C major—this is another way of identifying the relative minor of a major triad.

Figure 5.17 shows the circle of fifths/fourths again but this time the inside of the circle is filled with all the relative minor keys. The outer ring of upper case letters are the major keys. Following the red line to the lower-case letters shows each major key's relative minor key.

MEMORIZE ME!

Figure 5.17: The relative minor triads in the keys of the circle of fifths—up and down.

Circles

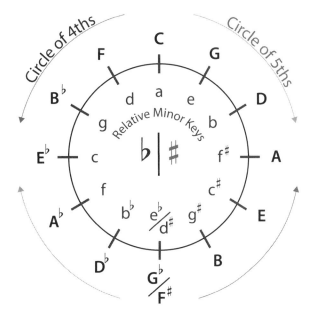

The relative minor is important to know because it presents the nearest emotional alternative to the major triad—and scale. Since they are so closely related, the two triads and the two scales are somewhat interchangeable.

For example, if we analyze the C major scale, we end up with the following triad sequence:

- ☛   C major

- ☛   D minor

- ☛   E minor

- ☛   F major

- ☛   G major

- ☛   A minor (the relative)

- ☛   B diminished

- ☛   C major (the octave)

If we do the same for the A minor scale, we end up with the following triad sequence. We'll dig into A minor more closely in the next sections…

- ☛   A minor

- ☛   B diminished

- ☛   C major (the relative)

- ☛   D minor

- ☛   E minor

- ☛   F major

- ☛   G major

- ☛   A minor (the octave)

As you can see, the quality of the triads are exactly the same as in C major—they just start and end the sequence at different positions. So, if you know the triads in one key (say, C major), you already know all the triads in the relative key (A minor in this case)!

You can see here, that while the triads are each the same, their order is different. This is important to recognizing that other scales outside of the major scale often relate back to the major scale. Simply find the relative major—or minor—note (up or down a minor third from the scale root) and you've found the relative major—or minor—scale.

Let's take a moment to define the relative minor scale, as it has a few qualities we should look at. The first is the quality of the scale degrees as they relate to the major scale. Remember that the major scale is built from the pattern WWHWWWH. The relative minor scale effectively starts at the sixth scale degree and follows the same pattern. In this case, we start the pattern with the last WH then wrap the pattern around until we land on the sixth scale degree again. The intervallic pattern of the relative minor is then WHWWHWW. This translates to scale degrees that follow this pattern in the minor scale:

☛ W—from the root to the second scale degree is a whole step. In the case of A minor, this yields B.

☛ H—from the second scale degree to the third is a half step. In the case of A minor, this yields a C, which is a half step up from B—the second scale degree. Notice that the third scale degree is flattened compared to the A major scale—C in the A minor scale instead of C♯ in the A major scale.

☛ W—from the third scale degree to the fourth is a whole step. In the case of A minor, this yields a D, up a whole step from C—the flattened third scale degree.

☛ W—from the fourth scale degree to the fifth is a whole step. In the case of A minor, this yields an E, up a whole step from D—the fourth scale degree.

☛ H—from the fifth scale degree to the sixth is a half step. In the case of A minor, this yields an F, up a half step from E—the fifth scale degree. Notice that the sixth scale degree is flattened compared with the major scale—F in the key of A minor instead of F♯ in the key of A major.

☛ W—from the sixth scale degree to the seventh is a whole step. In the case of A minor, this yields a G, up a whole step from F—the flattened sixth scale degree. Notice that the seventh scale degree is flattened compared with the major scale—G in the key of A minor instead of G♯ in the key of A major.

☛ W—from the seventh scale degree to the octave is a whole step. In the case of A minor, this yields the A again, up a whole step from G—the flattened seventh scale degree.

So the relative minor has three alterations from the major scale of the same note—the third, sixth, and seventh scale degrees are flattened when compared to the major scale of that key. In other words, A minor is just like A major except that the third, sixth and seventh scale degrees are flattened – C, F and G instead of C♯, F♯ and G♯. This definition has another name—the *natural minor* scale.

Natural Minor

The natural minor scale is one where the third, sixth, and seventh scale degrees are flattened when compared to the major scale of the same root note.

To make matters more confusing, there are in fact two other minor scales—the *harmonic minor* and the *melodic minor*—with different characteristics than the natural minor.

Harmonic Minor

The harmonic minor scale is one where the third and sixth scale degrees are flattened when compared to the major scale. The seventh remains natural.

Melodic Minor

A minor scale where the "up" of the scale consists of a flattened third and the "down" of the scale consists of a flattened third, sixth, and seventh scale degree.

The harmonic minor is an interesting one as there is a very large intervallic jump between the sixth and seventh scale degree. Take a look at **Figure 5.18** for a moment and see how the major, the minor (natural minor, a.k.a. relative minor), the harmonic minor, and the melodic minor compare. Hear them all in **Audio Track 61**.

Figure 5.18: A staff comparison between the major, the natural minor, the melodic minor, and the harmonic minor.

Audio Track 61: A comparison between the major, the natural minor, the harmonic, and the melodic minor in C.

Notice how the relative (a.k.a. natural) minor has a flattened third, flattened sixth, and flattened seventh, while the harmonic minor has a flattened third and a flattened sixth. A natural minor has a natural seventh, creating an interval of a minor third between the sixth and seventh.

In the key of C, you'll see the following notes that align between the minor scales:

- ☛ Major: C D E F G A B C

- ☛ Minor: C D E♭ F G A♭ B♭ C

- ☛ Harmonic minor: C D E♭ F G A♭ B C

The third kind of minor scale is called the melodic minor. It is a cross between the other two minor scales in that it behaves one way when ascending through the scale and another way when descending through the scale.

With the melodic minor, the scale is played upward with only the third flattened. This is enough to qualify it as a minor scale, but all other scale degrees are the same as the major. However, when played downward, the scale then includes the flattened sixth and seventh scale degrees—complementing the natural (a.k.a. relative) minor scale.

Note that as you progress upward through the circle of fifths, the relative minors also move in fifths—not a big surprise. The same holds true for the circle of fourths, where the relative minors also move in fourths. For the remainder of this book, we'll be looking exclusively at the natural (a.k.a. relative) minor. There are lots of other types of minor scales (called modes) that we'll see soon enough, but we will not spend more time on the harmonic or melodic minors.

Chops Test: Chromatic Scale, Circle of Fifths, and the Natural Minor

OK, now it's time to test yourself. Do not attempt this part of the book until you've been practicing for a week or so. Give yourself ample time to get going with the C major scale and get some confidence before attempting this.

That said, this chops test is really here to see how far you go on your own with your practicing. We did not discuss much of what's listed here, so we leave it to you to find these exercises on your own. You might have found these or others—you might not. Once you think you're comfortable with the C major scale, take the test. If there's a bunch you can't do, go practice that stuff for another week, then try again.

It's all good stuff and very important for later.

Let's see what you can do…

Basic Chops

By now, you should be able to do the following:

☞ Perform *all* of the basic chops test items from the previous sections.

☞ Recognize all of the starting notes of both the circle of fifths and the circle of fourths.

☞ Play the major scale in each hand separately throughout both circles—at least to two positions (G, D and F, B♭).

☞ Play the major scale in both hands together throughout both circles—at least to two positions (G, D and F, B♭.

☞ Play the intervals and triads of each major scale of the circle of fifths—at least two positions (G, D and F, B♭).

☞ Play the triads and their inversions of each major scale of the circle of fifths—at least two positions (G, D and F, B♭).

☞ Play the I-IV-V within each major scale of the circle of fifths—at least two positions (G, D and F, B♭).

Advanced Chops

By now you may be able to do the following:

☞ Perform all of the basic and advanced chops test items from the previous sections.

☞ Recognize all of the starting notes of both the circle of fifths and the circle of fourths—both as they go up the octaves and within a single octave.

☞ Play the major scale in each hand separately throughout both circles to at least five positions.

☞ Play the major scale in both hands together throughout both circles to at least five positions.

☞ Play the intervals and triads of each major scale of the circle of fifths to at least five positions.

☞ Play the triads and their inversions of each major scale of the circle of fifths to at least five positions.

☞ Play the I-IV-V and a few other progressions within each major scale of the circle of fifths in at least five positions.

Section 6
Beyond the Triads: Seventh Chords

RECAP

Using the interval relationship of the major scale, WWHWWWH, we can build major scales in keys beyond C by moving through the circle of fifths up or down. When we move up in fifths, each new key has a new sharp note (♯) that is natural to that key and as we move down in fifths, each new key has a new flat note (♭) that is natural to that key.

Every major scale has a relative minor scale that is a minor third below its major counterpart—also found at the sixth scale degree. This scale is known as both the relative minor (note) and the natural minor (scale built from the relative minor). Two other minor scales exist—the harmonic and the melodic—each of which has alterations from the natural minor at the sixth and seventh scale degree.

We have covered a large amount of information and in great detail. However, you might have noticed that we've restricted our conversations to notes, intervals (harmonic and melodic), and triads only. But there are other chords that can be made as well—and made from the *same scales* we've been covering.

Up until now, we've been working looking at chords exclusively with triads—three note chords made up of stacked third intervals. These are the basic building blocks of music and as you have seen, we can do a *lot* of good work with triads. It's possible that you'll write all of your music using triads and only triads. In fact, it's also possible that you'll write all of your music in only one key—using only seven triads for life (you know who you are…).

We're not going to cover all of music here—that would be nuts. But we are going to extend our knowledge of the major/minor worlds a bit by at least one note at a time. In other words, we're going to build bigger chords with more notes. This is much like learning words in another language that are bigger than just three, four, and five letters long. We call them *extended chords*.

> **Extended Chords**
> Chords built from third intervals with more than three notes in it.

> **Seventh Chords**
> Four-note chords built from third intervals where a third above the fifth is added. This note is usually a seventh in distance from the root of the triad.

The seventh chord is the most common extended chord as it adds another note, a seventh from the root, to the standard triad. There are a few types of seventh chords and like the triads, not all of them are natural to any particular key. Remember how the augmented triad didn't fit in the major scale? The same is true here; as an example, not all types of seventh chords belong to any major scale.

To keep things simple at first, we'll go back to our old friend C major to begin our work with seventh chords.

Let's revisit the scale and triads first shown here:

☛   C major scale (built from WWHWWWH)

CDEFGABC

☛   C major triads (MmmMMmd)

C-E-G:	**C major**
D-F-A:	**D minor**
E-G-B:	**E minor**
F-A-C:	**F major**
G-B-D:	**G major**
A-C-E:	**A minor**
B-D-F:	**B diminished**

Creating seventh chords is a simple process. You just add another third above the fifth of the triad. For the first chord, C-E-G (C major), we'd first look at the fifth of the triad, G, and then add a third to it.. The result is C-E-G-B, known as the major seventh chord. **Figure 6.1** shows the first seventh chord in C major (C-E-G-B), a.k.a., C major seventh. You can hear it in **Audio Track 62.**

Figure 6.1: C major seventh shown on the staff.

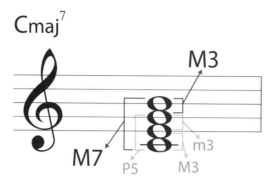

Audio Track 62: The C major seventh chord, showcasing the major triad and minor triads within it.

> **Major Seventh Chord**
> A chord is said to be a major seventh when it consists of a major triad and a major third interval above the fifth of that triad.

The C major seventh chord is spelled C-E-G-B. You'll notice that the first triad (C-E-G) is a major triad but there's another triad in the chord: E-G-B. This is a minor triad. You can think of the major seventh chord as either a major triad with a major third above the fifth (adding the seventh) *or* as a 4-note chord with the first three notes creating a major triad and the last three notes creating a minor triad. What's important is that you know what it is and how to build it.

Let's keep going and look at the next triad in the C major scale, D minor, and see what kind of seventh chord it makes.

We already know that we need to take D minor and add a third to the top of it, but what kind of third will we be adding—a major or a minor? Again, we don't have to think too hard about it—the notes of C major already tell us what notes are available, so we just need to choose the right one. Therefore, since we can *only* use the notes of the C major scale to build our chords (for now) we only need to leapfrog the next note to the correct third.

Let's take a look.

Remember that D minor is spelled D-F-A. Also remember that we need to add a third above the fifth of that triad to find the top note in the seventh chord. We could try a major third above A: C♯. Well, C♯ doesn't exist in C major, so we have to use the next logical note. Note that it can't be D as it's a fourth above A and not a third. Since it isn't D nor C♯, it must be C. So, our D minor triad, D-F-A, becomes D-F-A-C—our seventh chord. In this case, we define it as a minor seventh chord.

The Minor Seventh Chord
The minor seventh chord is defined as a minor triad with a minor third interval above the fifth scale degree of the triad.

The D minor seventh chord is spelled D-F-A-C. You'll notice that the first triad (D-F-A) is a minor triad but there's another triad in the chord—F-A-C. This is a major triad. So, you can think of the minor seventh chord as either a minor triad with a minor third above the fifth, *or* as a 4-note chord with the first three notes creating a minor triad and the last three notes creating a major triad. What's important is that you know what it is and how to build it. You can see it and hear it in **Figure 6.2** and **Audio Track 63**.

Figure 6.2: D minor seventh shown on the staff.

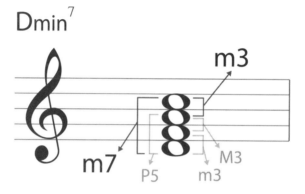

Audio Track 63: The D minor seventh chord, showcasing the two triads within it.

If we keep going through the next triads, we'll find that the next scale degree, E, yields a minor triad as well: E minor spelled E-G-B. Since we're not sure which third to add (major or minor), we can test by first adding a major third to B to get D♯. Since D♯ doesn't exist in C major we use the next closest note, D, which happens to be a minor third away from the fifth scale degree. Again we have a minor triad (E-G-B) with a minor third interval above the fifth (D on top of B), which is another minor seventh chord. So the third seventh chord in C major is E minor 7.

Next is F, which is a major triad (F-A-C). Adding the major third to C yields E (found naturally in the key of C major), which is a major third above the fifth of the triad F major. We've already defined this relationship as a major seventh chord. You'll also recognize that the chord has a major triad (F-A-C) under a minor triad (A-C-E), which is another defining characteristic of the major seventh chord.

So, the first four seventh chords of the scale are C major seventh, D minor seventh, E minor seventh, and F major seventh, shown in **Figure 6.3** and heard in **Audio Track 64**. You might recognize a pattern here—major 7, minor 7, minor 7, then major 7—very similar to the triad pattern—MmmM—which is the first half of the triad pattern of the C major scale. While it's nice that the seventh chords follow the triads in the first half of the scale, the pattern disrupts at the fifth chord. The fifth chord (G in this case) changes things a bit as we introduce a new kind of seventh chord—the *dominant* seventh.

Figure 6.3: The first four seventh chords of C major shown on the staff.

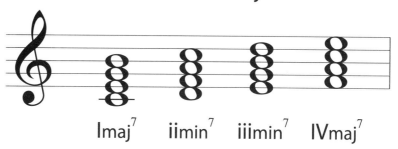

First Four 7 Chords of C Major

Audio Track 64: The first four seventh chords of C major.

> **Dominant Seventh Chord**
> The dominant seventh chord is defined as a major triad with a minor third interval above the fifth scale degree of the triad.

The G dominant seventh chord is spelled G-B-D-F (F is the next logical third that fits above the fifth scale degree, D). You'll notice that the first triad (G-B-D) is a major triad but there's diminished triad in the chord—B-D-F. This is a bit of an odd mix, blending the very "happy" major triad with the very "tense" diminished triad. The dominant seventh chord is unique in this regard and is prone to very strange behavior. We'll see that a bit later when we discuss the concept of dominance.

You can think of the dominant seventh chord as either a major triad with a minor third above the fifth, *or* as a four-note chord with the first three notes creating a major triad and the last three notes creating a diminished triad. What's important is that you know what it is and how to build it. You can see it and hear it in **Figure 6.4** and **Audio Track 65**.

Note that the major and minor seventh chords often have the moniker M (major) or m (minor) associated with the number 7 next to it. Not so with the dominant 7 chord. Its moniker is simply to have a 7 attached to the Roman numeral "V" so you'll see it as V7. When there is no M or m with the 7, know the chord as the dominant 7, sometimes referred to as the "five-7."

Figure 6.4: G dominant 7 shown on the staff.

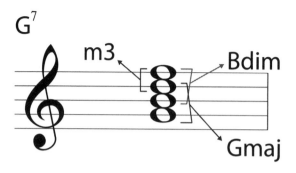

Audio Track 65: The G dominant 7 chord, showcasing the two triads within it.

The next chord in our C major scale is A. When we add the next logical third above the triad's fifth (which is G), the A minor triad becomes a minor seventh chord. This creates a minor triad in the first three notes and a major triad in the second three notes. The triad A-C-E has the note G added, making A-C-E-G, also known as A minor 7. Simple enough—it follows the same rules as D minor 7 and E minor 7.

The last note in the scale, the seventh, B, however, is unique and a bit more complex.

The seventh triad is naturally a diminished triad (B-D-F), so we must recognize that the seventh quality is going to be different from the previous six chords. Now, when we add the next third above the fifth (F) of the diminished triad, we get A, a major third interval above. So this last seventh chord, B-D-F-A has a diminished triad (B-D-F) in the first three notes and a minor triad in the last three notes (D-F-A). The name of this chord is a *minor 7/flat 5*. In some circles, it's known as a *half-diminished* chord.

> **Minor 7/Flat 5 (a.k.a. the half-diminished chord)**
> The minor 7/flat 5 chord is defined as a diminished triad with a major third interval above the fifth scale degree.

You can see it and hear it in **Figure 6.5** and **Audio Track 66**.

Figure 6.5: B minor 7/flat 5 shown on the staff.

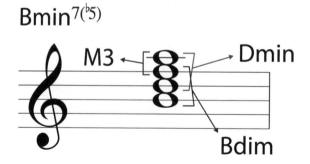

Audio Track 66: The B minor 7/flat 5 chord, showcasing the two triads within it.

Coach's Corner: The Chord with the Funny Name

The minor 7/flat 5 chord is a funny name for sure. Why such a weird name? Since the first triad is a diminished one, why not just call the chord a diminished seventh chord? Truth is, there's another seventh chord called the diminished seventh chord and it deserves the title more so than the minor 7/flat 5, which we'll see shortly…

So wrapping things up, we find that the major scale has three types of triads (major, minor, and diminished) but four types of seventh chords (major 7, minor 7, dominant 7, and half-diminished 7—a.k.a. minor 7/♭5). You can see them listed in order in **Figure 6.6** and hear them in C major in **Audio Track 67**.

Figure 6.6: C major scale harmonized in seventh chords.

7th Chords Analyzed with Roman Numerals

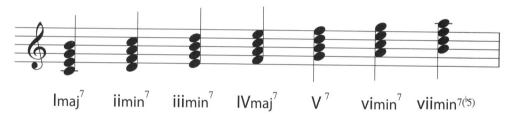

Imaj⁷   iimin⁷   iiimin⁷   IVmaj⁷   V⁷   vimin⁷   viimin⁷⁽♭⁵⁾

Audio Track 67: The C major scale harmonized in sevenths.

Coach's Corner: Fun with Seventh Chords

You might guess that the seventh chords are the same in all major scales. That is, as you travel through the circle of fifths and fourths, you'll find that the progression of the seventh chords is the same throughout each scale. Have some fun and go through each key in both circles and chart out each of the seventh chords to see if you've got them right. If not, take a look at **Figure CC6.1**—we've done the work for you… You can thank us later!

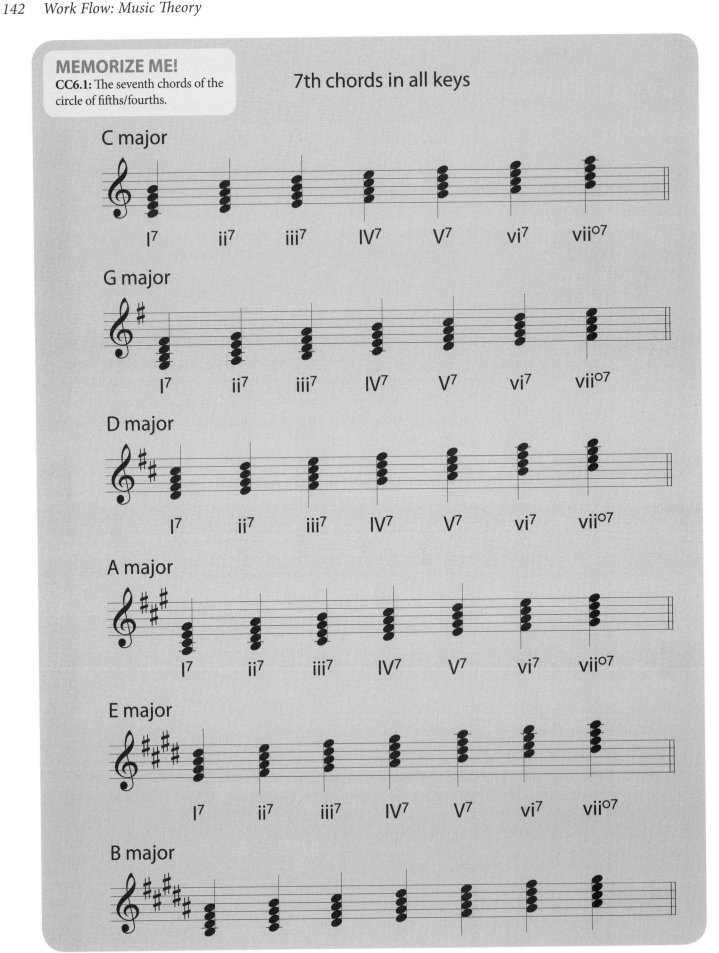

MEMORIZE ME!
CC6.1: The seventh chords of the circle of fifths/fourths.

7th chords in all keys

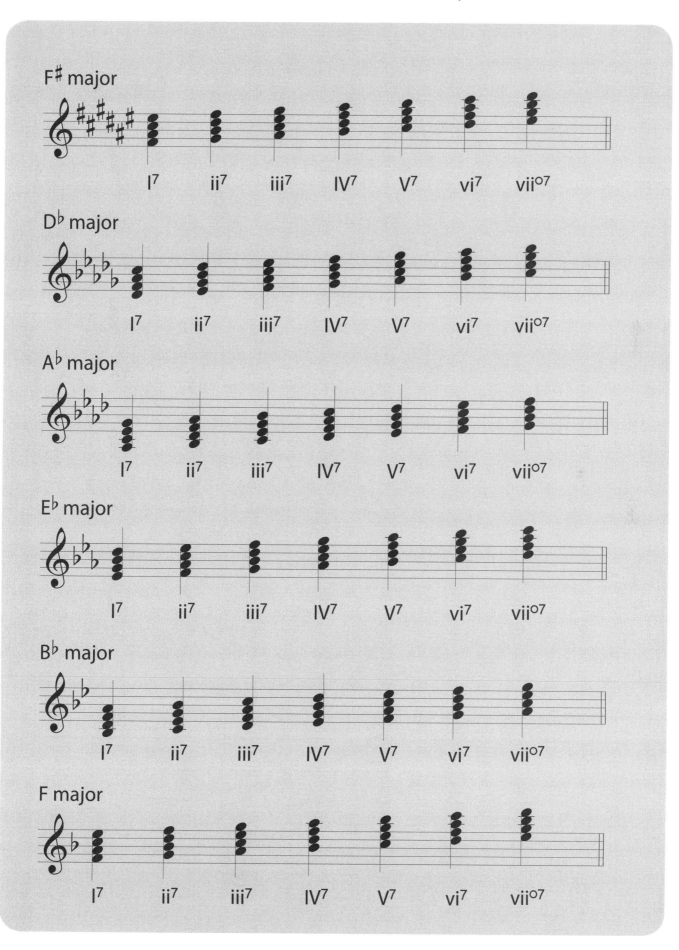

To review, here are some quick hints on the seventh chords of the major scale and some of their characteristics. Note that all versions of the seventh chords are spelled with C as the root note so you can truly see the side-by-side comparisons of the chords:

The *major* seventh chord (example is C major 7):

☛ The first three notes are a major triad.

☛ The last three notes are a minor triad.

☛ The third intervals "flip-flop"—the first interval is a major third (C-E), the second interval is a minor third (E-G), and the last third is a major third (G-B).

☛ Note its uniquely "soft" and "happy" sound (author's opinion).

The *minor* seventh chord (example is C minor 7):

☛ The first three notes are a minor triad.

☛ The last three notes are a major triad.

☛ The third intervals "flip-flop"—the first interval is a minor third (C-E♭), the second interval is a major third (E♭-G), and the last third is a minor third (G-B♭).

☛ Note its uniquely "soft" and "sad" sound (author's opinion).

The *dominant* seventh chord (example is C dominant 7):

☛ The first three notes are a minor triad.

☛ The last three notes are a diminished triad.

☛ The third intervals are all different but don't "flip-flop" exactly—the first interval is a major third (C-E), the second interval is a minor third (E-G), and the last third is also minor third (G-B♭).

☛ Note its uniquely "hard" and "tense" or "anticipated" sound (author's opinion).

The minor 7/flat 5 chord—a.k.a. the half-diminished (example is C minor 7/♭5):

☛ The first three notes are a diminished triad.

☛ The last three notes are a minor triad.

☛ The third intervals are all different but don't "flip-flop" exactly—the first interval is a minor third (C-E♭), the second interval is also minor third (Eb-G♭, and the last third is a major third (G♭-B).

☞ Note its uniquely "angular" and "spacey" sound (author's opinion).

Note that these four seventh chords are only the four types found in the major scale. There are some others, but we won't discuss them all here. We'll simply list a few and their characters and you can play with them if you like.

The *diminished* seventh chord (example is C dim 7):

☞ The first three notes are a diminished triad.

☞ The last three notes are a diminished triad.

☞ The third intervals are *all* minor thirds (C-E♭/E♭-G♭/G♭-B♭♭). Note the enharmonic equivalent of B♭♭ (double flat) is A. Double flats are strange territory for us and we'll try to avoid them from here on out.

☞ Note its uniquely "threatening" sound (author's opinion).

☞ The author usually describes this chord as the "Oh, S*&^T he's coming!" chord or the "tie-her-to-the-railroad-tracks" chord (referring to the sound of old silent films where the bad guy always ties the girl to the railroad tracks).

Coach's Corner: The "True" Diminished Seventh Chord

Remember when we mentioned that there was another seventh chord that was more deserving of the title *diminished seventh*? Here's why…

The diminished triad is a stack of minor third intervals. In the case of C major, it's B dim, or B-D-F. B to D is a minor third and D to F is also a minor third. Well, if you add another minor third to the already stacked minor thirds, we get the *true* diminished seventh chord—*all* stacked minor thirds. In the key of C major, when looking at the seventh scale degree B, we would add a minor third to the triad B diminished to get B-D-F-A♭ (F to A♭ is a minor third). This is a much more tense and angry chord than the relatively spacey minor 7/flat 5 and, as such, is more deserving of the name. Because the minor 7/♭5 chord has a natural seventh in A, it can only be called half-diminished. Note that the minor 7/♭5 title comes from the jazz world while the half-diminished is potentially a more common title in pop and other genres.

The minor/major seventh chord (example is C minor/major 7):

☞ The first three notes are a minor triad.

☞ The last three notes are an augmented triad.

☛ The third intervals partially "flip-flop"—the first interval is a minor third (C-E♭), the second interval is a major third (E♭-G), but the last third is also a major third (G-B).

☛ Note its uniquely "spacey" and "awkward" sound (author's opinion).

☛ The author often describes this chord as the "Mickey Spillane" chord as it seems to be used often in *noir*-ish private detective films.

The *augmented* major seventh chord (example is C augmented major 7):

☛ The first three notes are an augmented triad.

☛ The last three notes are a major triad.

☛ The third intervals partially "flip-flop"—the first interval is a major third (C-E), the second interval is also a major third (E-G♯), but the last third is also a minor third (G♯-B).

☛ Note its uniquely "angular" and "ugly" sound (author's opinion).

Seventh Chord Inversions

Now that we've seen all of the major scales through the circle of fifths and fourths, the relative minor scale, *and* seventh chords, you might wonder what's left. We assure you, there is still plenty to know—much more than we'll cover in this book. But before jumping into new territory, there is something from the past that we can reuse here to create new sounds with the chords we've learned, and that's inversions.

Do you remember when we took the three-note triads and made inversions from them? The root, first, and second inversions all used the same three notes but created the chord with different scale degrees on the bottom, middle, and top positions.

Well, seventh chords can become inverted as well but since there are four notes per chord, we now have four types of seventh chord inversions. Just like the triads, you can create them by simply shuffling the lowest note to the top of the chord as you move through the inversions.

You already know the first one: root inversion. In this case, the chord is spelled in a standard way, where the lowest note is the root of the chord and each subsequent third interval creates the next note in the chord. For example, dealing with our new friend C major 7, you'd spell the chord C-E-G-B, where the notes from lowest to highest are the root, major third, fifth, and major seventh. Notice that each note is a third away from each other note, just as you'd expect.

The next inversion, creatively called the first inversion, leads the chord with the third in the bottom as the root moves to the top of the chord—all other notes stay the same. In this case, the C major seventh chord would be spelled E-G-B-C. Note that the C is in the octave *above* the root and is not just the lower C played last. Take a close look at the intervals of this chord though; compared to the triads, they are different for sure.

We know that seventh chords are made out of stacked thirds just like triads but when you start inverting them, the third relationship is no longer consistent through the chord. This was true with triads (a fourth interval appeared in the first and second inversion) and is still true here in seventh chords. With the C major 7 chord first inversion, you'll notice that the first interval, from E to G, is still a third—a minor third. The second interval, from G to B, is also still a third, but the last interval, from B to C, is a minor second. So, while triads had third and fourth intervals in the inversions, seventh chords have thirds and second intervals. You can see all the inversions of Cmaj7 in **Figure 6.7** and hear them on **Audio Track 68**.

Figure 6.7: Cmaj7 harmonized in inversions.

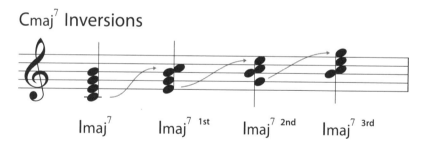

Audio Track 68: C major 7 harmonized in inversions.

Coach's Corner: Recognizing Seventh Chord Inversions

When dealing with chord inversions, there are a few easy mistakes that get made, especially when we deal with seventh chords. Remember when we first inverted triads? Do you remember how the intervals would change from stacked thirds to a third and a fourth? There is a shortcut to recognizing triad inversions by recognizing the fourth: if the fourth is between the first two notes, the triad is a second inversion triad and if it's between the second two notes, the triad is a first inversion.

Notice that the seventh chords have no fourth interval so we can't use this technique. However, you can use a similar one. Notice in the first inversion seventh chord, there is a second interval that is more like a cluster of notes than a gap. With seventh chords, you look for the cluster and its position. The root inversion has no cluster (it's all third intervals), but with the first inversion, the cluster is at the top—between the third and fourth notes of the spelling (which correspond to the seventh and first scale degrees: B and C). This is a good shortcut to recognizing this chord, E-G-B-C, as a C major 7 in first inversion and not some weird E minor triad with a flat sixth. Remember that as we respell chords, the names do *not* change. L-A-K-E still has the same musical meaning as K-A-L-E. Chords are the same; as we jumble the notes around, the name stays the same.

The next inversion of the seventh chord is the second inversion, where the fifth scale degree is the lowest note. Back to C major 7, the chord would be spelled G-B-C-E. The bass note is the fifth scale degree, the next note is the major seventh scale degree, then the root and the major third on top. Notice that the intervals are: major third (G-B), minor second (B-C), then a major third (C-E). Notice that there's a minor second interval (cluster) in the middle of the inversion, where B and C lie next to each other.

The third inversion seventh chord leads with the major seventh scale degree (B) then has the root (C) directly above it, a minor second away (cluster). Then come the major third scale degree (E) and the fifth, each a third interval above the note before. The chord is spelled B-C-E-G. Notice that there's a minor second interval in the bottom of the inversion, where B and C lie next to each other.

If we extend our view to the other seventh chords in the C major scale, we'll find a few slight variations.

The second chord in the C major scale is the D minor 7 chord, D-F-A-C. The four inversions are seen in **Figure 6.8** and heard on **Audio Track 69**. Notice that the inversions (only) have a second interval in it, much like the major 7 chord, although here it is a major second—a whole step apart.

Figure 6.8: D minor 7 harmonized in inversions.

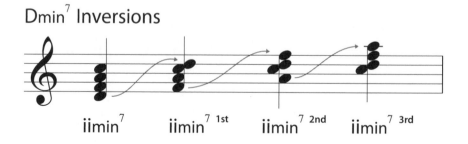

Dmin⁷ Inversions

Audio Track 69: D minor 7 harmonized in inversions.

The third chord in the C major scale is the E minor 7 chord, E-G-B-D. The four inversions are seen in **Figure 6.9** and heard on **Audio Track 70**. Notice that the inversions (only) have a major second interval as well.

Figure 6.9: E minor 7 harmonized in inversions.

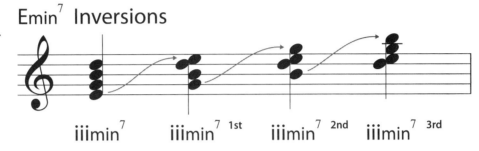

Audio Track 70: E minor 7 harmonized in inversions.

The fourth chord in the C major scale is the F major 7 chord, F-A-C-E. The four inversions are seen in **Figure 6.10** and heard on **Audio Track 71**. Notice that the inversions (only) have a second interval as well, although here it is a minor second as it is in C major 7.

Figure 6.10: F major 7 harmonized in inversions.

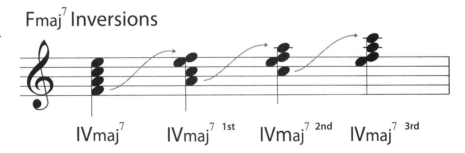

Audio Track 71: F major 7 harmonized in inversions.

The fifth chord in the C major scale is the G dominant 7 chord, G-B-D-F. The four inversions are seen in **Figure 6.11** and heard on **Audio Track 72**. Notice that the inversions (only) have a second interval as well, although here it is a major second—a whole step apart. This is interesting as the second interval is the same as it is in a minor seventh chord, even though the first triad is a major one.

Figure 6.11: G dominant 7 harmonized in inversions.

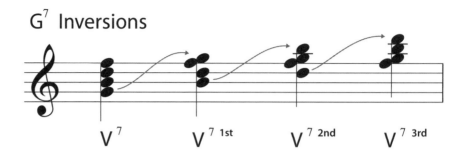

Audio Track 72: G dominant 7 harmonized in inversions.

The sixth chord in the C major scale is the A minor 7 chord, A-C-E-G. The four inversions are seen in **Figure 6.12** and heard on **Audio Track 73**. Notice that the inversions (only) have a second interval as well, although here it is a major second—a whole step apart.

Figure 6.12: A minor 7 harmonized in inversions.

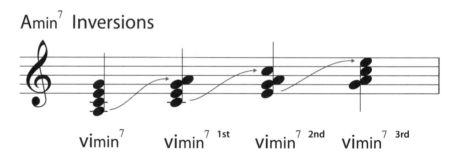

Audio Track 73: A minor 7 harmonized in inversions.

The seventh chord in the C major scale is the B half-diminished 7 chord, B-D-F-A. The four inversions are seen in **Figure 6.13** and heard on **Audio Track 74**. Notice that the inversions (only) have a second interval as well, although here it is a major second—a whole step apart.

Figure 6.13: B half-diminished 7 harmonized in inversions.

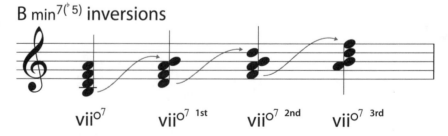

Audio Track 74: B half-diminished 7 harmonized in inversions.

Worksheet 6.1: Attaching Emotions to the Seventh Chords and Their Inversions

One of the things that should be familiar to you is the "emotional chart" process—we did it for two-note intervals, dyads, and triads, and we now do it for sevenths. As usual, build your emotional chart for the seventh chords of C major and write down the feeling that comes to you first when you hear it. This will help you memorize the sound of each seventh chord type and will help you recognize it when you hear it. To begin with, do this for the C major scale only, harmonized in sevenths but in root inversion only.

Once you've done the root inversion, add each other inversion to your chart to see if you can hear the difference while staying in C major. We suggest that you work on this by moving through each chord, one inversion at a time. Try to recognize by ear where the second interval is—the top, middle, or bottom—as a means to sonically identify the inversion of the chord. Then, try doing it through each inversion chord by chord. Start with C major 7 root inversion, then move to D major 7 root inversion, and so on. After B minor 7/♭5, go back to C and play the C major 7 chord in first inversion. Harmonize through the scale in all first inversion chords, then second, then third inversions.

It should go without saying that you can take this process further by moving it through each position on the circle of fifths and fourths. That is, do the emotional chart for the C major scale in all inversions, then reproduce the same chart for the G major scale, F major, D major, B♭ major, and so on. This will help you achieve the following:

☛ Learn to hear that the quality of the four types of seventh chords are the same no matter what key. That is, the third scale degree will always be a minor seventh chord and all minor sevenths sound similar. (Yet another example of how the interval relationships never change but the notes continue to change.)

☛ Learn how to play the seventh chords in all keys. This not only helps you "stick" the seventh chords and their sounds, it also helps you learn and "stick" the accidentals that belong in each key.

☛ Learn how to keep the accidentals constant as you invert the seventh chords. In G major, for example, you'll get very familiar with the fact that F is played as F♯ as you play through each seventh chord in all inversions.

Seventh Chords and Dominance

Earlier in the section where we introduced the four seventh chords, we said that one version of the seventh chord was special above the others. This chord represents one of the most tense relationships in music as well as one of the strongest ones. It holds both a major triad and a diminished triad at the same time—both happy and tense together—and holds many secrets to songwriting and key movement. Let's take a closer look at our new friend, the *dominant* seventh chord.

> **Dominant Seventh Chords**
> The dominant seventh chord is built from stacked thirds, such that the root inversion of the chord is a root, major third, perfect fifth, and flattened seventh of any major scale.

Let's look again at the C major scale harmonized in sevenths as listed in **Figure 6.6 repeat** (yep, we're showing you this figure twice, because it is that important).

Figure 6.6 repeat: The seventh chords of C major.

7th Chords Analyzed with Roman Numerals

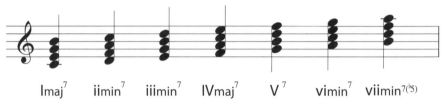

Imaj^7 iimin^7 iiimin^7 IVmaj^7 V^7 vimin^7 viimin$^{7(\flat5)}$

As you can see, the fifth chord of C major is G dominant 7. If we break the chord down into two parts (the bottom three and the top three notes in root inversion only), we find a major triad shared with a diminished triad. In the case of G7, we find that G-B-D-F contains the G major triad (G-B-D) and the B diminished triad (B-D-F). That's where the "happy" and the "tense" triads live next to each other.

Coach's Corner: The Dominant Chord Throughout History

Note that the description of the dominant chord as "holding the most tension" is a very old and subjective description. This was true with music up through the Classical period (the eighteenth century) and is somewhat true today. However, as the rules of music have been bending for several hundred years, many other chords are now used that arguably hold more tension than the dominant seventh. We still say it is the most tense though, as it has been so influential in many styles of music—from classical, orchestral, jazz, Latin, big band, swing, ragtime, and gospel to blues and even pop. The Beatles, for example, were big users of the dominant seventh chord.

One of the key functions of the dominant 7 chord is to establish that it is the V7 of the current major key and that right afterwards, you will likely hear a I chord—this was defined as the authentic cadence from earlier. So whenever you hear the V7 (or any dominant for that matter), you might expect that the root chord will follow soon. We like to say that the dominant chord "falls" to the I chord, implying that the dominant is somehow "above" the I and that gravity (emotional gravity in this case) will "pull" the V7 onto the I. The concept of dominance is so strong that really, any chord, whether naturally a V7 or not, can become a V7 which would then "fall" to the I below it. This process of the V7 predicting the I soon after is often referred to as *dominance* as the V7 "dominates" the I.

In C major, we would hear G7 "falling" to C major 7. If we wrote a triad progression with the following chords: I, ii, V, and I, but played it with seventh chords, we'd hear Cmaj7 (IM7), Dmin7 (iim7), then G7 (V7), repeating back to the root of Cmaj7 (IM7). In fact, no matter the progression, it's common for the V7 chord to immediately proceed the I chord (again, authentic cadence) whether at the beginning, middle, or end of the progression. The progression above (IM7-iim7-V7-IM7) looks and sounds like **Figure 6.14** and **Audio Track 75**.

Figure 6.14: Imaj7–iimin7-V7-Imaj7 cadence in C major.

I-ii-V-I Progression

Imaj⁷   iimin ⁷   V⁷   Imaj⁷

Audio Track 75: The I-ii-V7-I progression in C major, played as seventh chords.

This is about as clean a description of dominance as there is: the V7 "falls" to the I immediately afterwards. Note that there are times when the V7 will *not* fall to the I but for now, let's just take it as a general guideline that it does fall to I. For now, we'll call this rule *primary dominance*. *Secondary dominance* takes this simple V7-I relationship to another level.

Secondary Dominance
Secondary dominance occurs when a dominant chord progresses to another seventh chord a fifth below and not directly to the concluding I chord.

The basic concept of secondary dominance is nothing more than applying the basic concept of dominance to some circumstance other than the traditional V7-I relationship. One might ask, if *only* the V7 chord is dominant in the major scales, *can* there be secondary dominance here? The answer is no. For secondary dominance to occur, there must be a dominant chord in the progression that does *not* belong to the major key naturally.

Consider the following:

Secondary dominance can be applied to *any* chord at *any* time for *any* reason. In other words, *any* chord can *become* a dominant chord—just because. It's often categorized as *dealer's choice*; songwriters have the prerogative to alter any chord in the progression to a dominant 7 chord because they want to create tension. Remember that the V7-I relationship is strong one—perhaps the strongest chordal relationship. As such, we might want to use it in other places within the progression. Since dominance introduces tension, what would happen if we chose to create tension at another scale degree?

Coach's Corner: The "Matrix" Chord

Have you ever seen the legendary 1999 movie *The Matrix*? It's one of my favorite movies, as you might have heard me mention before. (If you're not a fan, keep your criticism to yourself. This is *not* a movie opinion forum and *I'm* in charge!) One of my favorite characters in the movie is Agent Smith. If you remember, Agent Smith was able to take over any human in the Matrix at any time for any reason. Usually, it was to chase Neo. Suffice it to say that in the Matrix, Agent Smith is everyone—and no one. (Thanks, Morpheus!)

Think of the Dominant 7 chord as Agent Smith. Any chord can simply (zzzzaaaapppp!) become dominant for any reason and in doing so, "up" the tension level. Think of the I chord as Neo (an aptly scrambled version of the "One")—always being chased by Agent Smith. Smith creates tension, while Neo creates the release of that tension. In this case, the dominant 7 chord creates the tension while the I chord releases that tension. That's the V7-I relationship in a nutshell: the V7 (Agent Smith) chases the One (I chord) and the I wins. (Wachowski Brothers—eat your hearts out!)

Let's look at the simplest execution of secondary dominance: extending the V7.

In the C major scale, we know that the V7 is G7 and the I is Cmaj7. Primary dominance says that whenever we play the V7 chord (G7), the Imaj7 (Cmaj7) is likely to be next in the progression. Let's take a closer look at G7 though—if it's the V7 of C, is there a V7 of G? In other words, can we say that there's a dom7 chord that dominates the dom7 chord a fifth below? In the key of G, the answer is yes, and it's found a fifth above the G itself—D7.

Lets look at the I-ii-V-I progression we saw earlier - still in the key of C major. Can D7 dominate G7 in C major? In this case, D7 acts as the V7 of the G7, which is the V7 of C. This makes D7 the V7 of the V7—a dominant chord dominating a dominant chord. One might ask at this point, "when does this end? What about A7 a fifth above D7—is that the V7 of the V7 of the V7 of C?" (author shakes head in dizziness…).

How far *can* this go?

Coach's Corner: The Dominance in the Mirror

Have you ever opened the medicine cabinet mirror and tried to find that spot where the inner mirror and the mirror at the back of the cabinet reflect each other? Have you see that reflection bending around the mirrors as if they were an infinite hallway of reflections? Eventually, if you see a reflection reflected in the reflection of the reflected mirror, you see that the image is the same, albeit smaller and smaller. Secondary dominance is something like this—as you increase the dominance level, the chords are still dominant but we get further and further from the original I, and the image of the primary dominance relationship gets harder to see.

Let's look at secondary dominance at the very next position, where a chord a fifth above G7 is also dominant—the V7 of the V7. In other words, let's take as a given that *every* chord has a V7 a fifth above it that dominates it, starting in this case with the V7 itself. This shouldn't be a stretch to you. As you go through the circle of fifths, you must have noticed that each key had a V triad that was a major triad that was also the next stop in the circle. You can easily extrapolate that each key has a V7 as the fifth chord if we look at that key in seventh chords.

Remember that we already know that the I chord has a dominant chord above it at the fifth scale degree called the V7. Secondary dominance is nothing more than taking *that* chord and assuming that there's a dominant chord at a fifth scale degree above *it*. In this case, we're stating that the secondary dominant is a fifth above the V7 chord—D7 in the case of C major.

Let's work with secondary dominance by altering the triad progression I-ii-V7-I from earlier. The first alteration will be to first state the ii as a natural minor 7 chord then alter it to the dominant 7 so you can hear how it shifts. In this case, you'll hear I, then iimin7, then II7 (dominant), *then* the V7 (a fifth below the II7) then resolution at the I again. In this case, the ii chord *becomes* dominant when right after it the II7 is played. This is an example of the ii chord becoming dominant as if Agent Smith has taken it over, increasing the tension level.

If the Agent Smith reference is lost on you, look back to "Coach's Corner: The Matrix Chord."

As an alternate version of the alteration, we'll dispense with the ii minor 7 and move directly to the II7 to show secondary dominance without the Agent Smith change. It will be the I-II7-V7-I progression. You can see and hear both in **Figure 6.15** and **Audio Track 76** to compare the differences.

Figure 6.15: Three versions of the IM7-iim7-V7-IM7 progression. The first is a straight performance in sevenths (root inversion). The second plays the ii *then* the II7, showing how the chord "morphs" into secondary dominance. The third plays the II7 *instead of* the previously written ii7 chord.

Secondary Dominance

Audio Track 76: I-ii-V-I played as shown in Figure 6.15.

There's a reason we're working with the cadence I-ii-V-I in the first place. It sets up the concept of secondary dominance quite well, as the ii "morphs" into the dominant chord beautifully and then "falls" right to the V below it (the V7 in this case) which, being dominant itself, falls right to the I. Let's make another "reflection" and see what happens (read "Coach's Corner: The Dominance in the Mirror" to understand the reference).

If we know that the primary dominant G7 has a secondary dominant a fifth above it at D7, then what is the secondary dominant above the D7? In other words, what is the tertiary (third) dominant? You could say "what is the secondary dominant of the secondary dominant" but that's just too many words…

As you remember from the circle of fifths, the fifth above D is A, yielding the tertiary dominant A7, which falls to D7, which falls to G7, which in turn falls to Cmaj7. This tertiary progression becomes VI7-II7-V7-I. Note that A is the vi (sixth) in the major scale—also the relative minor. Remember back when we were showing a few varieties of triad progressions? Well, one of them was the vi-ii-V-I (6-2-5-1). Now, if we play the same progression and apply dominance, you'll notice that it sets up the tertiary dominant discussion perfectly. **Figure 6.16** shows I-vi-ii-V-I in triads, sevenths then with secondary dominance. You can hear this tertiary dominance progression on **Audio Track 77**.

Figure 6.16: I-VI7-II7-V7-I in triads, sevenths, and secondary dominance shown on the staff.

Audio Track 77: The three versions of the progression from Figure 6.16.

So let's take the concept of secondary dominance and extend it further. As shorthand, we'll use the concept of V/V to imply the fifth of the fifth—hence, the V "over" V. We already know the following when it comes to dominance in C major:

I = C: root of the key (C)

V/I = G: fifth scale degree of the key (G)

V/V/I = D: second scale degree of the key (D)

V/V/V/I = A: sixth scale degree of the key (A)

Note that the VI7-II7-V7-IM7 (6-2-5-1) progression is very common in blues, classical, and gospel music too—tertiary dominance is a strong concept in these styles. Well just how far *can* this go? We're already at tertiary dominance—can it go to the quaternary dominance? Yup! In fact, there is no limit to the level of dominance available to us, although many styles go no further than this fourth step.

Knowing that the V/V/V/I = A, we can extend dominance one more level to E, or III7. The third chord of the mode, normally the minor 7, becomes dominant to increase tension and sets up the "falling" to a new I chord. In this case, E7 falls to A. However, as we are trying to get back "home" to C (in this case), E7 would fall to A7, then D7, then G7, *then* C. In Roman numeral analysis, this equates to III7-VI7-II7-V7-IM7 (or the 3-6-2-5-1).

You've heard this progression plenty of times before, from ragtime music to bluegrass, country, pop, and certainly in the blues and gospel. An excellent example of this chord movement can be heard in the song "Georgia on My Mind," by the great Ray Charles. It is emulated in **Figure 6.17** along with **Audio Track 78**, in solo piano both in all-root inversion and with voice leading so you can hear the dominance clearly (root) as well as the essence of the song (voice leading).

Figure 6.17: Quaternary dominance mimicking "Georgia on My Mind" by Ray Charles.

Audio Track 78: The use of secondary dominance mimicking Ray Charles' "Georgia on My Mind," first in root inversion, then with voice leading.

Coach's Corner: Examples of Dominance at Play

In Ray Charles' "Georgia on My Mind," there are some interesting twists to the multitudes of dominance at play. The first is that not *all* the chords in the progression are dominant. The actual chart calls for two rounds of dominance, the first of which is C major to E7, setting up the 3-6-2-5-1. However, notice that from E7, the song progresses to A minor—the natural vi chord in C major. We know we are back in the natural key because the A minor then falls to F major without any dominance. This sets up the half cadence IV-I back to C. This is a good example of a temporary departure from dominance returning to main key.

The second round involves the standard 6-2-5-1 progression where C moves directly to the VI7, then II7, then V7, then I. While not a strict interpretation of the 3-6-2-5-1 progression where all the chords are dominant, this aptly showcases how chords can simply become dominant and then progress either to the next I resolution (or I minor, in this case) *or* progress through the string of dominant chords to the final I.

This is all only one use of the dominant and secondary dominant chords—to extend the V7 relationship *within* the key and create a series of tension chords that slowly resolve downward to the existing I. However, there is another use of the secondary dominant function—to establish a *new* I, and change the key entirely.

Remember that primary dominance is the standard V7-I relationship. When we use secondary dominance to create a nonstandard V7, we imply that there *could be* a new I chord, thus changing the key. Let's look at the I-ii-V-I triad progression to see how this could work.

Remember that the I-ii-V-I progression in standard seventh chords is actually Imaj7-iimin7-V7-Imaj7. In the case of C major, this translates to Cmaj7-Dmin7-G7-Cmaj7. When played in secondary dominance, we get Imaj7-II7-V7-Imaj7 or Cmaj7-D7-G7-Cmaj7. Well we already know that the secondary dominant, II7 (D7) falls to the V7 (G7), which in turn falls to the Imaj7 of C major 7. However, knowing that a chord is dominant is enough for the chord a fifth below to become a new Imaj7. In our case, the II7 *could* fall to Gmaj7, *not* G7, making G major the new major key!

From another perspective, you could say that D7 is the *new* primary dominant of the *new* root key of G. Even though the D7 *was* a secondary dominant to G7 in the key of C, it does not *have to* pass through G7 to C—it can just be the primary dominant of the new I—G in this case.

If you look at **Figure 6.18**, you'll see this played out in two ways on the staff—one where we fall all the way down from the II7-V7-Imaj7, or D7-G7-Cmaj7. In the other version, the II7 only falls one step to the new Imaj7, or D7-Gmaj7. Note the staff and the key signature in the piece—as the key has changed from C major to G major, we need to introduce the sharp F♯ to the key signature at this point to reflect that the key has changed from C major to G major. You can hear these on **Audio Track 79**.

Figure 6.18: I-II7-V7-I versus I-II7-I (new) of the new key.

Original Progression

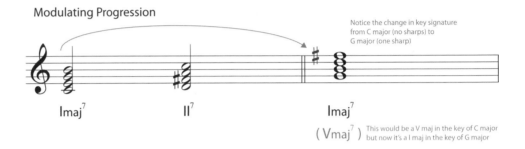

Modulating Progression

Notice the change in key signature from C major (no sharps) to G major (one sharp)

This would be a V maj in the key of C major but now it's a I maj in the key of G major

Audio Track 79: Two versions of the secondary dominance.

This is a great example of using secondary dominance to fall to a whole new key. Remember that any chord can become dominant at any time for just about any reason. Once that chord has become dominant, the chord the fifth below it is potentially the new key, or the new I.

Let's take a look at a different progression—I-IV-I-I or Cmaj7-Fmaj7-Cmaj7-Cmaj7—and use secondary dominance to create a key change. In this example, let's take the third I and transform it into a I7 chord—just for fun. We now have I-IV-I7-? In C major, this would translate to Cmaj7-Fmaj7-C7 - ? What chord is a fifth below the I? Can you figure this out without looking? I'll give you a hint—it involves interval inversions and the Rule of 9.

Right! The chord a fifth below the I is, in fact, the IV! So, where I-IV-I-I becomes I-IV-I7-IV (or the new I), Cmaj7-Fmaj7-Cmaj7-Cmaj7 becomes Cmaj7-Fmaj7-C7-Fmaj7. It would look and sound like it does in **Figure 6.19** and **Audio Track 80**.

Figure 6.19: I-IV-I-I versus
I-IV-I7-IV (new I).

Original Progression

Imaj⁷   IVmaj⁷   Imaj⁷   Imaj⁷

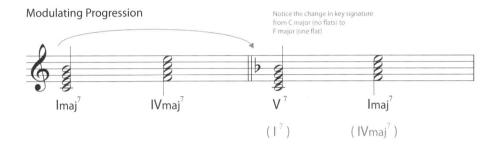

Modulating Progression

Notice the change in key signature
from C major (no flats) to
F major (one flat)

Imaj⁷   IVmaj⁷   V⁷   Imaj⁷

                  (I⁷)   (IVmaj⁷)

Audio Track 80: The two versions of the progressions I-IV-I-I.

Note that the C7 falls to Fmaj7 which is both the IV of the old key of C and the new I chord of F major. Also note how the key signature changes adding the B♭ to indicate that we've shifted keys to F major.

This move is very popular and can be heard in the Beatles classic "Hey Jude," right before the chorus. You can hear a mockup of this progression in **Audio Track 81**. Note that in this audio track, there's a melody added to help you recognize the song. The progression is I-I7-IV (new I) and you'll recognize the I7-IV when the song lyric "let it out and let it in" would be played. It happens twice in this example.

Look up the song if you're not familiar with it but if you're not familiar with it, you might also want to crawl out from under the musical rock you've been living under… Seriously…

Audio Track 81: A mockup of "Hey Jude" showing secondary dominance where Cmaj7 turns into C7 to "fall" to Fmaj as both the new I of the key and the IV of the existing key.

Keep in mind that any chord can become dominant at anytime for any reason. When this happens, it is most often secondary dominance at play and though the secondary dominant might eventually fall back to the original I chord, it can also be used to land on a new I chord, changing the key of the song at that point. The chart below is a good shorthand way of remembering the new I should each of the scale degrees become dominant.

Original Chord	Resulting Dominant Chord	Resulting "New" I
C or I	C7 or I7 (or V7 of IV)	F (formerly the IV)
D or ii	D7 or II7 (or V7/V7)	G (formerly the V)
E or iii	E7 or III7 (or V7/VI)	A (formerly the VI)
F or IV	F7 or IV7 (or V7/bvii)	Bb (formerly the b7)
G or V	G7 or V7 (or V7/I)	C (still the I)
A or vi	A7 or VI7 (or V/ii)	D (formerly the ii)
B or vii	B7 or VII7 (or V/iii)	E (formerly the iii)

Extended Chords (ninths, elevenths, thirteenths)

RECAP

Extended chords are ones where there are more than three notes, as in a triad. The seventh chord is the most common extended chord, consisting of stacked third intervals within that key. There are many types of seventh chords, four of which are naturally occurring in the major scales—maj7, min7, dom7, and the half-diminished (min7/b5). The dom7 chord can introduce tension to a progression and generally predicates a I chord after it. Secondary dominance occurs when a dominant chord moves to another dominant chord a fifth below it instead of a I chord.

Beyond the seventh chord are a few other chords within the extended chord family. They consist of the notes that are *above* the seventh chords although they take on other names when used this way. Let's explain more closely by looking at C major 7.

As we already know, the Cmaj7 chord consists of the first, third, fifth, and seventh scale degrees of C major. These are all made by flip-flopping the quality of the stacked third intervals—from a major third (1-3) to a minor third (3-5) and back to a major third interval (5-7). If we continue this pattern, we'd look for a minor third interval above the seventh—*as long as the resulting note is within the C major key*. In this case, the minor third interval above B is D—the second scale degree. The resulting chord would be spelled C-E-G-B-D.

As you might expect, the naming of this 5-note chord is going to be a question. The D is an interesting dilemma for the nomenclature, as you'd have to figure out a way to add the "second" to the title somewhere. Well you could just staple it onto the name calling the resulting chord a C major 7 add 2 (abbreviated as Cmaj7/2 or similar) but the impression is that the D should be played in the second scale degree position. For example, the D would be between the C and the E—and *not* above the higher B as it normally is. To make things less confusing this way, tradition has us call the D by a different name. Instead of calling it the two (or the second scale degree), we call it the ninth.

The Ninth Scale Degree
The ninth scale degree is the note that's next in the natural scale above the octave. It is tonally equivalent to the second scale degree an octave higher.

The convention of naming the second scale degree played an octave higher as the ninth is unfortunately a one-way street. No matter *where* the D is played (within the octave, above, or below the octave) we tend to refer to it as the ninth—except when it is a temporary suspension of the third as in a sus2 chord. So let's revisit our new five-note chord and give it a proper name—C major 7 add 9 (abbreviated as Cmaj7/9 or the super-abbreviated CM9). You can see it in a few spellings and inversions in **Figure 6.20** and hear it on **Audio Track 82**. Note that the CM9 chord doesn't require the seventh to be there at all. In this case, we could simply play C-E-G-D and it would work. If you really want that seventh in there, call the chord CM7/9 and you'll get C-E-G-B-D.

C Major⁷ ⁽ᵃᵈᵈ ⁹⁾

Figure 6.20: C major 7 add 9 in multiple spellings and inversions.

Audio Track 82: The resulting sound of each inversion and spelling of C major 7 add 9 from Figure 6.20.

If we continue the process of building larger chords, we'd have to add another third to our CM7/9 chord. We could do this by flipping the next third interval. Remember that the interval to get the ninth was a minor third so we'd have to add a major third to the ninth to get the next note—assuming that the flipping technique still holds.

In this case, we'd look at D (our ninth) and add a major third, resulting in F♯. F♯ is not in the key of C, so unfortunately, this doesn't work. So we have to abandon the flipping at this point and settle on another minor third as the next note—F. The point here is that the notes chosen on these extended chords *must* still live in the scale of the key!

Since F is the fourth scale degree, we could call the resulting chord a C major 7 add 9 add 4, but the same naming issue remains from before. After all, if the D can't be called the second, the F shouldn't be called the fourth and it isn't—we call it the eleventh. The resulting chord would be called a C major 7 add 9 add 11 (abbreviated as Cmaj7/9/11 or the super-abbreviated CM11).

Note that the CM11 chord doesn't require the seventh—or the ninth—to be there at all. In this case, we could simply play C-E-G-F and it would work. If you really want that seventh in there, call the chord CM7/11 and you'll get C-E-G-B-F. Continuing, if you really wanted the seventh and the ninth in there, call it CM7/9/11 and you'll get C-E-G-B-D-F. Also note that you could have the ninth and the eleventh without the seventh, which would be CM9/11 and played with notes C-E-G-D-F. These combinations are all up to you based on what notes you want to hear—or don't want to hear—in a particular chord. **Figure 6.21** shows a variety of eleventh chords and inversions with labels to help identify them. You can hear them in order on **Audio Track 83**.

Eleventh Chords
The eleventh chord is one where a triad or seventh chord has the fourth scale degree added to it. The fourth scale degree is referred to as the eleventh regardless of its octave position within the chord.

Figure 6.21: A variety of eleventh chords and inversions.

Audio Track 83: A variety of eleventh chords played in order as seen in Figure 6.21.

Coach's Corner: The Perils of the Eleventh Chord

Be careful when working with the eleventh here. There is a tendency to want to play the F♯ and not the F as the eleventh. There are a few reasons for this—one of which is the fact that the flipping of the third intervals no longer fits the key. As you spell the chord up from C (C-E-G-B-D), there's a tendency to keep flipping the intervals as our ears get used to that sound. Our ear will gravitate to the F♯ and not the F, as we expect another third.

Another reason is due to the nature of the chord we're building. Notice that as we move upward, there are other chords built within this one. We already know about the two triads—C major and E minor—that live naturally in Cmaj7 but now that we're going beyond the seventh chord, we start seeing other chords occur. G major is one that appears in CM7/9 as G-B-D above C-E-G. The tendency is to extend the G major triad to a G major seventh by adding the natural seventh of G major—F♯. Since F♯ doesn't belong in the scale of C major, we avoid the F♯ temporarily.

A third reason is the note F itself. Notice that it creates a minor second interval (nasty) between the E and the F—even though the F is an octave above it. To avoid that interval, jazz players often use the F♯ in eleventh chords but they don't call it a standard eleventh chord. They would call it a C major 7 add 9 add sharp 11 (CM7/9/♯11).

Jazz guys love to break the rules.

Extending our seventh chords some more, we find ourselves having to add yet another third above F. In this case, the only third above F that fits the C major scale is A—a major third above F. The resulting chord is C-E-G-B-D-F-A. Notice that *all* notes of the C major scale have been used! When we add the A to the chord, it isn't called the sixth, it is called the thirteenth. So this whole-scale chord would be called a C major 7 add 9 add 11 add 13 (Cmaj7/9/11/13, or the super-abbreviated CM13).

The Thirteenth Chord

The thirteenth chord is one where a triad or seventh chord has the sixth scale degree added to it. The sixth scale degree is referred to as the thirteenth regardless of its octave position within the chord.

Remember that the thirteenth chord doesn't require the seventh, ninth, or eleventh to be there to qualify as a thirteenth.

You can simply add it to a triad and call it a thirteenth. For example, we could just add the A to the C major triad. The result would be C-E-G-A and you'd have a C major add 13 (CMaj/13 or the super abbreviated CM13). You can see and hear the thirteenth chord in a few spellings and inversions in **Figure 6.22** and on **Audio Track 84**.

C Major⁷ ⁽ᵃᵈᵈ ¹³⁾

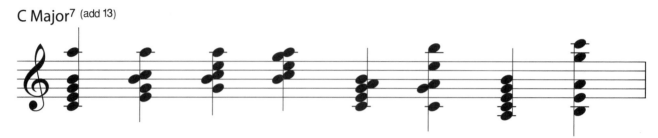

Figure 6.22: A variety of thirteenth chords and inversions.

Audio Track 84: A variety of thirteenth chords played in order as seen in Figure 6.22.

Piano Work—Dominance and the Blues

The blues was born out of a vocal tradition in the southern United States in the 1800s and evolved into a deep and varied instrumental music form throughout the early 1900s. The blues form was used in popular music making before the dawn of rock 'n' roll, the modern popular song form, and it directly influenced future jazz forms, rock, R&B, improvisational music, and more. It could be argued that the blues is the most influential form of modern and popular music,ever. The best part? It's actually quite simple!

The basic blues form consists of 12 measures and uses the I, the IV, and V chords of a scale and many artists, such as Elvis and the Beatles, wrote huge hits with *only* those three chords! The blues form repeats over and over, often starting with the main melody through the 12 bars and then breaking out into an improvisational track with each musician in the band taking a solo.

The basic 12-bar blues form is: I-I-I-I (group 1); IV-IV-I-I (group 2); and then V-IV-I-I (group 3). The blues also tends to use dominant seventh chords instead of triads, so if the blues is played in the key of C the chords would be C7 (C-E-G-B♭), F7 (F-A-C-E♭), and G7 (G-B-D-F). You can see this in **Figure 6.23**.

Figure 6.23: 12-bar blues form visual layout (Roman numerals, measure breakdown, three rows, etc.).

Often, the standard form gets altered slightly to make things interesting. Three places where alterations, or substitutions, are common include using the IV instead of the I as the second chord; using the V7 chord as the tenth chord (instead of the IV); and using the V7 as the last chord prior to repeating the form. Keep in mind that as the blues is heavily invested in dominant chords, secondary dominance is never far away.

For example, anywhere a V7 exists in the blues, you can precede it with a II7 to apply secondary dominance. Often, you'll hear what are called *turnarounds* in the last group of chords where secondary dominance applies directly. Instead of the common V-VI-I-I pattern seen in chord-group 3, you might see something like a VI7-II7-V7-I progression. Even more common is to cut the chord length in half (half notes instead of whole notes) and do the VI7-II7-V7-I progression, then throw in a V7 for good measure right before returning to the I at the head of the pattern.

You can see a version of the turnaround in **Figure 6.24** and hear a bluesy mockup on **Audio Track 85**. On the audio track, the full blues form is heard where the first 12 bars have a V7-IV7-I7-I7 conclusion. In the second 12 bars, the last 4 measures are played as the 6-2-5-1 turnaround. We've added a bass line and used voice leading for clarity of the form. Try to play along!

Figure 6.24: The VI7-II7-V7-I turnaround at the end of the blues form.

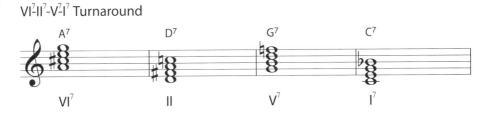

Audio Track 85: A full 12-bar blues progression with both a straight, then a turnaround.

The blues *scale* is a bit different from the form in the major and minor in that it is a five-note scale—not seven—and any five-note scale is called a *pentatonic* scale (meaning literally, five tones). The blues/pentatonic scale is universally recognized in cultural music around the world. In the key of C, the blues scale is: CE♭FGB♭. As you can see, there's a flattened third (minor) and a flattened seventh (also minor).

> **Pentatonic Scale**
> A musical collection of five notes consisting of the root, the flattened third, the fourth, fifth, and flattened seventh.

The pentatonic scale is easy enough but it gets slightly more complicated as there's an "optional" note that's often played in the blues to give it a richer character: the diminished fifth. In the key of C, this is F♯

The "optional" note F♯ that gives the scale its real bluesy sound is often called the *blue* note and forms a diminished fifth interval—also known as the *tritone*. Originally it was referred to in the Church as the *devil's interval* or, during the Italian classical period of the 1500s, *la musica diabla* (literally, the devil's music). Due to its sinister sound, it was actually outlawed in early Church music!

In the blues, it can either be a passing tone—one you "pass through" while playing the scale by temporarily landing on it but never hovering on it—or it can be used as a "mistake" note. In the latter case, you would strike the F♯ then immediately play the F as if in one sliding motion, creating the desired effect.

You can hear it used melodically on **Audio Track 86**.

Audio Track 86: The "accidental" tritone effect of the F♯ in a blues melody. Played with the bass, then the piano.

"Working out" on the piano with the blues is a great way to start songwriting. Likely you'll hear dozens (hundreds?) of songs already just by playing the I-IV-V in dominant in the 12-bar pattern. It's also a good exercise to use when practicing through the circle of fifths/fourths. It forces you to truly understand each key as you'll have to take the seventh note and flatten it. For most major sharp keys, this is a blessing as it's one less flat to remember!

You should certainly spend some time with the blues, if you haven't already. Again, it's the foundation of most popular music, so if you're a fan of rock, pop, hip-hop, R&B, soul, and even reggae, you'll hear the blues in there. Listen to the way the blues rhythm swings and the pace it uses. Also notice the pentatonic scale work in the melody and vocals—it should become pretty clear once you listen and try to play along with any blues tune.

Here's how you get started by playing the basic blues form:

☛ Play through the blues form with a metronome using I, IV, and V7 chords and whole notes—every chord is played over four beats. Note that in this example, you will play the I and IV in triads—only the V7 is dominant. Start with one hand at a time and then both hands playing the chords together. Start with root position chords and then try again with proper voice leading between chords. Alternate the starting inversion and subsequent inversions so you can also work out your voice leading skills.

☛ Expand this exercise by playing all seventh chords: I7, IV7, and V7, at first in root inversion, then using proper voice leading between chords. Start with a slow metronome and gradually increase the tempo as you get better at moving from chord to chord. Start by holding the chords as whole notes and then use smaller rhythmic values such as half notes, quarter notes, eighth notes, and eighth-note triplets. Continue to vary this by playing the chords in a rhythm along with and alternating against a component of the rhythm—the kick, snare, or hi-hat. Again, play this in a few inversions with different voice leadings.

Now, let's expand this exercise by introducing two concepts: splitting your hand function and working with the blues scale. By splitting the hand function, we mean that one hand will play chords and the other will either play the scale, some melody, or a melodic blues bass pattern. This widens the activity level significantly but makes the music fuller as there is twice as much to listen to at once.

☛ Play the blues scale with your right hand. Play the chords with the left. We'll start with the C blues scale. Use the fingering for the C blues scale shown in **Figure 6.25** as a starting point. As you practice more blues scales, and scales in general, you'll start to *jam* and *solo* over the chords and your playing will naturally evolve.

Figure 6.25: The finger pattern of the C blues scale: CE♭FF♯GB♭C.

Fingering of a C Blues Scale

Right Hand Fingering

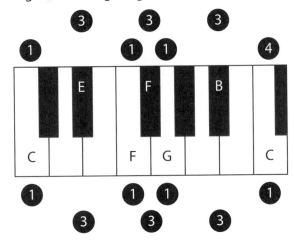

Left Hand Fingering

☛ First play the scale up and down and get used to the skips and jumps that make this scale, and make the sound of the scale unique. Play the scale at a slow pace—whole or half notes at first—to get used to the pattern.

☛ Try one octave up and down and then start to take the scale up the keyboard a couple octaves adjusting the fingering to make the transitions between octaves smooth. You'll likely start improvising on your own!

☛ Before moving on to the advanced techniques, practice the blues scale in the right hand over each chord in C in the left hand. Play the blues scale up and down over the C7 chord, and then repeat over the F7 and the G7 chords. Play without the metronome for a while here just to listen to the sound of the scale and the chords working together.

☛ Once you've got it, reintroduce the metronome. Notice that the five-note scale (six including the octave) doesn't quite fit the 4/4 blues structure. You'll have to improvise two notes somewhere to achieve eight notes of the blues scale to fill the space of each chord. Remember that each chord fills the bar (four beats) so you'll *need* to play the melody in eighth notes to match. Likely, you'll have to go slowly to make this work. As always, speed up and improvise as you go to add challenge and progress to your playing.

Now, let's vary the exercise to make it more musical. By now, you should have the chord structure down fairly well (in both hands, please!) and you should know how to play the basic blues scale too (also in both hands). What we're going to do now is assign different roles to each hand in each exercise. In the first exercise, we'll continue with the right hand as the melodic hand then we'll move to the left hand as the melodic hand.

☛ Continue your scale work in the RH while playing chords in the LH. For example, play the LH chords rhythmically while the RH starts playing more freely. Use a metronome, click track, or drum loop to stay in time and in the form of the blues as you jam.

☛ Start by repeating a single melodic motif twice—once each for chord groups 1 and 2. For chord group 3, vary the motif a bit to keep it interesting. We usually vary the first half, but repeat the same back half of the motif. Work on a few varieties until something feels right.

☛ Continue this process by increasing your speed and playing more complex melodies.

☛ Work this exercise through the circle of fifths/fourths.

Now, let's switch hands and have the LH play a bass melody while the RH comps chords. In the blues, we often use a *walking* bass line, where the notes always seem to move in a single direction.

☛ Start by outlining the notes of the I7, IV7, and V7 chords under the right hand block chord. For example, play the root note *only* in the LH while the RH comps chords. This is the simplest form of the blues bass.

☛ Now, let's create a walking bass line from there. Start by playing a four-note bass line in sync with each chord—the root, ♭3, 4, then 5. Note that when you switch to the IV chord, your LH will play the *same notes*. This reinforces the repetitious nature of the blues while letting you know that the scale works for all three chords.

☛ Increase complexity here first by moving the bass line with the chords. When you move to the F chord, move your bass line to now start on F but play the same intervals—the F, up a minor third, up another whole step then one more whole step. This mimics the original line, but moves it to the root of the new chord. You'll move it to G when the V chord plays. You can see and hear this in **Figure 6.26** and **Audio Track 87**.

C Blues Bass Line

Figure 6.26: The walking bass line moving with the chords of the blues.

Audio Track 87: The blues form with the moving and walking bass line from Figure 6.26.

☛ You can increase the complexity some more by varying the bass line to keep walking. Here, don't repeat the four-note phrase but keep moving the bass line all over the scale such that *no* phrase repeats itself! This will make the bass line more "jazzy" and will keep you *and* the audience guessing!

Chops Test: Compose a Unique Blues Piece

By this time, it's pretty clear what you should and should not be able to do. Scales, intervals, triads, inversions, circle of fifths/fourths, seventh chords, and dominant chords should all be at your fingertips. Even if you're not the fastest player out there, if someone calls for a particular key, it should take you no more than five minutes to chart your scale, intervals, triads, and (at least) the V7 chord.

You should be able to play the I-IV-V in this key with some degree of musicality. If not, keep practicing.

A lot.

Assuming you can do all the above, let's move on to your new chops test by working through the blues. Since the blues incorporates everything we've done up to now, it's the perfect exercise to bring it all home.

Compose your own blues piece. From scratch.

Students at Pyramind are required to compose a piece using the 12-bar blues form. The piece doesn't have to sound like a traditional blues pieces as far as style, tempo, and instrumentation—we've heard Christmas blues, vacation blues, drum 'n' bass blues, country blues—you name it!

Your mission (should you choose to accept it!) is to compose a 12-bar blues piece in *any* style or genre with the parameters outlined as follows.

Basic Chops

- Use at least two chord substitutions—one of which introduces secondary dominance.

- Play the blues piece four times through—live! Sequencing it in your DAW is great, but defeats the purpose of getting good at *playing* the piano.

- Within the four rounds, play at least one of them with a walking bass line in the LH while comping chords in the right.

- Within the four rounds, play at least one of them with an improvised melody in the RH while comping chords in the left. Remember, the blues is often most successful when the melody is somewhat repetitive and the motif shines through consistently.

Advanced Chops

- Don't be lame. Choose a key *other than* C.

- In fact, play the song in at least four other keys—two from the circle of fifths and two from the circle of fourths.

- Play it out somewhere. Yes, we said it—play outside! Where people can hear you. There's gotta be an open mic night somewhere near you—give it a shot. It's no more nerve wracking than karaoke—and no one expects you to be great… it's an open mic!

Section 7
Way Beyond C Major: An Introduction to Modes

RECAP

The major scale consists of seven notes whose intervallic distances are WWHWWWH. The major scale can be played note by note in melodic fashion (melodic intervals) or in two-note clusters called *dyads* (harmonic intervals). Three note clusters where each note within the cluster is spaced by thirds are called *triads*.

The qualities of the collection of triads in the major scale follow the pattern MmmMMmd. Triads can be spelled in root inversion (1-3-5), in first (3-5-1 octave) inversion, or second inversion (5-1-octave 3). Triads can be strung together as either *cadences* (two triads) or *progressions* (more than two triads). Songs are written using a combination of triad progressions and inversions through a process known as *voice leading*. Voice leading helps keep the individual notes close to each other while the triads move in potentially larger distances.

Each major scale has a relative minor scale that is located starting at the sixth scale degree— or a minor third interval *below* the major scale. C major (and the relative minor, A minor) each have no sharps or flats within the key. Accidentals are introduced to the major scales in order of increasing fifths (all sharps) or decreasing fifths (all flats). These are called the circles of fifths (sharps) and fourths (flats).

Triads can be extended to four-note chords by adding another third—called seventh chords. A special seventh chord—the dominant 7—lives at the fifth position in the scale and is unique in that it often precedes the I chord. This is called dominance. Other dominant chords can dominate the V7, usually a fifth above. When this occurs it is called secondary dominance. Dominance is the main function of the blues—arguably the most influential song form in all of popular music. Other chords (called extended chords) besides the seventh exist by adding thirds above the seventh. These are often the ninth, the eleventh, and the thirteenth.

The Major Modes

Welcome to the next level in music theory—the major modes.
Modes are scales of music that unlock a wider range of emotionality than the major scales. If you think of the major scale

as decidedly "happy," and the minor as "sad," these new modes allow you a much more detailed and complex range of emotional expression. Believe it or not, you already know two of the modes of music: the major scale (we'll call it the *major mode* from here on out) and the relative minor mode.

When learning the modes, the first thing to learn is the names of the modes. We'll describe them one at a time after we learn their names. The modes are named after their Greek origins so don't be worried if the names don't make sense. Like some of the earlier concepts, it's fine to just memorize them. Please note that we'll be looking at the modes in terms of their triads primarily.

Listed in order from the root through each scale degree of the major scale (C major as the reference scale), the modes are in the memorize me box to the left.

Yes, the names are funny—it does not absolve you from memorizing them though. The name of the mode calls up the *entirety* of the sound being used in a composition—the scale, the triads, and, usually, the whole *feel* of the song being written. As a first introduction to *how* to work with the modes, let's relate each to our starting mode: the C Ionian.

☞   C Ionian is the standard C major scale.

☞   D Dorian contains the *exact same notes* as C Ionian, but is a different scale in terms of the interval pattern. DEFGABCD is the scale of D Dorian. Note that the Dorian scale *is* the Ionian scale beginning and ending on the second scale degree—D instead of C.

☞   E Phrygian contains the *exact same notes* as C Ionian, but is a different scale in terms of the interval pattern. EFGABCDE is the scale of E Phrygian. Note that the Phrygian scale *is* the Ionian scale beginning and ending on the third scale degree, E.

☞   F Lydian contains the *exact same notes* as C Ionian, but is a different scale in terms of the interval pattern. FGABCDEF is the scale of F Lydian. Note that the Lydian scale *is* the Ionian scale beginning and ending on the fourth scale degree, F.

☞   G Mixolydian contains the *exact same notes* as C Ionian, but is a different scale in terms of the interval pattern. GABCDEFG is the scale of G Mixolydian. Note that the Mixolydian scale *is* the Ionian scale beginning and ending on the fifth scale degree, G.

MEMORIZE ME!

Ionian (I-owe-nee-an)—you already know this as the major scale

Dorian (dor-ee-an)

Phrygian (fridge-ee-an)

Lydian (lid-ee-an)

Mixolydian (mix-o-lid-ee-an)

Aeolian (a-o-lee-an)—you already know this as the relative minor

Locrian (low-kree-an)

☛   A Aeolian contains the *exact same notes* as C Ionian, but is a different scale in terms of the interval pattern. ABCDEFGA is the scale of A Aeolian. Note that the Aeolian scale *is* the Ionian scale beginning and ending on the sixth scale degree. Also note that this is the relative minor to C Ionian, A.

☛   B Locrian contains the *exact same notes* as C Ionian, but is a different scale in terms of the interval pattern. BCDEFGAB is the scale of B Locrian. Note that the Locrian scale *is* the Ionian scale beginning and ending on the seventh scale degree, B.

Notice that each of the modes is listed in order as they relate to the scale degrees of C major. This is only one way to know the modes. It is the easiest to remember in terms of the *order* or scale degrees of the modes, but it's not nearly the best in terms of understanding their emotional power. To do that, we need to dig into each of them one at a time and see them for what they are in and of themselves. Since they represent "shades" of happy and sad, let's take them one-at-a-time, from the happiest to the saddest.

Coach's Corner: Simple Description, Big Changes

Don't be fooled by the simplicity of this first description. On the surface, you won't see the differences—they *are* the same notes, after all. As we dig in deeper and study the intervallic relationships, you'll find that they are *very* different from each other. As we already know, the scale determines the triads and their qualities. So by altering the intervallic relationship in a mode from the Ionian starting place, we also alter the triads, their quality, and how those qualities affect standard chord progressions—resulting in some *big* differences.

Lydian Mode

We'll start with the Lydian mode for two reasons: it's one of the easiest to learn *and* it's considered to be the brightest, or happiest of the modes (yes, it's happier than the Ionian mode/major scale!). As you recall from the previous section, the Lydian mode is built on the fourth scale degree of C major. This means that it's effectively the same scale as C major except that it starts on and ends on F.

You can see the F Lydian scale in **Figure 7.1** and hear it on **Audio Track 88**.

F Lydian

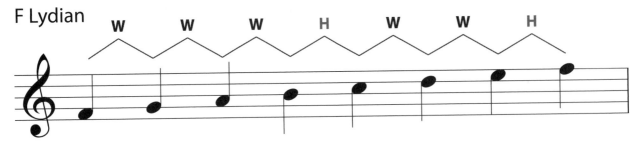

Figure 7.1: The F Lydian scale (FGABCDEF).

   **Audio Track 88:** The F Lydian scale as heard on the piano.

At first inspection, you might ask "what's the difference between F Lydian and C Ionian (major)?" You'd be right to ask this—after all, there isn't one note difference between F Lydian and C Ionian. However, there is a big difference in the sound of the Lydian mode when you compare it to the Ionian in intervals and in triads.

Remember WWHWWWH? Let's take a closer look at the Lydian mode to see how the mode is constructed in intervals.

Since we've been working for so long on the major scale, it's easy to have taken for granted that the underlying relationship in all of music is based on WWHWWWH. After all, the major scale was the first thing we learned, and all of the triads and cadences we've seen up until now have all revolved around it. The modes change *all* of that, starting with the Lydian. We'll start with F Lydian since it holds no accidentals and then we'll compare apples to apples —C Ionian versus C Lydian, *not* C Ionian versus F Lydian.

Looking at F Lydian again, the notes are:

F G A B C D E F

Looking deeper, the relationship between the notes is as follows:

F to G: whole step

G to A: whole step

A to B: whole step

B to C: half step

C to D: whole step

D to E: whole step

E to F: half step

or, in linear terms, WWWHWWH. Seen horizontally versus the Ionian mode, it looks like this:

Lydian: W W W H W W H

Ionian: W W H W W W H

Notice how the third and fourth intervals are different but the others are the same? In the Ionian mode, the third interval between the third scale degree and the fourth scale degree is a half step. In C major, this is the interval between E and F. In the Lydian mode, the third interval is a whole step. So, in C Lydian, this would yield an F♯, not an F. Also, since the next interval (from the fourth to the fifth scale degree) is a half step in Lydian (not a whole step like in Ionian) the next note is still G, just like the Ionian. Therefore, the Lydian is recognized by the fourth scale degree being sharpened.

So the C Lydian scale is:

C D E F♯ G A B C

as opposed to

C D E F G A B C

in Ionian mode.

Did you get all of that? No? Here it is in simpler terms:

MEMORIZE ME!
The Lydian mode is recognized by the *sharp fourth scale degree* as compared to the Ionian.

Coach's Corner: Knowing the Modes

How you choose to remember the modes is up to you. You can certainly just remember that the Lydian, for example, is nothing more than the same collection of notes as the major scale starting and ending from the fourth scale degree. *Or* you can remember the modes by the relationships in the intervals (WWWHWWH in Lydian as opposed to WWHWWWH in the Ionian). Lastly, you can remember them by the alteration from the Ionian mode—sharp the fourth scale degree to get Lydian from the Ionian. In the end, you'll definitely do best by knowing *all three ways*.

So now we know that the Lydian mode is different from the Ionian mode because it has a sharp fourth scale degree. But, what we don't know (yet!) is how that affects the triads of the mode. As with the Ionian mode, the Lydian has a series of triads that are built from each scale degree. These triads are the same as before—major, minor, and diminished—but each triad is different from the Ionian triads at each scale degree.

In other words, the Lydian triad sequence is different from the Ionian triad sequence. Let's look at the Lydian mode in C to really compare it to the Ionian in triads.

Remember that when we build triads from *any* scale, the triads are always and *only* built from the notes in the scale. With C Lydian the first triad is still C major—C-E-G. The second triad, normally D minor in Ionian mode, changes. In this case, it's D *major*—D-F#-A. Continuing onward, you'll see the triad sequence of C Lydian in **Figure 7.2**. You can hear it on **Audio Track 89**.

C Lydian Triads

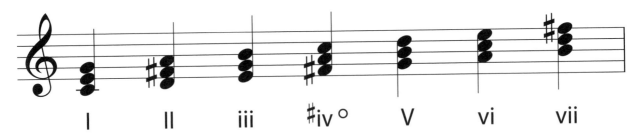

Figure 7.2: The C Lydian triad sequence.

Audio Track 89: The C Lydian mode played on the piano in triads.

Notice in Figure 7.2 how the second triad, the fourth, and the seventh triads are all different from the Ionian due to the sharpened fourth (F# instead of the Ionian F). The second triad, normally a minor triad, is now major while the fourth triad, normally a major, is now diminished. Similarly, the seventh triad, normally a diminished, is now minor. This is the definition of the Lydian mode in triads.

Another way to know the Lydian is to recognize that the Lydian triad sequence is *the same* as the Ionian sequence, just shifted by a fourth. It shouldn't be a big surprise—after all, the Lydian mode *is* built off of the fourth scale degree of the Ionian. To look at this another way let's compare the Ionian and Lydian in two ways: in triads C Ionian to F Lydian and in triads C Ionian to C Lydian. You can see them both in **Figure 7.3** and **7.4**, respectively. **Audio Track 90** plays the triad comparison seen in Figure 7.3 only.

> **MEMORIZE ME!**
> The Lydian mode, defined as a sharpened fourth scale degree, has a triad sequence of: I Major, II Major, iii minor, #iv diminished, V Major, vi minor, and vii minor.

C Ionian Triads vs. C Lydian Triads

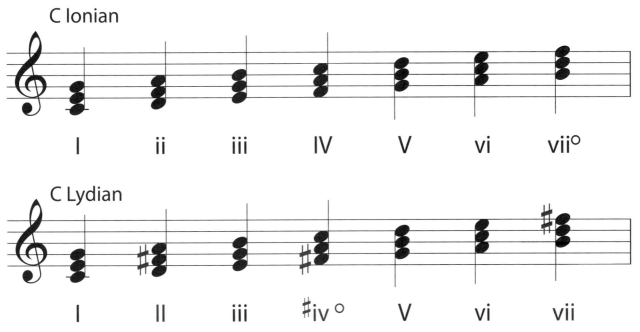

Figure 7.3: The triad sequence of C Ionian versus C Lydian.

C Ionian Triads vs. F Lydian Triads

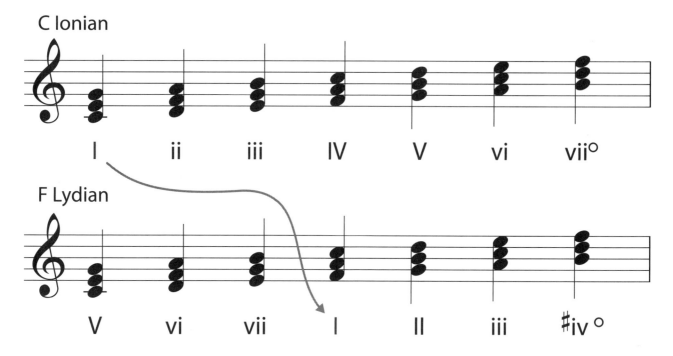

C Ionian Triads vs. F Lydian Triads

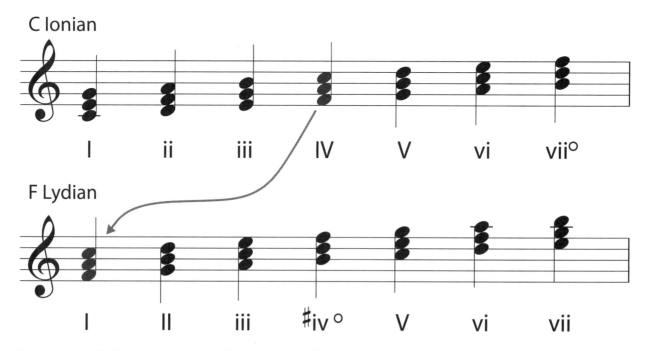

Figure 7.4a and b: The triad sequence of C Ionian versus F Lydian, shown in two different ways for comparison.

Audio Track 90: The triads of C Ionian versus C Lydian.

Mixolydian Mode

Next on the list of modes is the Mixolydian. We're learning this one next for three reasons—it's easy to learn, it's the next brightest after the Ionian, and it's one of the more popular modes. In terms of "brightness" or "happiness," so far (from brightest down) the brightest is Lydian, then Ionian (already covered), and now, Mixolydian.

The Mixolydian mode is built from the fifth scale degree of the Ionian mode in the same way that the Lydian mode is built from the fourth scale degree of the Ionian mode. So, similar to the Lydian mode, you *could* simply start on G and run through the notes of the C major mode back to G, as seen In **Figure 7.5**. You can hear it on **Audio Track 91**.

G Mixolydian

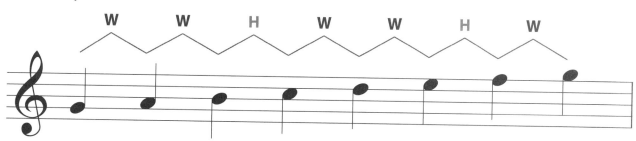

Figure 7.5: The notes of G Mixolydian

 **Audio Track 91:** The G Mixolydian scale.

Looking at G Mixolydian again, the notes are:

GABCDEFG

Looking deeper, the relationship between the notes is as follows:

G to A: whole step

A to B: whole step

B to C: half step

C to D: whole step

D to E: whole step

E to F: half step

F to G: whole step

or, in linear terms, WWHWWHW. Seen horizontally versus the Ionian mode, it looks like this:

Mixolydian: **W W H W W H W**

Ionian: **W W H W W W H**

See how the sixth and seventh intervals are different but the others are the same? In the Ionian, the sixth interval between the sixth scale degree and the seventh scale degree is a whole step. In C Ionian, this is the difference between A and B. However, in the Mixolydian mode, the sixth interval (from the sixth to the seventh scale degree) is a half step. So, in C Mixolydian, this would yield a Bb not a B. Therefore, the Mixolydian is noted by the seventh scale degree being flattened.

So the C Mixolydian scale is:

C D E F G A B♭ C

as opposed to

C D E F G A B C

in Ionian mode.

Did you get all of that? No? Well, the Memorize Me! box at the left puts it simpler terms…

So now we know that the Mixolydian mode is different from the Ionian mode because it has a flattened seventh scale degree. But what we don't know (at least, yet) is how that affects the triads of the mode. As with the Ionian mode, the Mixolydian has a series of triads that are built off of each scale degree. These triads are the same as before—major, minor, and diminished—but each triad is different from the Ionian triads in each scale degree.

In other words, the Mixolydian triad sequence is different from the Ionian triad sequence. Now, let's look at the Mixolydian mode in C to really compare it to the Ionian in triads.

Remember that when we build triads from *any* scale, the triads are *always* and *only* built from the notes in the scale. Therefore, the first triad is still C major—C-E-G. The second triad is also the same—D minor (D-F-A). When we get to the third scale degree on E, we see the first triad change—E minor (E-G-B) in Ionian becomes E diminished (E-G-B♭) in Mixolydian. Continuing onward, you'll see the triad sequence of C Mixolydian in **Figure 7.6**. You can hear it on **Audio Track 92**.

MEMORIZE ME!
The Mixolydian mode is denoted by the flat seventh scale degree. All other notes are the same as the Ionian mode.

C Mixolydian Triads

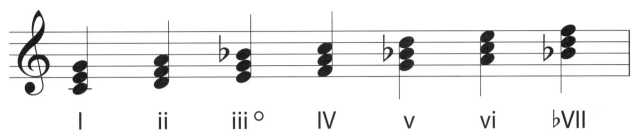

Figure 7.6: The C Mixolydian triad sequence.

Audio Track 92: The C Mixolydian mode in triads.

> **MEMORIZE ME!**
> The Mixolydian mode, defined as a flattened seventh scale degree, has a triad sequence of: I Major, ii minor, iii diminished, IV Major, v minor, vi minor, and ♭VII Major.

Notice in Figure 7.6 how the third, the fifth, and the flat seventh triads are all different from the Ionian due to the flattened seventh. The third triad, normally a minor triad, is now diminished; the fifth triad, normally a major, is now minor; and the seventh triad, normally a diminished, is now major, but starting at the flattened seventh scale degree. The Memorize Me! box to the left provides the definition of the Mixolydian mode in triads.

Another way to know the Mixolydian is to recognize that the Mixolydian triad sequence is *the same* as the Ionian sequence, just shifted by a fifth. It shouldn't be a big surprise—after all, the Mixolydian mode *is* built off of the fifth scale degree of the Ionian.

To look at this another way, let's compare the Ionian and Mixolydian in two ways: in triads C Ionian to C Mixolydian *and* in triads C Ionian to G Mixolydian. You can see them both in **Figures 7.7** and **7.8**, respectively. **Audio Track 93** plays the triad comparison shown in Figure 7.7 only.

C Ionian Triads vs. C Lydian Triads

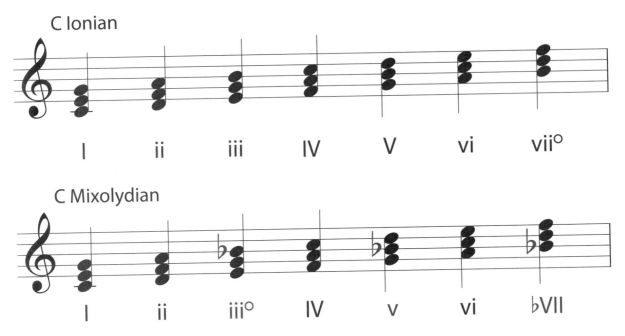

Figure 7.7: The triad sequence of C Ionian versus C Mixolydian.

C Ionian Triads vs. G Mixolydian Triads

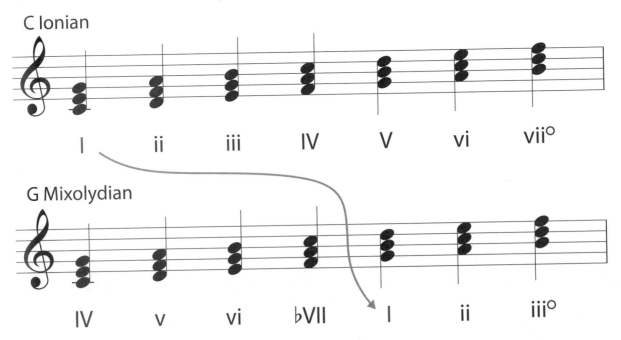

C Ionian Triads vs. G Mixolydian Triads

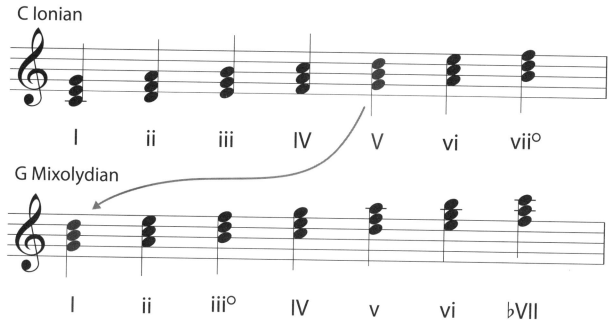

Figure 7.8a and b: The triad sequence of C Ionian versus G Mixolydian, shown in two different ways for comparison.

Audio Track 93: The triad comparison between C Ionian and C Mixolydian.

Dorian Mode

Next on the list of modes is the Dorian. We're learning this one next for three reasons—it's easy to learn, it's the next brightest after the Mixolydian, and it's still one of the more popular modes. In terms of "brightness," so far (from the brightest downward) is Lydian, Ionian, Mixolydian, and now, Dorian. Note that Dorian is the first of the minor modes whereas Ionian, Lydian, and Mixolydian are all major modes.

Coach's Corner: More than Simply Happy or Sad

Up until now, the three modes we've explored are all considered to be *major* modes. This is due to the fact that the first triad in each is major. However, to assume that "major" means simply "happy" and "minor" means "sad" is a gross underestimation of the modes' real emotional power. Both the Mixolydian and Dorian modes are heard in funky grooves and both express a combination of happy and sad variations. There is a solid mixture of happy and sad in both modes, but the expression of it is different in each.

While none of the subjective descriptions added here are to be taken as gospel, you can say that the Mixolydian mode is more of a happy mix—think of it as a summer barbeque party—while the Dorian is a bit more of the rainy-day indoor gathering. Dorian adds a certain "bittersweet" element to the emotional equation, which one would have to define overall as being more sad than happy. Again, these are not rules but guidelines; the key is to start thinking of these modes as emotionally more complex than just "happy" and "sad." Just like we did with the dyads and triads, you should start thinking of assigning your own emotions to these modes as you start putting together triad sequences with them.

The Dorian mode is built from the second scale degree of the Ionian mode in the same way that the Lydian mode is built from the fourth scale and the Mixolydian is built from the fifth. So, just as with the other modes, you *could* simply start on D and run through the notes of the C major mode back to D, as seen in **Figure 7.9**. You can hear it on **Audio Track 94**.

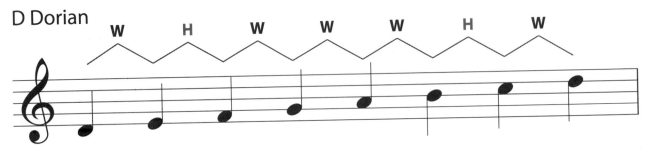

Figure 7.9: The notes of D Dorian.

   **Audio Track 94:** The D Dorian scale.

Looking at D Dorian again, the notes are:

D E F G A B C D

Looking deeper, the relationship between the notes is as follows:

D to E: whole step

E to F: half step

F to G: whole step

G to A: whole step

A to B: whole step

B to C: half step

C to D: whole step

..or, in linear terms, WHWWWHW. Seen horizontally versus the Ionian mode, it looks like this:

Dorian: W H W W W H W

Ionian: W W H W W W H

See how the second, third, sixth, and seventh intervals are different, yet the others are the same? In the Ionian mode, the second interval is a whole step and here, it's a half step. The third interval—normally a half step—becomes a whole step. And note the sixth interval whole step in Dorian versus the half step in Ionian, along with the changed seventh interval (whole in Dorian vs. half in Ionian).

Coach's Corner: Know the Modes—Your Way

This process of comparing intervallic relationships can start to be confusing. You might want to think about building a chart of intervals as we go through the modes so you can visually reference the differences in intervallic relationship. Of course, you can simply skip over this part and just learn the modes by shifting the start positions of the Ionian mode based on your knowledge of the mode and the scale degree it's built from. Just like before, it doesn't matter *how* you know the modes, only that you know them. You might have heard this before.

These differences show up in the third, and seventh scale degrees. For example, C Dorian would have an E♭ (third scale degree) instead of the Ionian E. This is a result of the second interval (the interval between the second and third scale degree) being a half step—not a whole step. On the other side of this, the fourth scale degree, normally F, is *still* F, although the third interval (between the third and fourth scale degrees) has changed from a half step to a whole step. The resulting note, F, is the same, but the interval needed to get there has changed.

The other changes, at the sixth and seventh intervals, yield similar results. The sixth interval (between the sixth and seventh scale degrees) is now a half step, down from the Ionian whole step. As a result, in C Dorian the seventh scale degree yields a B♭, not the Ionian B. As before, the seventh interval (between the seventh scale degree and the eighth scale degree, or octave) has changed to a whole step from the Ionian half step. This yields a C (up the whole step from B♭), just like in the Ionian mode.

The C Dorian scale is built by altering the C Ionian scale with a flattened third and seventh scale degree. So the C Dorian scale is:

C D E♭ F G A B♭ C

as opposed to

C D E F G A B C

in Ionian mode.

Did you get all of that? No? The Memorize Me box at the left shows it in simpler terms…

So now we know that the Dorian mode is different from the Ionian mode because it has a flattened third and seventh scale degree. But, what we don't know—yet—is how that affects the triads of the mode. As with the Ionian mode, the Dorian has a series of triads that are built off of each scale degree. These triads are the same as before—major, minor, and diminished—but each triad is different from the Ionian triads in each scale degree.

In other words, the Dorian triad sequence is different from the Ionian triad sequence. Let's look at the Dorian mode in C to really compare it to C Ionian in triads.

Remember, when we build triads from *any* scale, the triads are *always* and *only* built from the notes in the scale. Therefore, the first triad is *no longer* C major—C-E-G, but rather C minor—C-E♭-G. By definition, this makes the Dorian mode a minor mode. The second triad is the same—D minor (D-F-A). When we get to the third scale degree on E♭, we see the second change—E minor becomes E♭ major (E♭-G-B♭). Continuing onward, you'll see the triad sequence of C Dorian in **Figure 7.10**. You can hear this on **Audio Track 95**.

> **MEMORIZE ME!**
> **The Dorian mode is recognized by the flat third and the flat seventh scale degree.**

C Dorian Triads

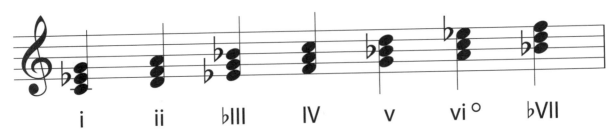

Figure 7.10: The C Dorian triad sequence.

   **Audio Track 95:** The triads of C Dorian.

Coach's Corner: Building Triads in C Dorian

A *big* mistake at this point is missing the fact that the third scale degree is E♭—*not* E—when building triads in C Dorian. It's possible that you already made this mistake in Lydian (assuming that F was still the fourth and not F♯) or in Mixolydian (assuming that the flattened seventh scale degree B♭ was still B). Remember that once you alter a scale degree in the modes, that note is *forever* altered in that mode. E *no longer* exists in the C Dorian mode and it never will again—as long as you stay in that mode.

Another mistake that is commonly made with modes is forgetting to change the name of the scale degree as well as the note. In C Dorian, we recognize that the third scale degree is E♭ and not E but what do we call this? It is the third note in the mode but from here on out, we wouldn't just call it the third, we would call it the *flat* major third. With Lydian, we'd describe the fourth scale degree as the *sharp* fourth diminished triad, and with Mixolydian we'd describe the seventh scale degree as the *flat* seventh major triad.

MEMORIZE ME!

The Dorian mode, defined as a flattened third and seventh scale degrees, has a triad sequence of—i minor, ii minor, ♭III Major, IV Major, v minor, vi diminished, and ♭VII Major.

Notice in Figure 7.10 how the first triad, the third, the fifth, the sixth, *and* the seventh triads are all different from the Ionian due to the flattened third and seventh. The third triad—normally a minor triad—is now a flat 3 major. The fifth triad (normally a major) is now minor. The sixth triad, normally a minor, is now diminished, and the seventh triad (normally a diminished) is now a flat 7 major. To the left is the definition of the Dorian mode in triads.

Another way to know the Dorian is to recognize that the Dorian triad sequence is *the same* as the Ionian sequence, just shifted by a second. It shouldn't be a big surprise—after all, the Dorian mode *is* built off of the second scale degree of the Ionian.

To look at it another way, let's compare the Ionian and Dorian in two ways: in triads C Ionian to C Dorian *and* in triads C Ionian to G Dorian. You can see them both in **Figure 7.11** and **7.12** respectively. **Audio Track 96** plays the triad comparison shown in Figure 7.11 only.

C Ionian Triads vs. C Dorian Triads

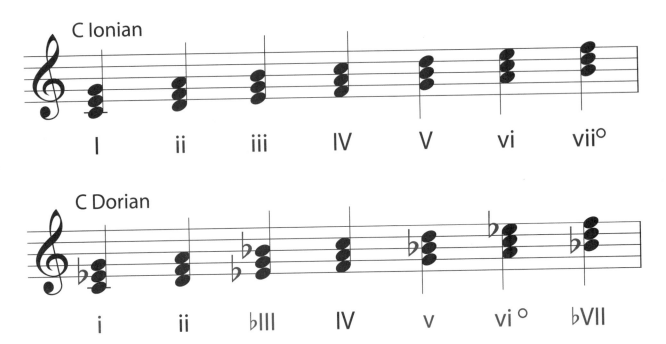

Figure 7.11: The triad sequence of C Ionian versus C Dorian.

C Ionian Triads vs. D Dorian Triads

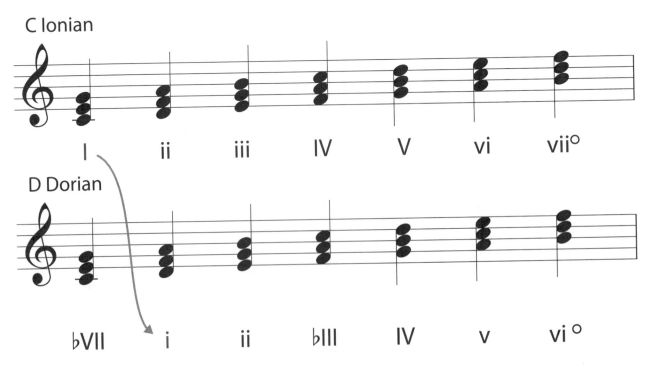

C Ionian Triads vs. D Dorian Triads

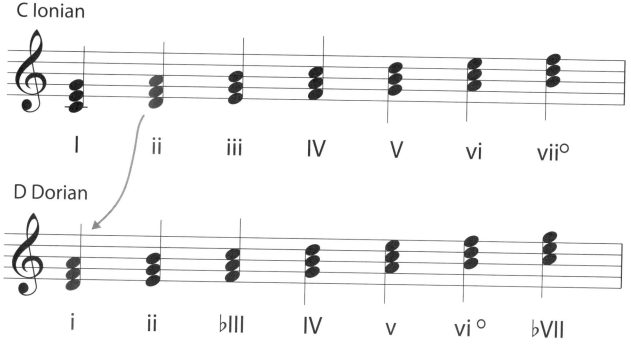

Figure 7.12a and b: The triad sequence of C Ionian versus D Dorian, shown in two different ways for comparison.

Audio Track 96: The triad comparison between C Ionian and C Dorian.

Aeolian Mode

Next on the list of modes is the Aeolian. Clearly by now, you've recognized that we're introducing the modes to you in order of darkness—brightest to darkest. The Aeolian mode is the next darkest after the Dorian mode and it's safe to say that the "happiness" that was still hanging on in Dorian has officially left the building. Aeolian is just plain sad. Good news? You already know this mode—it's the relative minor compared to the Ionian mode. Mind you, there are three versions of the minor scale, as we saw earlier—the natural, the harmonic, and the melodic minor; the Aeolian mode is the natural minor. This is the only minor scale of the three that we consider in this book.

The Aeolian mode is built from the sixth scale degree of the Ionian mode in the same way that the Lydian mode is built from the fourth scale, the Mixolydian is built from the fifth, and the Dorian is built from the second. So, similar to the other modes, you *could* simply start on A and run through the notes of the A major mode back to D, as seen in **Figure 7.13**. You can hear this on **Audio Track 97**.

A Aeolian

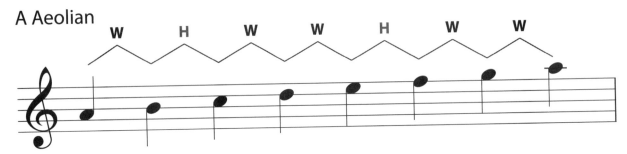

Figure 7.13: The notes of A Aeolian.

Audio Track 97: The A Aeolian mode.

Looking at A Aeolian again, the notes are:

A B C D E F G A

Looking deeper, the relationship between the notes is as follows:

A to B: whole step

B to C: half step

C to D: whole step

D to E: whole step

E to F: half step

F to G: whole step

G to A: whole step

or, in linear terms, WHWWHWW. Seen horizontally versus the Ionian mode, it looks like this:

Aeolian: W H W W H W W

Ionian: W W H W W W H

See how the second, third, fifth, and seventh intervals are different? In the Ionian, the second interval is a whole step and in Aeolian, it's a half step. The third interval—normally a half step—becomes a whole step. The fifth interval (normally a whole step) becomes a half step, while the seventh interval, normally a half step, becomes a whole step.

Coach's Corner: Know, Know, Know the Modes

This process of comparing intervallic relationships can start to be confusing. You might want to think about building a chart of intervals as we go through the modes, so you can visually reference the differences in intervallic relationship. Of course, you can simply skip over this part and just learn the modes by shifting the start positions of the Ionian mode based on your knowledge of the mode and the scale degree it's built from. Just like before, it doesn't matter *how* you know the modes—only that you know them. Well. You might have read this already… again.

These differences show up in the third, sixth, and seventh scale degrees. For example, C Aeolian would have an E♭ third scale degree instead of the Ionian E. The fifth interval (between the fifth and sixth scale degrees) is now a half step, down from the Ionian whole step. So, in C Aeolian, the sixth scale degree yields A♭, not the Ionian A. Notice here that the sixth interval (between the sixth and seventh scale degrees) hasn't changed—it's still a whole step.

However, since the sixth scale degree *has* changed, the *result* of the same sixth interval does change. So, the sixth scale degree of the Aeolian mode is an A♭. A whole step up from there is a B♭—flattened as compared to the Ionian seventh scale degree of B. Lastly, the seventh interval is now a whole step as compared to the Ionian half step. The result, C, is the same as the C Ionian scale, even though the interval is different.

The C Aeolian scale is built by altering the C Ionian scale with a flattened third, sixth, and seventh scale degree. So the C Aeolian scale is:

C D E♭ F G A♭ B♭ C

as opposed to

C D E F G A B C

in Ionian mode.

Did you get all of that? No? The box to the left shows it is in simpler terms…

MEMORIZE ME!

The Aeolian mode is recognized by the flat third, sixth, and flat seventh scale degrees.

So now we know that the Aeolian mode is different from the Ionian mode because it has a flattened third, sixth, and seventh scale degree. But, what we don't know (yet!) is how that affects the triads of the mode. As with the Ionian mode, the Aeolian has a series of triads that are built off of each scale degree. These triads are the same as before—major, minor, and diminished—but each triad is different from the Ionian triads in each scale degree.

In other words, the Aeolian triad sequence is different from the Ionian triad sequence. Let's look at the Aeolian mode in C to really compare it to the Ionian in triads.

Remember that when we build triads from *any* scale, the triads are always and *only* built from the notes in the scale. Therefore, the first triad is *no longer* C major—C-E-G, but rather C minor—C-E♭-G. By definition, this makes the Aeolian mode a minor mode. The second triad is also different—D diminished (D-F-A♭)—as opposed to the normal D minor. When we get to the flattened third scale degree on E♭, we see another triad change—E minor becomes E♭ major (E♭-G-B♭)—the same as the Dorian mode. Continuing onward, you'll see the triad sequence of C Aeolian in **Figure 7.14**. You can hear this on **Audio Track 98**.

C Aeolian Triads

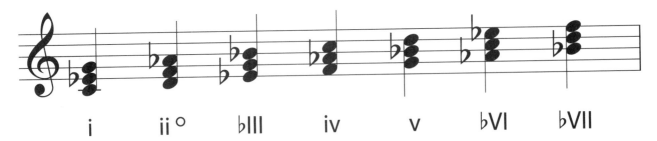

Figure 7.14: The C Aeolian triad sequence.

 **Audio Track 98:** The C Aeolian mode triad sequence.

MEMORIZE ME!

The Aeolian mode—defined as a flattened third, sixth, and seventh scale degree—has a triad sequence of i minor, ii diminished, ♭III Major, iv minor, v minor, ♭VI Major, and ♭VII Major.

Another way to know the Aeolian is to recognize that the Aeolian triad sequence is *the same* as the Ionian sequence, just shifted by a sixth—or moved to the relative minor position. It shouldn't be a big surprise—after all, the Aeolian mode *is* built off of the sixth scale degree of the Ionian.

To look at this another way let's compare the Ionian and Aeolian in two ways: in triads C Ionian to C Aeolian *and* in triads C Ionian to A Aeolian. You can see them both in **Figure 7.15** and **7.16**, respectively. **Audio Track 99** plays the triad comparison shown on Figure 7.15 only

C Ionian Triads vs. C Aeolian Triads

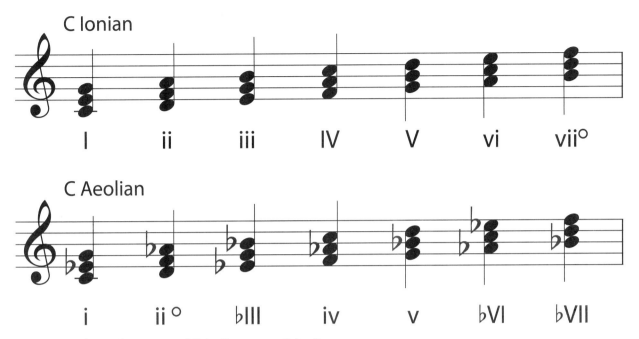

Figure 7.15: The triad sequence of C Aeolian versus C Aeolian.

C Ionian Triads vs. A Aeolian Triads

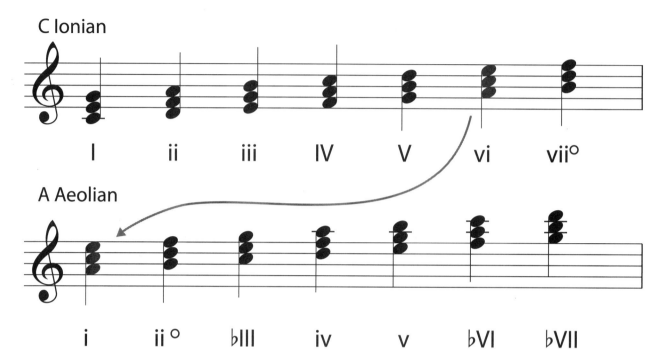

C Ionian Triads vs. A Aeolian Triads

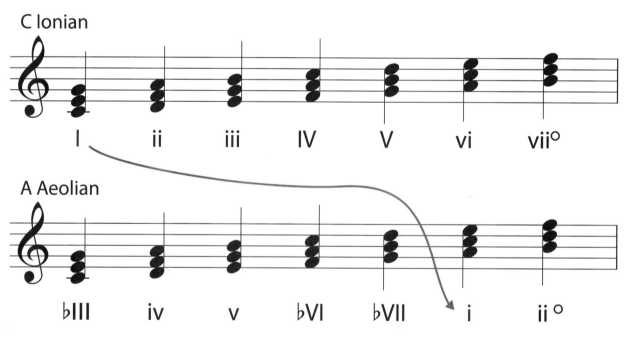

Figure 7.16a and b: The triad sequence of C Ionian versus A Aeolian, shown in two different ways.

Audio Track 99: The triad comparison between C Ionian and C Aeolian.

Phrygian Mode

Next on the list of modes is the Phrygian. Clearly by now, you've recognized that we're introducing the modes to you in order of darkness—brightest to darkest. The Phrygian mode is the next darkest after Aeolian and it's safe to say that the "sadness" that defined the Aeolian mode is still here. Now, it starts getting angry.

The Phrygian mode is built from the third scale degree of the Ionian mode in the same way that the Lydian mode is built from the fourth scale, the Mixolydian is built from the fifth, the Dorian is built from the second, and the Aeolian is built from the sixth. So, similar to the other modes, you *could* simply start on E and run through the notes of the C major mode back to E, as seen in **Figure 7.17**. You can hear it on **Audio Track 100**.

E Phrygian

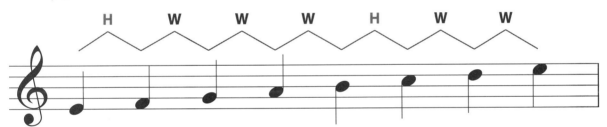

Figure 7.17: The notes of E Phrygian.

 **Audio Track 100:** The E Phrygian mode.

Looking at E Phrygian again, the notes are:

E F G A B C D E

Looking deeper, the relationship between the notes is as follows:

E to F: half step

F to G: whole step

G to A: whole step

A to B: whole step

B to C: half step

C to D: whole step

D to E: whole step

or, in linear terms (seen horizontally vs. the Ionian mode) it looks like this:

Phrygian: H W W W H W W

Ionian: W W H W W W H

Coach's Corner: The Payoff

See how only the second, fourth, and sixth intervals are the same between Phrygian and Ionian? By this time you should recognize that as the intervals change, the notes that they create change *but* don't always create different scale notes when compared to the Ionian mode. What's important to note here is that you need to know *both* the intervallic relationships of the modes *and* the actual notes created of a mode given any key. Knowing both does two things—it makes sure that you have creative freedom when finding melody within a mode *and* it ensures that you end up playing the right notes. Both are good things.

Coach's Corner: This Might Sound Familiar, But…

This process of comparing intervallic relationships can start to be confusing. You might want to think about building a chart of intervals as we go through the modes so you can visually reference the differences in intervallic relationship. Of course, you can simply skip over this part and just learn the modes by shifting the start positions of the Ionian mode based on your knowledge of the mode and the scale degree it's built from. Just like before, it doesn't matter *how* you know the modes—only that you know them. Well. You might have read this already… a few times… there might be one more…

These differences show up in the second, third, sixth, and seventh scale degrees. For example, C Phrygian would have a D♭ instead of the Ionian D as the second scale degree as well as an E♭ third scale degree instead of the Ionian E. As with the Dorian and Aeolian modes, this flattened third immediately identifies this mode as a minor mode. Comparing the Phrygian mode to the Aeolian mode, you'll see that all the other alterations from the Ionian mode to the Aeolian mode persist to the Phrygian mode with the addition of the flattened second scale degree.

The C Phrygian scale is built by altering the C Ionian scale with a flattened second, third, sixth, and seventh scale degree. So the C Phrygian scale is:

C D♭ E♭ F G A♭ B♭ C

as opposed to

C D E F G A B C

in Ionian mode.

Did you get all of that? No? The Box to the left shows it in simpler terms…

So now we know that the Phrygian mode is different from the Ionian mode because it has a flattened second, third, sixth, and seventh scale degree. But, what we don't know (yet!) is how that affects the triads of the mode. As with the Ionian mode, the Phrygian has a series of triads that are built off of each scale degree. These triads are the same as before—major, minor, and diminished—but each triad is different from the Ionian triads in each scale degree.

In other words, the Phrygian triad sequence is different from the Ionian triad sequence. Let's look at the Phrygian mode in C to really compare it to the Ionian in triads.

Remember that when we build triads from *any* scale, the triads are always and *only* built from the notes in the scale. Therefore, the first triad is *no longer* the Ionian C major—C-E-G—but rather a C minor—C-E♭-G. By definition, this makes the Phyrgian mode a minor mode. The second triad is also different—D♭ major (D♭-F-A♭)—as opposed to the Ionian D minor. When we get to the third scale degree on E♭, we see another triad change—E minor becomes E♭ major (E♭-G-B♭)– the same as the Dorian and Aeolian mode. Continuing onward, you'll see the triad sequence of C Phrygian in **Figure 7.18**. You can hear it on **Audio Track 101**.

C Phrygian Triads

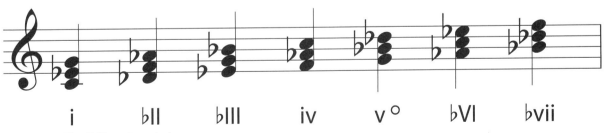

i   ♭II   ♭III   iv   v°   ♭VI   ♭vii

Figure 7.18: The C Phrygian triad sequence.

Audio Track 101: The triads of C Phrygian.

MEMORIZE ME!

The Phrygian mode, defined as a flattened second, third, sixth, and seventh scale degree, has a triad sequence of i minor, ♭II Major, ♭III Major, iv minor, v diminished, ♭VI Major, and ♭vii minor.

Another way to know the Phrygian is to recognize that the Phrygian triad sequence is *the same* as the Ionian sequence, just shifted by a third. It shouldn't be a big surprise—after all, the Phrygian mode *is* built off of the third scale degree of the Ionian. To look at this another way let's compare the Ionian and Phrygian in two ways: in triads C Ionian to C Phrygian *and* in triads C Ionian to E Phrygian. You can see them both in **Figure 7.19** and **7.20**, respectively. **Audio Track 102** plays the triads found in Figure 7.19 only.

C Ionian Triads vs. C Phrygian Triads

Figure 7.19: The triad sequence of C Ionian versus C Phrygian.

C Ionian Triads vs. E Phrygian Triads

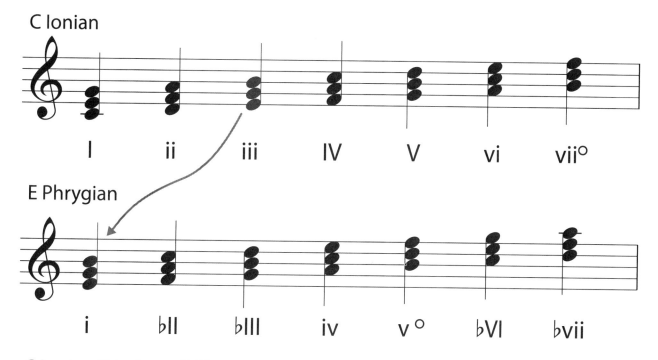

C Ionian Triads vs. E Phrygian Triads

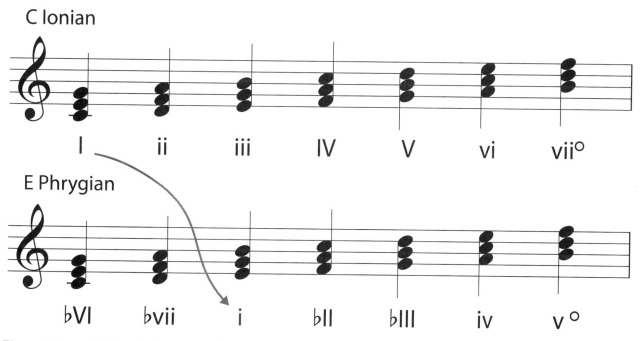

Figure 7.20a and b: The triad sequence of C Ionian versus E Phrygian, shown in two different ways.

Audio Track 102: The triad comparison of C Ionian to C Phrygian.

Locrian Mode

Next on the list of modes is the Locrian. Clearly by now, you've recognized that we're introducing the modes to you in order of darkness—brightest to darkest. The Locrian mode is the next darkest after Phrygian, and it's safe to say that this mode has a *very* angry sound.

The Locrian mode is built from the seventh scale degree of the Ionian mode in the same way that the Lydian mode is built from the fourth scale, the Mixolydian is built from the fifth, the Dorian is built from the second, the Aeolian is built from the sixth, and the Phrygian is built from the third. So, similar to the other modes, you *could* simply start on B and run through the notes of the C major mode back to B, as seen in **Figure 7.21**. You can hear this on **Audio Track 103**.

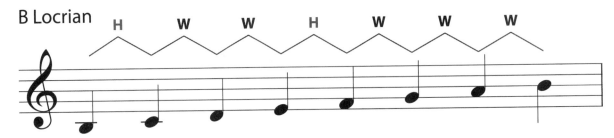

Figure 7.21: The notes of B Locrian.

   **Audio Track 103:** The B Locrian mode.

Looking at B Locrian, the notes are:

B C D E F G A B

Where the notes of C Ionian are:

C D E F G A B C

Looking deeper, the relationship between the notes is as follows:

B to C: half step

C to D: whole step

D to E: whole step

E to F: half step

F to G: whole step

G to A: whole step

A to B: whole step

or, in linear terms, seen horizontally versus the Ionian mode, it looks like this:

Locrian: H W W H W W W

Ionian: W W H W W W H

Coach's Corner: Noting the Differences

See only the second, fifth, and sixth intervals are the same? By this time you should recognize that as the intervals change, the notes they create change *but* don't always create different scale notes when compared to the Ionian mode. What's important to note here is that you need to know *both* the intervallic relationships of the modes *and* the actual notes created in a mode given any starting note. Knowing both does two things—it makes sure that you have creative freedom when finding melody within a mode *and* it ensures that you end up playing the right notes. Both are good things.

Coach's Corner: The Last Time—We Promise!

This process of comparing intervallic relationships can start to be confusing. You might want to think about building a chart of intervals as we go through the modes so you can visually reference the differences in intervallic relationship. Of course, you can simply skip over this part and just learn the modes by shifting the start positions of the Ionian mode based on your knowledge of the mode and the scale degree it's based on. Just like before, it doesn't matter *how* you know the modes—only that you know them. Well. You might have read this already… a few times… yet there will be no more. Whew!

These differences show up in the second, third, fifth, sixth, and seventh scale degrees. In other words, only the root and fourth scale degrees are the same between Locrian and Ionian. For example, in addition to all the other alterations we've seen through Phrygian, C Locrian would have a G♭ instead of the Ionian G as the fifth scale degree. As with the Dorian and Aeolian modes, the flattened third immediately identifies this mode as a minor mode, but the flattened fifth takes it to another level—this is actually a diminished mode.

The C Locrian scale is built by altering the C Ionian scale with a flattened second, third, fifth, sixth, and seventh scale degree. So the C Locrian scale is:

C D♭ E♭ F G♭ A♭ B♭ C

as opposed to

C D E F G A B C

…in Ionian mode.

Did you get all of that? No? The box to the left shows it in simpler terms…

So now we know that the Locrian mode is different from the Ionian mode because it has a flattened second, third, fifth, sixth, and seventh scale degree. But, what we don't know (at least not yet) is how that affects the triads of the mode. As with the Ionian mode, the Locrian mode has a series of triads that are built off of each scale degree. These triads are the same as before—major, minor, and diminished—but each triad is different from the Ionian triads in each scale degree.

In other words, the Locrian triad sequence is different from the Ionian triad sequence. Let's examine the Locrian mode in C to really compare it to the Ionian in triads.

Remember, when we build triads from *any* scale, the triads are *always* and *only* built from the notes in the scale. Therefore, the first triad is *no longer* the Ionian C major—C-E-G—but rather a C diminished—C-E♭-G♭. By definition, this makes the Locrian mode a diminished mode. Continuing onward, you see the triad sequence of C Locrian in **Figure 7.22**. You can hear this on **Audio Track 104**.

> **MEMORIZE ME!**
> The Locrian mode is recognized by the flattened second, third, fifth, sixth, and seventh scale degrees.

C Locrian Triads

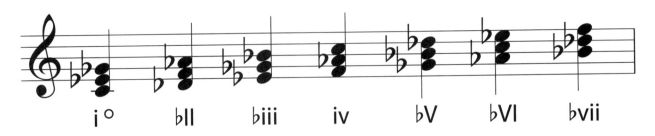

i°   ♭II   ♭iii   iv   ♭V   ♭VI   ♭vii

Figure 7.22: The C Locrian triad sequence.

Audio Track 104: The C Locrian triads.

Another way to know the Locrian is to recognize that the Locrian triad sequence is *the same* as the Ionian sequence, just shifted by a seventh. It shouldn't be a big surprise—after all, the Locrian mode *is* built off of the seventh scale degree of the Ionian.

To look at this another way, we can compare the Ionian and Locrian in two ways, in triads C Ionian to C Locrian *and* in triads C Ionian to B Locrian. You can see them both in **Figure 7.23** and **7.24**, respectively. **Audio Track 105** plays the triad comparison shown in Figure 7.23 only.

C Ionian Triads vs. C Locrian Triads

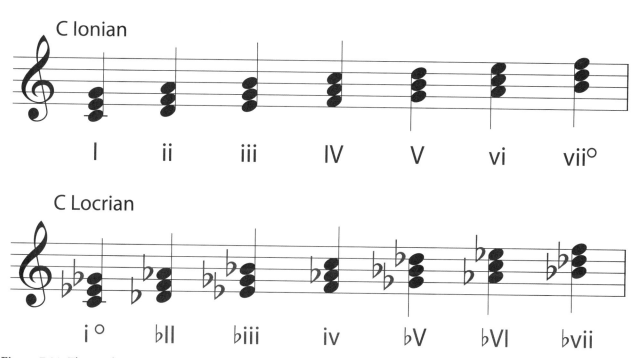

Figure 7.23: The triad sequence of C Ionian versus C Locrian.

C Ionian Triads vs. B Locrian Triads

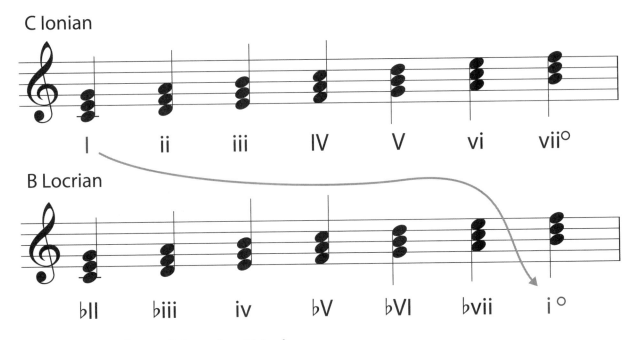

C Ionian Triads vs. B Locrian Triads

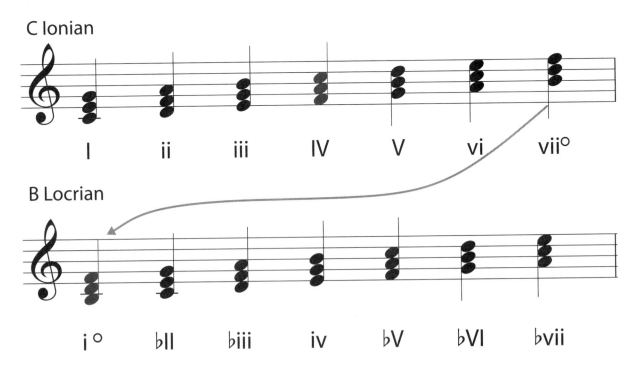

Figure 7.24 a and b: The triad sequence of C Ionian versus B Locrian, shown in two different ways.

Audio Track 105: The triad comparison between C Ionian and C Locrian.

Worksheet 7.1: Modes

The modes are certainly different from and more difficult to understand at first compared to the major scale. They have a set of rules all to themselves and knowing them is effectively the same as learning five new scales beyond the Ionian (major) and Aeolian (natural minor). When learning them for the first time we can simply compare the other modes to the Ionian mode *or* we can memorize the modes as they are—in and of themselves. Both are good ideas.

This worksheet is just the beginning of the work we do with modes at Pyramind. In our more advanced classes, we dig deeply into each mode and use their emotional strengths to build songs within the modes. For our purposes here, it is enough to simply know them and start working with them at their triad level. To do this, we'll revisit some of our old friends: cadences, progressions, inversions, and voice leading. Here are some quick-hints on working with modes.

The first thing we need to do is practice the modes. We suggest working with a different mode each night. As you've likely spent a *lot* of time on the Ionian, we'll assume you have it down and ask that you concentrate your Monday through Saturday workouts on modes.

☞ Pick a mode of the day and apply it to C.

☞ First, cycle through the scale of the mode with the standard five-finger techniques—first up and down the first five notes, then expanding to the whole scale. *Verify your work*—make sure that you get the accidentals right in the mode of choice. If you choose to practice Phyrgian, for example, what scale degrees should be changed as compared to Ionian to make sure you're actually playing Phrygian correctly? …insert pause to see if you know the answer… Right: the flattened second, third, sixth, and seventh.

☞ Play the scale with the metronome at first then add your favorite beat as you move along. Speed up your pace as you get better and faster but don't trade speed for accuracy. Getting it right is more important than doing it fast. Remember to vary the scale in a few ways—leapfrog, intervals, dyads, and so on.

☞ As an advanced technique, play the mode's scale three times perfectly in C then move directly to the next sharp in the circle of fifths—G. Then, move to the first flat key of F—*all* in the same mode. Continue this throughout the circles until you've gotten all stops on the circle of fifths and fourths through that one mode. Then do the next mode all the way through.

☛ Then, move through this mode in triads—root inversion at first. Do this to the metronome then with your favorite beat. Speed up as you get better and faster.

☛ As an advanced alternative, cycle through the modes in C using all three triad inversions.

☛ As another advanced alternative, cycle through both circles playing the triads perfectly in each, three times before moving onward.

☛ Lastly, cycle through all the modes and both circles starting each new key in all three inversions. In other words, start on C Ionian root, first, then second inversions. Then move to Lydian, Mixolydian, and so on—all in C. Then, move through the sharp keys, then the flat keys, and repeat. This will take a while.

We suggest that, at first, you chart out each mode in each key so you have a reference to play with. Odds are, managing the inversions, the triads, the accidentals, the finger position, and executing this exercise will be *plenty*! To move through each key will take time—and lots of practice.

Worksheet 7.2: Songwriting with Modes

As you practice your modes, keep in mind that the goal for now is familiarity, finger memory, and ear training. Use this goal to achieve a second goal: writing songs with the modes.

Remember some of the progressions we listed way back in the major scale? No? Well they looked like **Figure 7**.

Various Progressions

Figure 7.25: Various four-chord progressions.

Note that the Roman numeral analysis in this list only applies to the Ionian mode. It's virtually guaranteed that the quality of each triad will be different in each mode. For example, the I-IV-V-I won't be all major triads in the Mixolydian mode as it is in Ionian. Take these progressions and apply them to *each* mode. Start in one key (one in which you're comfortable—C is fine to start), but be sure to challenge yourself by moving through the circles to at least two positions each. That means C, G, D, F, and B♭.

Let's do an easy one together—the ever-present 1-4-5. Let's start in something easy, such as Mixolydian in G.

Remembering Mixolydian, you'll recognize the flattened seventh scale degree. That means that our Mixolydian scale consists of the following:

G A B C D E F G

See? It's easy! No sharps or flats. Did you miss the flattened seventh in this list? Remember that G major (Ionian) has an F♯ as the seventh scale degree. It's the first stop on the circle of fifths and has one sharp. However, in Mixolydian, the seventh scale degree is flattened—F as opposed to F♯.

Now, remembering the triad sequence, we have the following:

- ☞ G major

- ☞ A minor

- ☞ B diminished

- ☞ C major

- ☞ D minor

- ☞ E minor

- ☞ F major

So, our 1-4-5 looks like **Figure 7.26** and sounds like **Audio Track 106**.

Progression in G Mixolydian

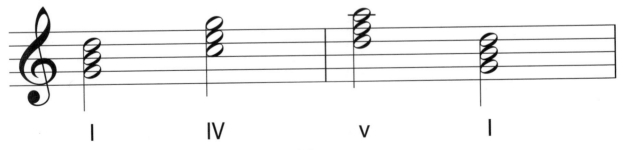

Figure 7.26: The I- IV- v- I progression played in G Mixolydian.

Audio Track 106: The 1-4-5 of G Mixolydian.

Notice how the V triad in this progression is minor (v)? Remember how it used to be major in the Ionian mode? Let's compare the two in the same key—that's where the real modal differences show up. Let's use C Ionian versus C Mixolydian as an example, and first build the two scales.

C Ionian consists of:

C D E F G A B C

While C Mixolydian (flat seventh) consists of:

C D E F G A B♭ C

So, the triads look like **Figure 7.27** which we're revisiting from earlier.

C Ionian Triads vs. C Mixolydian Triads

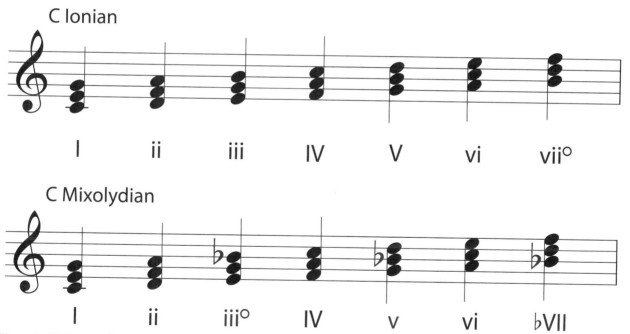

Figure 7.27: The triad sequence of C Ionian versus C Mixolydian.

Now, we'll see the two played back to back using the familiar 1-4-5 progression. **Figure 7.28** shows the two bars written back-to-back with the accidental written in on the second bar when B becomes B♭. Listen to it on **Audio Track 107.** You should notice the last v triad being played as a minor versus being major in the first bar.

C Ionian vs. C Mixolydian

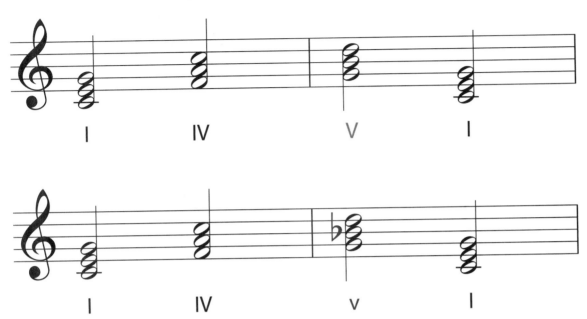

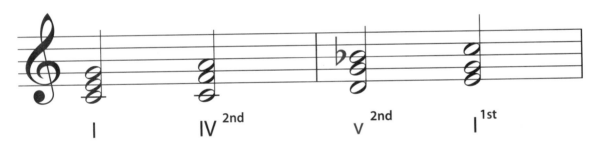

with Voice Leading

Figure 7.28: The 1-4-5 written once as Ionian and the second time as Mixolydian.

Audio Track 107: The triad progression shown in Figure 7.28.

Coach's Corner: A Mixolydian Frat Rock Classic

Working with modes is often just a simple matter of taking common chord progressions and trying them out in different modes. Many times, simply by making the modal change, the progression will take on a whole new emotional meaning. In the example shown previously in Figure 7.28 (Mixolydian in G), you might recognize the triad progression as an old classic from the 1960s. If you've ever seen the film *Animal House*, you know the song. It's "Louie Louie" by The Kingsmen. Look it up and recognize it by its I-IV-v-IV progression—a pure Mixolydian frat rock favorite!

Let's try one more mode example… How about the I-ii-vi-V? Let's try it in F Lydian.

First build your scale. Write it down on a separate paper—preferably on staff paper—then proceed to play it a few times using proper finger positions. Be sure to verify your work! Now that you have your scale, build your triads. Write them down on staff paper before committing them to your fingers. Then write the progression above and begin playing it—first in all root inversions then by using voice leading.

What inversions did you use? Did you remember to use voice leading or did you just write them in root inversion? If you chose to start in root inversion, it should look like **Figure 7.29** and sound like **Audio Track 108**. Note that the flat symbol at the head of the image is indicating the key—F—not calling for an accidental of the first chord. Notice that the flat remains in the head of the staff for the second line as well but the accidental is now a natural note as altered by the mode. In this case, B♭ (natural to Ionian) is played as a B, notated as such in the chord.

F Ionian vs. F Lydian

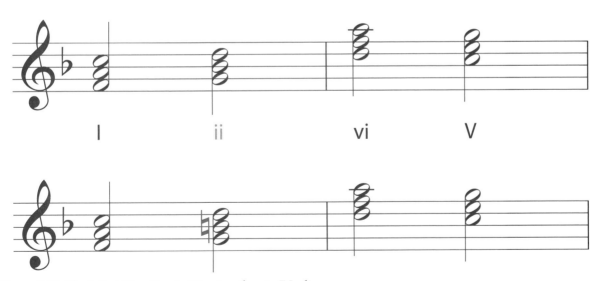

Figure 7.29: The I-ii-vi-V written in F Ionian, then in F Lydian.

 **Audio Track 108:** The triad progression written in Figure 7.29.

Try the above progressions *all* in at least five keys—C, G, D, F, and B♭.

Now, take one last deep breath. We're almost at the end of our journey together and there's only one more thing to look at with modes before we wrap it up and call it a day. It's the collection of all those progressions *without* the I in them.

Remember these from way back in the section on the major triad progressions?

vi-IV-V-ii

iii-IV-vi-V

V-IV-V-IV

ii-iii-IV-V

Remember how we said that these didn't really belong to the C major scale because there was no I in them? Well, here's why.

As the I is never stated in these progressions as written, there's no solid way to know what the key is—they never settle down and just play the I. This is a very big clue that we are not dealing with the major scale but rather one of the modes. Let's inspect and see.

Take, for instance, the first progression—vi IV V ii. Let's assume for now that the first triad determines the mode. The first triad, the vi minor, tells us that this is an Aeolian progression starting with the root at the Ionian vi, or Aeolian i. Since it's not written as a i, we'd need to rewrite the progression assuming that the vi is actually the Aeolian i. Applying this to the key of C, we'd have the triads seen in **Figure 7.30** and heard on **Audio Track 109**.

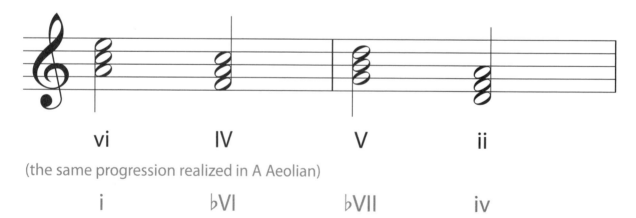

vi-IV-V-ii in C

| vi | IV | V | ii |

(the same progression realized in A Aeolian)

| i | ♭VI | ♭VII | iv |

Figure 7.30: The vi-IV-V-ii (A-F-G-D) progression applied in the key of C.

Audio Track 109: The triad progression shown in Figure 7.30.

Let's remember the comparison between C Ionian and A Aeolian. We know that they contain the same notes and the same triads—A Aeolian is the relative minor of C Ionian after all. The chart below shows the two compared scale to scale, triad-to-triad, and Roman numeral analysis to Roman numeral analysis.

C Major I (Ionian starts)

D minor ii

E minor iii

F Major IV

G Major V

A minor vi	A	I	(Aeolian starts)
B diminished	vii	B	ii
C Major I	C	bIII	
D minor ii	D	iv	
E minor iii	E	v	
F Major IV	F	♭VI	
G Major V	G	♭VII	
A minor vi	A	i	

In this case, we see that the leading triad is A. So one has to then ask a question—is this progression in the key of C major without the I or is it in the key of A Aeolian?

While technically, the answer is "both" as the triads belong to both keys, the *real* answer is A Aeolian. After all, you can't have a key or a mode without a I.

Let's take a closer look and see why.

We can't describe this progression as being in the key of C because the C triad never even shows up in the progression—but we can call this A, because it leads with A. This is not always the case, but is a good clue. But what kind of A progression is this? Let's analyze.

The first step is to re-categorize the first triad. Since the first triad (A) is now no longer the vi but now the i, we need to rewrite the first triad as a i. Note that since it is minor, it is a good clue that whatever mode we're in, it's not a major mode, thus eliminating Ionian, Lydian, and Mixolydian. Locrian is out as well because the first triad is not diminished.

The second step is to re-categorize the other triads. Starting with the second one, F major, we must recognize that it is no longer the IV, but something else—but what is it? Let's go all the way back to the intervals to figure it out. The interval from A down to F is a major third. A major third down from the i is a ♭VI. Let's keep using this process to uncover the other triad relationships.

We continue this process at the third triad, G major. G is a major second up from F and since F is now a ♭VI, the G must be a ♭VII. Lastly, we need to go down from the flat seventh to the last triad, D minor. D is a perfect fourth down from G and a fourth down from the flat VII is the iv.

Let's review—

☞   A minor, the former vi, is now the i.

☞   F major, the former IV, is now the ♭VI.

☞   G major, the former V, is now the ♭VII

☞   D minor, the former ii, is now the iv.

So, written now in A Aeolian mode, the progression iv-IV-V-ii becomes i-♭VI-♭VII-iv.

Confused?

Let's try another one: iii-IV-vi-V.

Let's do the same thing—start as if it were the key of C Ionian, then determine the transposition and the new mode.

If we're in C Ionian, then we have a iii as the first triad—E minor. Then the IV in F major, the vi in A minor, and, lastly, the V in G major. That's great, but as C major is not even in the triad sequence, we know it can't be C Ionian.

Assuming the E minor is the new i, starting with a minor triad also eliminates Ionian, Lydian, and Mixolydian as possible modes because they all start with a I major. It also eliminates Locrian as the first triad is not diminished. Since our progression begins with a iii and we know that the mode that starts on the iii is Phyrgian, we should start there.

Consider the chart below as a comparison between C Ionian and E Phrygian.

C I	**Major**	**(Ionian starts)**			
D	**ii**	**minor**			
E iii	**minor**	**E**	**i**	**(Phrygian starts)**	
F IV	**Major**	**F**	**♭II**		
G V	**Major**	**G**	**♭III**		
A vi	**minor**	**A**	**iv**		
B vii	**diminished**	**B**	**vdim**		
C I	**Major**	**C**	**♭VI**		
D	**ii**	**minor**	**D**	**♭VII**	
E iii	**minor**	**E**	**i**		

Let's look at the intervals in play here. From the i to the next chord is a minor second interval. Knowing this, the second chord should be a flat II. And since the second chord's quality is major, we'd say it's a ♭II. Up from there is another major third, which should yield a minor iv chord. From a ♭II chord up a major third, we'd get a iv chord. Then down a whole step to a major, we'd get a ♭III.

So, going through the same process, we find that the iii-IV-vi-V in Ionian becomes i-♭II-iv-♭III—still E minor, F major, A minor, then G major. Notice the first two triads for a moment—i minor and ♭II. There are only two modes with a ♭II chord: Phrygian and Locrian. Since the i is minor and not diminished, this progression is Phrygian.

See it in **Figure 7.31** and hear it on **Audio Track 110**.

iii-IV-vi-V in C

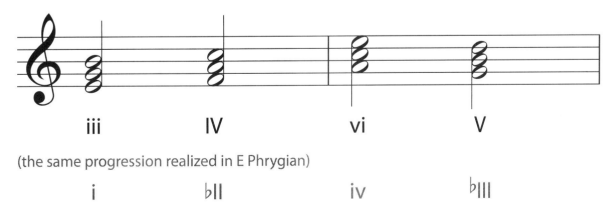

(the same progression realized in E Phrygian)

Figure 7.31: The iii-IV-vi-V (E-F-A-G) progression applied in the key of C.

Audio Track 110: The triad progression shown in Figure 7.31.

Chops Test: The Modes

Now it's time to test yourself—one last time.

If the modes are beyond your comfort zone, that's OK. We've given a *lot* of information here and it will take time to get it all under your fingers—even if it's still trying to get into your head. Besides, you have the rest of your life to work on it. Try to enjoy the work of playing and practicing. Eventually it'll all click for you and your music will progress to a whole new level.

In the meantime, let's see what you can do…

Basic Chops

By now, you should be able to do the following:

☛ Find the notes of the Ionian mode to at least two positions of each circle up and down the scale with both hands—separate and together.

☛ Play *each* of the modes in scale form to at least two positions of each circle up and down the scale with both hands—separate and together.

☛ Play all the dyads of the Ionian mode up to two positions of each of the circles with both hands—separately and together in root inversion.

☛ Play *each* of the modes in triads to at least two positions of each circle up and down the scale with both hands—separate and together.

☛ Play *each* of the modes in triads through each inversion to at least two positions of each circle up and down the scale with both hands—separate and together.

☛ Play a variety of triad progressions in each mode across at least five keys—C, G, D, F, and B♭ (to two positions on each circle).

Advanced Chops

By now you *may* be able to do the following:

☞ Find all the notes of the Ionian mode to *all* positions of *each* circle up and down the scale with both hands—separate and together.

☞ Play *each* of the modes in scale form to *all* positions of each circle up and down the scale with both hands—separate and together.

☞ Play all the dyads of the Ionian mode to *all* positions of each of the circles with both hands—separately and together in root inversion.

☞ Play *each* of the modes in triads to *all* positions of each circle up and down the scale with both hands—separate and together.

☞ Play *each* of the modes in triads through each inversion to *all* positions of the circle up and down the scale with both hands—separate and together.

☞ Play a variety of triad progressions in *each* mode across each of the keys of the two circles.

And let me just tell you—if you can do this, you're more than capable of writing great songs. You have *all* the tools necessary to match some of the greatest songs written in popular music.

And I'm not joking.

Section 8
Where to Go from Here?

Welcome to the end of the book. Hopefully, this is not the end of the musical road for you, but rather the beginning. We like to think of this book as the "driver's manual"—it's important to learn the rules of the road before trying to jump on the freeway. It may not have been fun at every turn, but if you read it in detail *and* did all the work, we'll bet that you can sit at a piano anywhere in the world and play something that people will enjoy hearing. Best of all, you can sit at your studio MIDI keyboard and *produce* recordings and compositions that everyone will enjoy hearing!

Learning to play music and the piano is hard work. It requires discipline and consistent effort, just like learning any language, going through physical therapy, or sticking to a diet or exercise regimen. The results are only going to be as good as the effort you put into it. There's no "red pill" for this, no shortcut, no digital download. You've got to put in the time and the hours.

Music is a language. Like any language, there are the essentials you need to survive in a foreign country and there are the details that allow you to excel in a foreign country. And like with any language, there are eloquent public speakers, bumbling fools, and all ranges in-between. The contents of this book should get you most of the way to a public speaking circuit—but again, it all depends on the work *you* put in.

We suggest that you tackle these items section by section or page by page if the content gets too heady for you. We also suggest that you practice, practice, and practice for a minimum of one hour every night—*every* night. When you think you've practiced enough, go practice some more. Rest assured, your video-game console, social networking site, and DVR will wait for you. Be sure to check back with us regularly at both *www. pyramind.com* and *www.pyramindonline.com* to see what's new in our training series and to keep sharp with your chops.

We'll see you in class soon…